Llewellyn's 1997
Magical Almanac

Featuring:

D. J. Conway

Marguerite Elsbeth

Edain McCoy

Silver RavenWolf

Bernyce Barlow

Estelle Daniels

Jim Garrison

Ken Johnson

Sirona Knight

Ann Moura (Aoumiel)

Gwydion O'Hara

Rachel Raymond

deTraci Regula

Cerridwen Iris Shea

Lilith Silverhair

Patricia Telesco

Donald Tyson

With Contributions By:

Jen Besemer, Jane Callard, Rhiannon Cameron,
Roslyn Reid, Starr, and Jack Veasey

LLEWELLYN'S MAGICAL ALMANAC

Editor/Designer:	Cynthia Ahlquist
Cover Art:	Merle S. Insinga
Cover Design:	Maria Mazzara
Photos, pages 233, 249, 256-7, 294:	Bernyce Barlow
Photo, page 289:	Oz Johnson
Drawings, pages 1, 10-11, 13, 20, 23, 58, 60, 62, 72, 74, 93, 102, 222, 254, 264, 268, 292, 308, 311, 313, 315, 328, 334-5:	Carrie Westfall
Drawings, pages 4-6, 34-35, 37, 75-7, 114, 196:	Tom Grewe
Calendar Art:	Robin Wood
Clip Art:	Dover Publications

Merle S. Insinga, this year's cover artist, would like to dedicate her work to the memory of her mother, Helen Stott.

Special thanks to Amber Wolfe for the use of daily color and incense correspondences. For more detailed information, please see *Personal Alchemy* by Amber Wolfe.

Moon sign and phase data computed by Matrix Software.

ISBN 1-56718-925-3

Llewellyn Publications, A Division of Llewellyn Worldwide, Ltd.
P.O. Box 64383, Dept. 925-3, St. Paul, MN 55164-0383

G reetings, and welcome to the *1997 Magical Almanac*. I'm going to start this year's *Almanac* off with a heartfelt thank you to all of our 1997 writers. It would be impossible to produce this book year after year without their insights, ingenuity, and their willingness to share the many creative ways in which they weave magic into their lives. I am proud to announce that our dynamic magical team of D.J. Conway, Marguerite Elsbeth, Edain McCoy, and Silver RavenWolf is back with us for 1997, and that once again Bernyce Barlow, Jim Garrison, Ann Moura (Aoumiel), deTraci Regula, Lilith Silverhair, Patricia Telesco, and Donald Tyson have graced our pages with articles. In addition, we have several authors who are new to the *Almanac* (although many are not new to writing), including Estelle Daniels, Ken Johnson, Sirona Knight, Gwydion O'Hara, Rachel Raymond, and Cerridwen Iris Shea. Last, but definitely not least, I have included some pieces submitted by our readers, including Jen Besemer, Jane Callard, Rhiannon Cameron, Roslyn Reid, Starr, and Jack Veasey.

Next, thank you to all of the artists who contributed to the *Magical Almanac* this year. Merle S. Insinga has created a fabulous cover painting, and Carrie Westfall and Tom Grewe have captured the spirit of the *Almanac* with magical (and sometimes downright funny) spot illustrations. Thank you also to Bernyce Barlow for saving me all of the good photos.

Finally, a personal thank you to Bernyce and Silver. I treasure your friendship, feedback, and well-timed humor. And now (drumroll, please!) a word about our authors!

D. J. CONWAY has been involved in many aspects of New Age religion. Although she is an ordained minister in two New Age churches and holder of a Doctor of Divinity degree, Conway claims that her heart lies within the Pagan cultures. No longer actively lecturing and teaching, she has centered her energies on writing. She is the author of the Llewellyn books *Celtic Magic; Norse Magic; The Ancient and Shining Ones;*

Maiden, Mother, Crone; Dancing with Dragons; Animal Magick; Moon Magick; Flying Without a Broom; By Falcon Feather and Valkyrie Sword; Astral Love; and *Dream Warrior* (fiction). She is also the author of *Magical, Mythical, Mystical Beasts; Lord of Light and Shadow; Soothslayer* (volume two of the *Dream Warrior Trilogy*); and co-creator of the *Shapeshifter Tarot* with Sirona Knight and Lisa Hunt, all forthcoming from Llewellyn.

MARGUERITE ELSBETH has studied and practiced astrology and tarot since 1973. She has facilitated healing and ritual groups, as well as publishing numerous articles in *Dell Horoscope* and *The Mountain Astrologer.* Her book *The Grail Castle: Male Myths and Mysteries in the Celtic Tradition,* co-authored with Kenneth Johnson, has been published by Llewellyn Publications, and she and Ken have collaborated on the forthcoming *The Silver Wheel.* Marguerite is a hereditary Strega.

EDAIN McCOY is part of the Wittan Irish Pagan Tradition and is a Priestess of Brighid within that tradition. She has taught classes in guided meditation and automatic writing, and occasionally works with students who wish to study Wiccan and Celtic Witchcraft. She is a member of The Authors Guild and The Wiccan/Pagan Press Alliance. Edain is the author of *Witta: An Irish Pagan Tradition; A Witch's Guide to Faery Folk; The Sabbats; How To Do Automatic Writing; Celtic Myth and Magick; In A Graveyard At Midnight; Lady of the Night;* and two forthcoming titles, *Entering the Summerland* and *Secrets of a Witches' Coven.*

SILVER RAVENWOLF is the Director of the International Wiccan/Pagan Press Alliance, a network of Pagan newsletters, publishers, and writers, and the editor of the organization's mouthpiece, *The MidNight Drive.* She is also the National Director of WADL, the Witches Anti-Discrimination League. Silver is a degreed Witch, receiving her Eldering from Lord Serphant from the Serphant Stone Family (Gardnerian lineage), and is Clan Head for the Black Forest Traditional Witches. She is the author of the books *To Ride A Silver Broomstick, HexCraft, Beneath A Mountain Moon, To Stir A Magick Cauldron,* and the

upcoming *Angel Magick*. She is also the co-author with Nigel Jackson of the *Rune Mysteries Book,* which is part of the *Rune Oracle Kit,* forthcoming from Llewellyn.

BERNYCE BARLOW is the author of *Sacred Sites of the West,* forthcoming from Llewellyn. She researches and leads seminars on the sacred sites of the ten western states. She is currently excavating sites in the Great Basin, and she insists that Dot from the *Animaniacs* television show is her totem "animal."

ESTELLE DANIELS is a professional part-time astrologer and author of *Astrologickal Magick,* a book written for people who are interested in using astrology in the Craft, and astrologers who are interested in exploring magical topics. She has studied astrology since 1967, and has been practicing professionally since 1972. She is also an initiate into eclectic Wicca, and teaches the Craft with her High Priest. If you would like to purchase a copy of her book, you can contact her by mail care of Llewellyn. Please specify if you want an autographed copy.

JIM GARRISON is just some guy who has studied magic for too long and now writes too much about it. Just kidding. Jim is really an independent Pagan with a background ranging from Wicca and Post-Modern Shamanism to Heretical Thelema, and beyond. Although he was initiated into an offshoot of the Lady Sheba tradition of Wicca, he is very busy being a writer, artist, and new dad, and prefers to remain a non-affiliated Pagan, following his own path and helping others to find theirs as best he can.

KEN JOHNSON holds a degree in comparative religions with an emphasis in the study of mythology. He has been a professional astrologer since 1975, and is co-author of *The Grail Castle: Male Myths and Mysteries in the Celtic Tradition* and *The Silver Wheel* with Marguerite Elsbeth, and co-author of *Mythic Astrology* with Ariel Guttman. He is also the author of *North Star Road* and the forthcoming *Jaguar Wisdom*.

SIRONA KNIGHT is the author of *Greenfire* and *Moonflower,* and co-creator with D. J. Conway and Lisa Hunt of the forthcoming *Shapeshifter Tarot.* She is also a contributing editor for *Magical Blend Magazine,* and a third degree Master of the Craft of the Gwyddonic Druid Tradition.

ANN MOURA (AOUMIEL) has been a solitary Witch for over thirty years. She is the author of the Llewellyn books *Dancing Shadows* and *Green Witchcraft,* and has recently completed work on a book about the dark aspects of the Lady and the Lord. She conducts seminars on Green Witchcraft and enjoys working in her herb garden.

GWYDION O'HARA has been an avid student of the ways of past cultures for many years. His research has taken him through the ancient arts and sciences, including herbology and aromatherapy, and the old legends, as reflected in his book *Moonlore,* pulished by Llewellyn. He is also the author of *Sunlore* and *Pagan Ways,* both forthcoming from Llewellyn, and is working on a full-length manuscript on the use of essential oils in aromatherapy magic.

RACHEL RAYMOND is an artist, herbalist, astrologer, psychic, bookkeeper, architect, and teacher. She says that having tried everything else, she has determined that "writing is the only occupation I am truly fit for." She lives with her husband, two small children, assorted pets, and lots of books in a tiny house with a big herb garden in the hills of southern California.

DETRACI REGULA is a priestess of Isis, the author of *The Mysteries of Isis,* and the co-author, with David Harrington, of *Whispers of the Moon: A Biography of Scott Cunningham.* Both books are published by Llewellyn. She speaks Chinese, and has travelled in China and Japan, where she did some of the research for her article on Asian vampires.

CERRIDWEN IRIS SHEA is an urban witch who writes in many genres under several different names. Her plays have been produced in New York, Los Angeles, London, Edinburgh, and Australia. Her writing has appeared in numerous publications, including *Circle Network*

News, Thema, Poet's Choice, and *Playgirl.* She is currently working on a series of novels featuring urban witch Skye Taylor as protagonist.

LILITH SILVERHAIR is a solitary practitioner of an eclectic Pagan path, living in what has been dubbed "weird central" with her husband and two children. She is co-editor of the newsletter *Coll of the Goddess,* and editor of the Pagan fiction annual *MoonDreams.* Her articles have appeared in several newsletters, including *Silver Chalice* and *Witches' Brew.* She is currently putting the finishing touches on her first novel, *Miranda's Children,* about reincarnation and Goddess worship.

PATRICIA TELESCO is the author of *A Victorian Grimoire, Urban Pagan, Victorian Flower Oracle, A Kitchen Witch's Cookbook, A Witch's Brew,* and *Folkways* from Llewellyn. She participates in historical recreation, Star Trek writing, has a mail-order business, and loves to hear from readers. She is currently working on several self-help and dream image books.

DONALD TYSON is the author of *The Truth About Runes, The Truth About Ritual Magic, Rune Magic, The Rune Magic Deck, The New Magus, Ritual Magic, The Messenger* (fiction), *Three Books of Occult Philosophy, The Power of the Runes* (divination kit), and *Tetragrammaton,* all from Llewellyn. He is also the author of the forthcoming *The Tortuous Serpent* (fiction), and *Scrying for Beginners,* as well as *New Millenium Magic,* a revised version of *The New Magus.* He lives in Nova Scotia, where he devotes his life to the attainment of a complete gnosis of the art of magic in theory and practice.

JEN BESEMER holds a BA and MA in creative writing, both from Antioch University. She is a Wiccan priestess and a founding member of the White Horse Tribe. For Jen, creative expression is one way to both manifest and worship the divine, and she feels that every person is an artist at heart. Currently, Jen lives with her husband, dog, and three cats. When she isn't writing, she enoys reading, cooking, painting, and movies.

JANE CALLARD has been a Wiccan solitare for the last four years. She has worked as a nurse, and is now a tarot teacher and counselor, specializing in grief and bereavement issues. She is also a poet and writer, and is currently working on a science fiction trilogy.

RHIANNON CAMERON has been dedicated to the Craft for more than two decades. The history, legends, lore, and uses of food and herbs have held lifelong interest for her. Rhiannon also offers correspondence training for newcomers to the Craft.

ROSLYN REID is a Druid and member of the Morning Shadow Institiute (a Pagan spirituality organization which offers ordination, among other things). She has been a yoga practitioner and body-builder for ten years, studies and teaches tarot, and has been a regular contributor of articles and art to several Llewellyn publications. She has also been published in *Sage Woman* and *Harvest*.

STARR is a second degree initiate in the NorthWind tradition of American eclectic Wicca. She holds a BA in English with an emphasis in creative writing. She has taught classes on Wicca at her local community college and Unitarian fellowship. Ritual, ritual as theater, and writing rituals are some of her special interests.

JACK VEASEY is a member of the Black Forest Tradition of Celtic Wicca, in which he was initiated and is being trained by Silver RavenWolf. He is the author of seven published books of poetry, two plays that have been produced, and articles for such publications as *The Philadelphia Inquirer*. He teaches adult education courses in poetry and creative writing.

I hope you enjoy the *1997 Magical Almanac*. Any questions or comments about the *Magical Almanac* may be directed to me, care of Llewellyn Publications. Have a magical year!

—Cynthia Ahlquist, Editor

TABLE OF CONTENTS

THE SILVER MAID

BY MARGUERITE ELSBETH

Siberian shamans believe that stars are the "windows of the world." These are sky openings which provide air for the various celestial bodies. The Milky Way is one such "hole" of light. So, when the northern lights shimmer across the blackened sky, this Siberian folktale of how the milky way came into being is often told.

There was once a Saami maid who ran very fast. Many youths came courting, but she would run into the forest and none could catch her. Yet there was one boy who was sure he could catch her and made up his mind to marry her.

When he came calling, she ran into the forest as usual, and he gave chase. This time, the chase continued through the forest and across the plain. Realizing that she was harder to catch then he thought, he forced the maid to run uphill. The maid reached the top and disappeared into a dark puff of cloud.

The young man lay on the frozen ground, his energy spent. When the maid saw that he was helpless, her fear turned to pity and she came out of her cloud to tend him.

"What can I bring you?" she asked.

"Water," he replied with rasping breath.

There was no water on the hill, so the maid thought to revive him by squeezing several drops of breastmilk onto his lips. But the wind spread the milk across the sky and covered the maid also, turning her into a silver block of ice.

When the youth opened his eyes, he saw the maid standing over him. She was as beautiful, graceful and bright as always, but solid as stone. Sad and confused, he returned to his village and there passed the days until his heart broke. You can still see the Silver Maid mirrored in the cold night sky, and her milk splashed by the wind across the Milky Way.

1

A Solitary New Moon Ritual

By Jack Veasey

You will need: Kitty litter in the cauldron; a white candle (to represent the Maiden); an herbal oil appropriate to what you wish to manifest; two other herbs appropriate to what you wish to manifest; a silver coin to offer to the Maiden; slips of paper and a pen (it is better that the ink be some color other than black: red, blue, or green, depending on what you wish to manifest). If you substitute olive oil for an appropriate essential oil, use three herbs instead of two.

To begin, ground and center, devote your altar, cast a circle, call the quarters, perform a working salute, and raise power with *A Black Forest Verse to Raise Power*, below.

A Black Forest Clan Verse to Raise Power

From the Earth and from the sky, Energy, I call Ye nigh.
From the Moon and from the Sun, let the holy power run
Through my body and my mind; Earth, Sky, Moon, and Sun be kind!
Stag and Bull, Horse, Bear, and Raven, let my circle be your haven;
Fill my tools and fill my hands with Your might at my command.
Till the circle is undone, let my life and Yours be one;
While your life beats in my breast, what I will, will manifest!
Let what starts now in this sphere go on when I'm gone from here;
Let the rhythm of this verse be that of the universe;
Let the power I now draw turn my wishes into law!
Seven times three; Wing! Hoof! Paw!

Invoke the Maiden Goddess, Macha, saying:

O, Macha, Maiden temptress, enchantress;
You who start the pounding in the breast and set the hand to reaching;
You whose beauty opens wide the bloodshot eye,
Who make the battle-weary male fit for the teaching;
You who spread the raven's wings across the sky;
You Whose crop of acorns is the heads of vanquished enemies;
You who win our wars of life with small gestures

2

That please and devastate those who would hold us back;
Who bring unease to their complacency with your disarming charms;
You who need only say the Word, and any would give All;
You before whom all resistant minds must fall;
Let Your Seductive Power flow into my arms
As I embrace Your fervent worship.
Mania, Mana, Mene, Minne — Your names on my lips—
Let now their utterance draw light from my small fires,
And bring manifested Form to my Desires.

Anoint the white candle, rubbing oil from the ends to the middle; energize by pressing between thumb and forefinger until fingers start to throb, while concentrating on the manifestations you wish to draw toward you. Place the candle in the cauldron and light it.

Sprinkle herbs appropriate to your desires around the base of the candle. Say:

Paper will give way to flame; the essence of the sord remains.
Fire destroy and fire create; let what's written be my fate.
Fly to the Maiden, fiery bird; bring back the fact behind the word.

Write the things you wish to manifest on slips of paper, visualizing yourself already having them. Ignite the slips in the flame of the candle, and let them fall into the mix in the cauldron. As they burn, say:

Truth released from word by fire, take your shape as I desire!
Maiden fire, bright, new, and warm, bring my wishes into form!

Sit for a few moments meditating, visualizing yourself as having and enjoying what you wish for. Say:

Lovely Maiden, thank Thee for Thine aid.
In love and trust, this offering is made.

Pass the silver coin three times through the flame of the candle, then drop or push it into the mixture of the cauldron.

To finish, perform the reverse salute, dismiss the quarters, and open the circle. Leave the candle burning in the cauldron until it is all gone. Save the mixture until your desires have manifested, then return it to the elements.

Moon Phase Timing

By Estelle Daniels

The most ancient astrology had to do with the Moon as she moved through the sky, starting as a small sliver, growing to bright fullness and then diminishing to a small sliver, only to appear three days later as a small sliver again. As the centuries progressed, people came to find that the Moon could be a marker for certain activities.

A basic type of astrology and timing is based upon the Moon and her cycles. There are three cycles of time markers which can be used effectively to time activities in accordance with the Moon's cycles. These are based upon a two-fold cycle (waxing/waning), a three-fold cycle (new, full, old) and a four-fold cycle (new, first quarter [waxing], full, third quarter [waning]).

When timing with the Moon, it is important to be as precise as possible in determining when the cycles change. An almanac or calendar will show the Moon phases (new, first quarter, full and last quarter), and these should be carefully noted. The exact time of the Moon phases signals the culmination, or highest energy, of that cycle, and the minute after the exact phase is the start of the next cycle. As an example, the Moon is waxing (increasing in light) when it is between New and Full. The Moon is waning (decreasing in light) when it is between Full and New. At Full it is considered "most waxed," and the influences of a waxing Moon are most potent. At new it is "most waned," and the influences of a waning Moon are most potent. After new is exact it is waxing, after full is exact it is waning. With this type of astrology, you are using very precise rules, and exact timing is one thing you have to be aware of.

Two-Fold Cycle

Mandala for this cycle is the yin-yang

Waxing Moon is good for starting things, new things (experiences, ideas, people, places, tangible items etc.), things which need to increase or grow, planting, planting above-the-ground crops, leaving on a trip, things which will be brought out into the open, bringing together, building, binding, gathering, summoning, action, birth and growth, heightened vitality, subjective awareness, building form, and developing structure.

WANING MOON is good for ending ventures, things which should decrease, wither, or die, dieting, harvesting, planting below-the-ground crops (root crops), things which should remain secret, banishing, loosing, sending away, returning home from a trip, reaction, loss, letting go, give-away, death and decay, lessened vitality, objective awareness, fulfilling purpose, and releasing meaning.

THE THREE-FOLD CYCLE

Mandala for this cycle is the triskelion

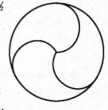

NEW MOON (from New to first trine, about 2 ½ days after first quarter) is the time for starting plans, projects, relationships; for getting ideas, gathering resources, planting seeds, starting research, leaving on a trip, entering an arena or coming out, enthusiasm, and high spirits. New Moon corresponds to the Maiden.

FULL MOON (from first trine through Full to second trine, about 4 ½ days after Full Moon) is the time for being in the public eye, the implementation and culmination of plans or projects, dissemination and application of ideas, application of research, harvesting the fruits of labors, doing business on a trip, taking a vacation, enjoying life, and just being. Full Moon corresponds to the Mother.

OLD MOON (from second trine to New Moon) is the time for wrapping up plans, projects, and relationships; reevaluation of ideas and their applications, refinement and storage of research, weeding and plowing crops under, planting and harvesting root crops, saving for the future, returning from a trip, hiding and being reclusive, evasion and secrets, endings, and winding down. Old Moon corresponds to the Crone.

THE FOUR-FOLD CYCLE

Mandala for this cycle is the Sun wheel

NEW MOON (from New Moon to first quarter) is the time to start projects and bring ourselves or ideas into the open. It is beginning, impulsive, emerging, initiating, subjective, instinctual, new, innovative, active, aspiring, and young. It corresponds to east, spring, and the rising Sun.

FIRST QUARTER (from first quarter to Full Moon) is the time to build, continue, change, perfect, and modify our projects and ideas. It is creative, active, adolescent, struggling, challenging, outgoing, vital, powerful, strong, and culminating will. It corresponds to south, summer, and the noontime Sun.

FULL MOON (from Full Moon to last quarter) is when our projects, plans, and ideas are released into the world. It is accomplishing, fulfilling, objective, conscious, and aware, relating, emotional, and mature. It corresponds to west, autumn, and the setting Sun.

LAST QUARTER (from last quarter to New Moon) is when we evaluate what we have done, see what worked and what did not, and take that and prepare for the next cycle; evaluating the past in the present with an eye to the future. It is releasing, assimilating, old, breaking down, letting go, consolidating, introspective, dreaming, silent, wise, renewing, and final. It corresponds to north, winter, and the midnight (invisible) Sun.

When using these Moon cycles, each element does stand alone, but it is also just a part of the greater cycle as a whole. Each cycle is one of birth, becoming, realization, actualization, culmination, examination, reevaluation, release, and then death, preparing for rebirth. Seeing your actions and activities as a part of the larger cycles around us, those of the Moon, Sun, or even the other planets, is a way of tuning yourself into the universe. If you time your important activities to these cycles, you can become more effective and aware in your daily life.

Spells for Paying Bills

By Silver RavenWolf

Pendulum Divination

Lay out all the bills on the altar face down. Light a silver or blue candle for mental clarity. Relax. Ground and center. Take your pendulum and ask which direction means yes. Then ask which direction means no. Now ask which bill you should pay first. When you receive the "yes" response, set that bill aside and mark down on a piece of paper which bill was chosen. Take your pendulum and ask which bill you should pay second and repeat the same procedure. Follow through with the successive bills.

Angels

Two angels, Anauel and Barakiel, are the positive energies of success. Call on them to help you pay your bills in a timely manner.

Zodiac Colors

Burn your zodiac color candle along with a green candle for one hour every day for seven days. As you light the candles, specifically intone what you want to draw toward you. Zodiac colors are: Aries—white or pink; Taurus—red or yellow; Gemini—light blue or silver; Cancer—green or brown; Leo—red or green; Virgo—gold or black; Libra—red or black; Scorpio—brown or black; Sagittarius—gray or silver; Capricorn—orange or brown; Aquarius—green or blue; and Pisces—white or green.

Symbols

Pass your personal checks through frankincense incense before you pay your bills. Draw a symbol of prosperity on your checkbook. Useful symbols are the triskele or the the pentacle. Draw these symbols in clove oil on all dollar bill increments.

Empower Your Paycheck

Empower your paycheck to stretch to meet all your needs. Anoint with clove oil before you cash it.

The Magic Money Jar Spell

By Silver RavenWolf

When March winds blow, and skies are bleak
And your checking account looks like welfare week
Go to your kitchen with a dash
Find a jar to bring some cash.

Get a tea bag, mint for sure
Brew a cup, you need no more.
In your little witches pot,
Add vervain, not a lot.

In goes dragons' blood and cinquefoil
Bring it all to a rolling boil.
Mix ingredients, stir it thrice
Cut the heat, throw in some ice.

On paper virgin, write your need
Be specific, ignore the greed.
Put the paper in the jar
To bring in riches from afar.

Call the Fates, yes all three
Ask them for prosperity
Here's the chant, it's easy now
Take your time to give it pow.

Three great ladies crossed the land
Each held prosperity in their hand
The first said, "She needs some."
The second said, "She has some."
The third said, "There is more to come."
"We turn three times, the way of the Sun."

Raise your energy, clap three times
Then seal the brew with a magical sign.
When it cools, pour in the jar
Close it tight, mark with a star.

A minor magic, I call this
To bring you monetary bliss
For extra punch, choose a planetary hour
Full Moon's good, for extra power.

When money comes, thank the Gods
Pour the contents on the sod
Return in like the gifts you got
And remember all the blessings brought.

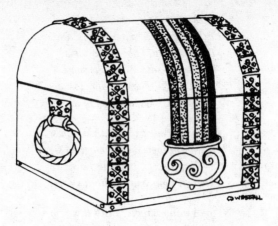

THE MAGIC MONEY BOX

BY EDAIN MCCOY

Chinese folklore stresses the importance of clearing debts before the beginning of the new year. This stems from a belief that what you take into the year with you will follow you out of it again. To this end, the first day after the last New Moon of the Chinese year is set aside as a time to make pilgrimages to the shrines of the deities of prosperity, to pay them homage and to ask their blessings in the year to come. The focus of the trek is often the shrine of Tsai Shin, a deity of prosperity and wealth, who may have been a pre-Shinto goddess of abundance.

At home, mothers help their families construct a wealth box, a magical portal for allowing wealth to come from the divine realms and manifest in the physical world of the home. The imagery which is the catalyst for the magic is that the box never runs dry, so some money must be left in it at all times. Remember the old magical adage: like attracts like.

To make a magical wealth box, start with a simple, box-like structure. This can be a cardboard box—easy to get at packaging stores—or a jewelry box, or something you make out of scrap wood.

When you have your box, consecrate it to your purpose by visualizing all previous energy or "programming" which the object may have absorbed being removed from it and sinking into the ground. Consecrate the box to its purpose by declaring it the domain of Tsai Shin, or of any other deity who represents monetary gain to you. Also, make a statement out loud declaring the box's purpose:

Magical Wealth Box, sacred of Tsai Shin, blessed be your task to keep me in money when it is needed and to assist in bringing me good luck. I ask only as much as I need as it is needed, no more and no less. That which comes to me shall not take away from the need of another, as by my will it harms none.

With paints, stickers, or any other means you like, decorate your box to taste. You might want to draw dollar signs or the sigil of your own country's currency on it. You might choose to draw the money itself, carve pentagrams or spirals, paste on pictures relating to wealth, or write on it the name(s) of deities you feel can help you in this quest. In China, the bat is considered an animal of good fortune and its image is used liberally on wealth boxes and other talismans of prosperity.

Start the box off on its task by placing one single dollar bill inside. This is the imagery of like attracts like—sympathetic magic which will help the box draw more wealth to you. Close and re-open the lid a few times just to get the idea across to your subconscious mind that this box can indeed produce money.

To make the box an even stronger talisman for prosperity, you might consider keeping various amounts of "mad money" in it, odd bits of cash which you can draw on for fun when it is needed. For example, you might pull out a little some night when you have had some exceptionally good news and want to celebrate by taking your family or friends out to dinner. This single act will strengthen the link between the box and its task, and will make it an excellent conduit for positive monetary gain.

CREATING MAGICAL SNOW PEOPLE

BY EDAIN MCCOY

Like Frosty the Snowman of the popular children's Christmas song, who comes to life when his icy head is topped with a magical chapeau, potent magical snow people can be crafted by today's creative magicians. The very act of molding the snow with one's own hands, time, interest, and personal energy sets in motion a sympathetic bond between crafter and creation which can be harnessed for magical purposes.

Perhaps the most common use for a magical snow person is as a ward, or guardian, of your home or property. As you roll the giant snowballs which will become the body of your guardian, be sure to visualize the snow person's intended function as a protector of the area on which it sits. You might even want to place a protective stone, herb, or talisman as the center of the snowball before you begin rolling, to strengthen this link.

When the snow guardian's shape is completed, dress it up with symbols of protection, either made from more snow, or with other items. Try a pentagram necklace, a sword or knife, a wand made out of the fallen branch of a protective tree, or a talisman of protection which you have made yourself.

When your ward is complete, verbally and visually charge it to remain on guard for you until it melts away.

You can also use the snow person as a conduit for personal magic, using it as a model for change. For example, as you roll the snow person, invest it with the energy of yourself, building as many links between you and the energy in the snow as possible. Adding some of your own hair to the snow person can help strengthen this bond.

As you craft your snow creature, mold it into a shape or image of some change you desire in your life. The most obvious use of this is for those who wish to gain or lose weight. Shape the snow to reflect the outward appearance you wish to have. For those who wish to lose weight, the image of the snow melting, which must eventually happen unless you live at the South Pole, can help boost this spell's effectiveness.

You can also use "your" snow image to intensify a spell for a desired job, success in an exam, or to help draw to you a possession you want to obtain. For example, add some item which reflects the job you want to the snow person. As you make this addition, view this image as representing current success, since present tense imagery always makes the best magic. To help bring a possession to manifestation, give your snow person a token of that item, such as a set of car keys for a new car.

If you have no immediate magical goal, but still want a way to connect with the power and enchantment of the snow, get your halloween finery out of storage and dress your snow creation up as a Witch or wizard. You will definitely be making a unique statement that will be the talk of your neighborhood!

Snow Magic

By Silver RavenWolf

So there you sit. The snow falls in rich flakes, then turns into a blinding fury. Is there magic in snow? You bet there is!

The snowflake epitomizes the crystalline magical womb of the All Mother—Holda or Hela. She represents the unity of all patterns. Within the structure of the snowflake all things form and evolve. Mother Holda has the mysterious powers of death and life. Her wild and destructive energies undulate in chaotic patterns, yet command deep respect.

Snowflakes crystallize in the shape of the ancient "hex star" symbol, which stands for cosmic wholeness and complete structure. This symbol, called the "hexefus," means Witches' cauldron or Witches' foot (the root of the witches' power). Therefore, snow magic can be a blessing or a bane, depending on how you use it.

Dame Holda commands and uses the "roads between the worlds." She flies among the "ghost roads" at night with the Gandreid, her ghostly company of witches and spirits. The goose flies beside her, an emblem of this spirit-flight. Snowflakes fall from the bird's wing feathers upon the world below, as the goose passes overhead at midnight. Mother Holda directly represents

Crone magic and the wisdom of grandmothers. Therefore, snow magic falls under the auspices of the Dark Mother. Here are some simple magics to try with snow:

* To melt hard feelings against you, gather snow that has fallen in a gentle storm. Write the name of the person who is giving you a hard time on a piece of paper. Put it in the middle of a glass plate. Take the snow and pile it on top. Add a dash of sugar. As the snow melts, the person in question will loosen his or her hold over you.

* To banish someone or something that has given you a lot of pain, take snow from a wild storm and follow the same procedure as in number one. Be sure to ask for Dame Holda's blessing and that the spell not reverse or place upon you any curse.

* Snow poppets are fun to make. If a friend is sick, fashion a tiny snow person, add something that belongs to him or her, such as a lock of hair. As the snow melts, your friend will get better.

* Instead of using your athame, cast a circle with one of those splendid icicles.

* Make snow wishes. With your staff or wand, carve your wishes in the snow. Ask Dame Holda to grant your wishes. Trace the hex star beside the wishes to seal them.

* Make a snow bottle. Write your wishes on a piece of paper and put the paper in a bottle packed with snow. As the snow melts, your wishes will be granted.

MAGICAL QUICKIES FOR INNER AND OUTER BEAUTY

BY SILVER RAVENWOLF

Many of us practice beauty regimes. Sometimes we pamper ourselves to improve our looks, other times we focus on raising our self esteem. Whatever the reason for practicing those beauty treatments, here are some fun magics to add as an extra ingredient.

◊ When taking a shower, imagine that each drop of water contains universal love that cleans and energizes your aura as well as your body.

◊ Is there something you want to draw toward you? Braid your hair. As you braid the hair, add a statement of positive affirmation. You can also braid enchanted flowers, ribbon, or yarn into your hair for a bigger magical punch.

◊ Enchant hair rollers and all makeup for prolonged beauty, universal love, higher self-esteem, spirituality, etc. Enchant lipstick to allow honesty and integrity to fall from your lips. Enchant perfume for thought and memory, and put it on your temples. Enchant eye makeup for clear vision into difficult problems. Enchant body lotion and soap to protect you throughout the day.

◊ Empower nail polish to bring abundance to you through everything you touch.

◊ Cleanse, consecrate, and empower all jewelry. Use special pins for unusual occasions, such as job hunting, interviews, house buying, solving a crisis, healing family disputes, etc.

These are just a few ideas to get your mental motor running. I'm sure you can come up with interesting magical ingredients to add to your beauty regime.

A Mirror in Candlelight

By Jim Garrison

S crying is quite simple and easy to do. Scrying is basically looking past the here and now to see things from another perspective. It is a magical application of the human faculty for visualization, in order to acquire information in a non-linear manner. You could call it an active form of meditation, as opposed to the usual receptive/passive mode that is commonly taught.

Instead of using the tarot—which does work very well for this sort of work—I want to share another way to begin exploring the possibilities of scrying. This will require a candle, a mirror, and a dim/dark space in which to experiment.

As with most magical practices, first you need to relax. Once you have relaxed a bit, set the mirror in front of you. Flat on the floor or a table top is fine. Now set the candle on the floor or table top at the top of the mirror and light the candle. You should sit so that you can easily and comfortably see the candle flame in the mirror. Relax.

Look into the candle flame reflected in the mirror. Relax.

Look past the reflection, through the reflected flame. Feel yourself flowing into the flame within the mirror. Let the flame fill your vision completely.

You are now in a place where you can see anything you wish—you have but to direct your vision and you will see what there is to see.

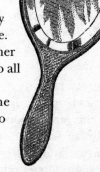

When the contact is broken, or your focus returns to your body, do a simple grounding and centering. Try eating something—that helps, usually.

I suggest writing in your journal. You may find that you "saw" much more than you realize. This can be a very subtle process, at times, other times it can be overwhelming—it varies due to all sorts of factors.

Now that you've tried fire, consider the ways you might use the rest of the elements to scry into the secrets of the universe.

Candles Talk To Me

By Silver RavenWolf

When you perform a magical application involving candles, there are various ways to tell not only the outcome, but the flavor of the present situation. Here's how you do it.

IF YOUR ILLUMINATOR CANDLES LIGHT THE FIRST TIME and have a strong flame, your workspace is conducive to your magic. If you have difficulty lighting your illuminator candles (or lamp), then outside influences may weaken your work. Do a thorough cleansing of the area, then re-light the candles. If the candles still carry a weak flame, check your astrological correspondences. Something may be amiss. For example, the Moon may be void of course. Or, perhaps doubt nibbles at the hem of your robe, and you worry about the magic you are planning.

IF YOUR ILLUMINATOR CANDLES (OR LAMP) PRESENT A WEAK FLAME throughout the magical operation, you may be facing some sort of barrier to your work. Weak flames can indicate instability, loss, and obstacles. Learn to feed the flame with south energy. Do this by drawing energy from the south with your receptive hand and feeding it into the flame with your dominant hand. Be sure to add an incantation to your work that will dissolve barriers and strengthen your cause. This rule holds true of focused candles—those candles that you are using for a specific magic.

IF YOUR ILLUMINATOR CANDLES (OR FOCUSED CANDLES) POSSESS A JUMPING FLAME, then things are certainly hot around the situation. Energy pumps with a steady rhythm in your environment. You must determine the desirability of this energy, and use this force accordingly.

IF YOU ARE USING TWO FOCUSED CANDLES where each candle stands for a particular person, watch the flames carefully. Is one flame stronger than the other? Does this mean that one person carries more authority, or has the winning hand in the emotional game? If both flames are jumping, both parties carry strong feelings about the other. You must determine if the situation refers to hatred or passion.

IF ANY CANDLE FLAME DANCES IN A DEOSIL PATTERN, your magic builds with the blessing of the elements and divinity. If any candle flame dances in a widdershins pattern, a banishing activity is at hand. If you don't want the banishing energy, use the appropriate incantation to correct this energy and send it in the proper direction.

IF ANY CANDLE FLAME CARRIES A PREPONDERANCE OF A SPECIFIC COLOR, then check your color correspondence charts to divine the meaning. For example, a greenish tint would indicate healing energy, or blue could mean a more spiritual benevolence. A rainbow flame indicates the presence of angels/spiritual helpers/or higher spiritual beings.

CANDLES OFTEN TALK TO YOU. The softer "chatter" denotes the purest energy. Frequent, mid-range chatter indicates the blusterings of an individual in authority. Harsh, strong chatter speaks of chaos.

THE DIRECTION OF THE CANDLE FLAME SHOWS YOU FROM WHENCE ENERGY WILL COME, and what kind of energy will surround your work. If the flame points to the north, the work is encompassed by stability, fertility, and a physical manifestation. If the flame points to the east, more mental pursuits will follow. Clarity of mind surrounds the working, and energies manifested will include hidden knowledge, ideas, and force of will. If the flame points to the south, daring and passion are afoot. Here, creativity and harvest will manifest, as well as possible physical lust and passion. If the flame points to the west, the energies surrounding you are more emotional in nature. Love, transformation, and emotive energies all fall under the auspices of west energy. If the flame burns straight up, then the higher spiritual planes plan to involve themselves in your working, and smooth sailing in the situation is assured.

Watch your candle flames carefully. I'm sure you can come up with additional divinatory meanings that you can tailor to your magical applications.

The Wizard and the Spring Maiden

A Children's Story for Imbolc

By D. J. Conway

The winter snows still lay thick over the frozen ground and the cold wind whistled through the bare limbs of the trees. Even the new Sun felt cold to the little birds, who huddled together in the trees to keep warm.

"The wizard isn't awake yet, is he?" asked a tiny chickadee.

"No, the door to his house is still closed." A bluejay cocked her head and stared down at the little hill in the meadow below. "I haven't seen so much as a hair of his beard at the window either."

"I wish the Maiden would awake. Then we would know spring will soon arrive." The chickadee fluffed his feathers as he looked off across the snow-covered fields.

A gray squirrel suddenly poked his head out of a hole in the tree and chattered at the birds in a grumbling voice. "What is all the noise out here?" he asked. "I'm trying to sleep, you silly birds!"

"The wizard is still asleep, and the Maiden hasn't awakened yet,"

the chickadees answered all at one time. "Perhaps there will be no spring this year." The bluejay flew to a limb nearer the squirrel and looked at him with her black eyes.

"Nonsense," the squirrel answered as he squeezed out of his hole to sit on the bare branch. "Spring always comes." He rubbed the sleep from his eyes, then fluffed his tail with his paws.

"We're so hungry," chirped the chickadees. "If the Maiden does-n't wake up soon, we will starve." The squirrel cocked his head, lis-tening for the sweet song of the Maiden as She calls everything in the forest to begin waking up. He heard nothing but the whistle of the cold wind and the rattle of the bare tree branches.

"This is the right time of year for the Maiden to wake and the young Sun King to dance through our forest," the squirrel said. He scratched his head as he thought. "I'll go wake the wizard and ask him if he knows why the Maiden still sleeps."

The squirrel dashed down the tree trunk and jumped out across the snow. In long leaps he ran across the ground until he reached the rocks surrounding the hidden door to the wizard's home. He stopped and listened, but he heard no movement within the hill-house.

"Wake up! Wake up, wizard!" The squirrel pounded on the door. "Sleepy old wizard," he grumbled to himself. "We need your help." He pounded again on the door with both paws.

Green Leaf, the little gnome wizard, stirred restlessly in his downy bed. Someone was pounding on his door, making a terrible racket that echoed through the rooms and halls of his snug little hill-house. He opened one eye and looked around the room.

One beam of pale sunlight crept through a crack in the shutters and lit up the face of the strange clock beside the wizard's bed. In-stead of hours and minutes, the clock face had the names of the sea-sonal festivals: Imbolc, Spring Equinox, Beltane, Summer Solstice, Lunasad, Autumn Equinox, Samhain, and Winter Solstice.

Green Leaf yawned, then opened both eyes to stare at the clock. "It's Imbolc!" he said as he sat up suddenly in bed. "I've overslept. Oh my, oh my."

The little gnome wizard scrambled out of his warm nest of blan-kets and hurriedly dressed. The pounding on his door kept banging through the hill-house.

"I'm coming," Green Leaf shouted as he hopped toward the door, pulling on his boots. He fumbled with the lock, finally opening the little door.

"The Maiden is still asleep!" exclaimed the squirrel. "There are no lambs in the fields! The young Sun King hasn't arrived! Hurry, wizard, hurry!"

Green Leaf sighed as he put on his heavy green cloak and his tall pointed red hat. With his wooden staff in one hand, he trudged out into the snow and headed for the thickest part of the forest. Soon he was deep inside the bare tree trunks and snow-covered firs and pines.

"I wish the Maiden would sleep in the same place each year," he grumbled, but he knew She didn't. It was his job each Imbolc to find Her sleeping place and wait there until the young Sun King arrived.

Green Leaf searched and searched for the sleeping Maiden until he at last found Her curled up in the shelter of a hawthorn thicket. She looked so beautiful, Her long hair falling down over Her arms, that Green Leaf couldn't be grumpy anymore. He smiled, then raised his arms and began to sing his Imbolc greeting to the Sun King.

The forest suddenly lit up with brilliant sunbeams as the young Sun King danced through the trees toward the gnome. The glow about Him was so bright that Green Leaf had to squint his eyes to see.

"Blessed Imbolc, Green Leaf." The deep voice and loving smile of the Sun King warmed the little gnome wizard. "Blessed Imbolc, Lord," Green Leaf answered as he bowed to the Sun King. "I thought I was late."

"No, my little friend. Everything in this world knows when Imbolc comes, all the animals and plants and even gnomes." The Sun King's smile lit up the trees around them. "Awake, my Lady," He said as He knelt to kiss the sleeping Maiden.

The Maiden sat up, stretched Her arms, and smiled. "It is time for all the world to wake," She said, and the Sun King nodded as He helped Her to Her feet. They went off together through the forest, dancing to awaken the life-energy of the Earth.

As Green Leaf trudged back through the snow to his hill-home, he could still hear the wake-up song of the Maiden and feel it spreading out through the world. Around him, the life-energy in the trees began to stir. Deep in the ground he could feel the little burrowing

creatures starting to wake from their winter sleep. The gnome wizard crossed the meadow where the sheep were and found the first of the newborn wobbly-legged spring lambs blinking in the sunlight.

"Welcome to the world," Green Leaf said to the little lamb. "Soon everything will be wide awake and growing. The grass will be sweet and green, and you will have other little lambs to play with." The lamb and its mother looked at the gnome wizard and blinked their eyes.

"Yes, the life-energy from the Maiden is once more running through the world, making everything new," Green Leaf said as he tramped down the path to his house. Suddenly, he felt the energy flowing through his own body. He leaped into the air and clicked his heels together in joy. "The Maiden is awake!" he shouted to the squirrel and the birds waiting for him near his door.

Green Leaf went back inside his hill-house and hung up his cloak and hat. "Now I am going to have a cup of tea, then go back to bed and have a nap until Spring Equinox." And the little gnome wizard did just that.

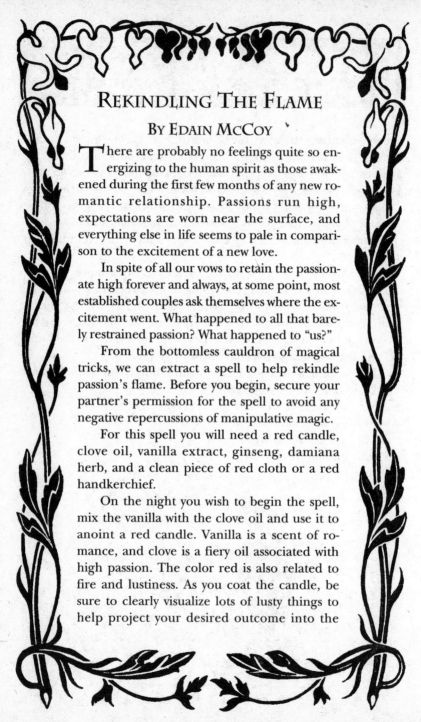

REKINDLING THE FLAME

By Edain McCoy

There are probably no feelings quite so energizing to the human spirit as those awakened during the first few months of any new romantic relationship. Passions run high, expectations are worn near the surface, and everything else in life seems to pale in comparison to the excitement of a new love.

In spite of all our vows to retain the passionate high forever and always, at some point, most established couples ask themselves where the excitement went. What happened to all that barely restrained passion? What happened to "us?"

From the bottomless cauldron of magical tricks, we can extract a spell to help rekindle passion's flame. Before you begin, secure your partner's permission for the spell to avoid any negative repercussions of manipulative magic.

For this spell you will need a red candle, clove oil, vanilla extract, ginseng, damiana herb, and a clean piece of red cloth or a red handkerchief.

On the night you wish to begin the spell, mix the vanilla with the clove oil and use it to anoint a red candle. Vanilla is a scent of romance, and clove is a fiery oil associated with high passion. The color red is also related to fire and lustiness. As you coat the candle, be sure to clearly visualize lots of lusty things to help project your desired outcome into the

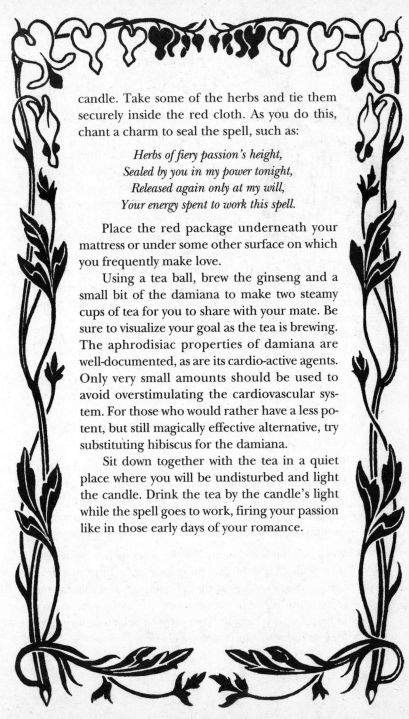

candle. Take some of the herbs and tie them securely inside the red cloth. As you do this, chant a charm to seal the spell, such as:

Herbs of fiery passion's height,
Sealed by you in my power tonight,
Released again only at my will,
Your energy spent to work this spell.

Place the red package underneath your mattress or under some other surface on which you frequently make love.

Using a tea ball, brew the ginseng and a small bit of the damiana to make two steamy cups of tea for you to share with your mate. Be sure to visualize your goal as the tea is brewing. The aphrodisiac properties of damiana are well-documented, as are its cardio-active agents. Only very small amounts should be used to avoid overstimulating the cardiovascular system. For those who would rather have a less potent, but still magically effective alternative, try substituting hibiscus for the damiana.

Sit down together with the tea in a quiet place where you will be undisturbed and light the candle. Drink the tea by the candle's light while the spell goes to work, firing your passion like in those early days of your romance.

LET ANGELS HELP YOU WITH UNREQUITED LOVE

BY SILVER RAVENWOLF

It's true. We've all been through it. Someone doesn't love you anymore. What an ego blaster. You experience a compendium of emotions—you hate him or her, your self-esteem plummets; you hate the other woman, or man, as the case may be; you hurt deep inside—that awful aching thing. You don't want to eat, or you are eating non-stop. Life is the pits. If people tell you to forget it and go on, you get angry at them. If you've had mutual friends, chances are you've lost their attention too, as they wander off to the Benedict Arnold's circle. Bring in the angels.

- Talk to your guardian angel. Let it all out. Your fears, your hatreds, your hurt and pain.

- Let the other person go. Yes, let him or her go. If he or she really cares about you, he or she might, maybe, possibly, come back (but don't count on it). Clean out the place. Get rid of memorabilia that makes you sad. Pack or give it away.

- Do nice things for yourself. Go out and eat dinner with a friend, visit an amusement park, go swimming—get out of the house! Take up a new hobby or sport where you will meet other people. You don't have to be romance shopping, just bring new life into your people network.

- Work on your self-esteem. When someone leaves you it is your pride that is the first thing to tumble. Buy some new clothes, work on a goal that pleases you and makes you feel worthwhile, donate some time to charity (that always helps). Do anything that makes your self-esteem rise, as long as it doesn't hurt anyone else.

- Looking your best, go have your picture taken. You think I jest? You can get nice pictures for under twenty dollars. Set this picture on a tray on your altar.

- Go to the kitchen and make some angel sugar. That's right—angel sugar; two cups of white sugar and one teaspoon of vanilla. Mix it together, then spread it out on tin foil or wax paper to dry for four hours (or more depending upon the climate of your area). Smash out the lumps with a spoon. Empower all of the sugar, then put some in an airtight container and take some to your altar. Spread the sugar on the tray around your picture in circle.

- Ask the angels to heal your pain and empower you to continue your mission in life. Be specific and concentrate on what you feel you really need. Is it a change of scenery, a new job, new friends? Be fair and honest in your assessment of your life.

- Leave your picture on your altar with the sugar until you start feeling better, and can see that the pain is moving away, and healing has begun. Use the sugar in the container on your cereal, in your coffee, or on a dessert. Every time you take it into your body remember that the angels are with you and you are being healed.

The angel sugar also works well in other occasions. For example, if someone is giving you a rough time at work, in the family, in your circle of friends, etc., you can sprinkle a little angel sugar on his or her desk, in his or her food, or whatever, and ask the angels to take a special look at the problem to help you resolve your differences. Call the angel Balthial to help you overcome feelings of jealousy and bitterness.

You can also take a bowl of angel sugar, put the disagreeable person's name on a piece of paper, bury it in the bowl, then stick a brown candle in the bowl and burn it, asking the angels to promote harmony. This worked so well for one of my clients that her on-the-rocks-relationship did a complete turnaround and she married the guy. They are happy and comfortable in their new life.

Bringing Love Into Your Life
With the Angels

By Silver RavenWolf

There is nothing worse in the world than feeling lonely and unloved. Every time these feelings come close to you, don't forget that you are never alone—your guardian angel is always with you and you are loved by all the angels and divinity combined. To bring love toward you try this simple seven day magic.

Day to Perform: Friday (the Venus Day).

Angelic Hour to Perform: Uriel.

Moon Phase: New (Reminder: Do not perform when the Moon is void of course).

Supplies: Two pink taper candles, a picture of yourself, and a red heart cut out of construction paper.

Angels to Call: Hahaiah, who inspires positive and loving thoughts; or Anael, who is in charge of love, passion and romance; Hael who inspires art, kindness, mercy and beauty; or Mihr, who will find you a loyal friend or heal a broken friendship, or you may prefer a chant of angelic names: Raphael, Rahmiel, Theliel, Donquel, Anael, and Liwet.

- Begin by working at your altar. Cleanse, consecrate, and empower the pink candles. On the back of the heart write your desire. Warning: Do not call a specific person. That is against free will and the angels will not help you. Instead, call loving thoughts toward you, friendship, companionship, etc. Please be specific. Ground and center.

- In a ritual, call your Guardian Angel and invoke both divinity and the angel you have chosen to help you. Be honest and forthright. Don't ask for what you don't really want. Operate only in harmony with the Universe.

Set the two pink candles about one foot apart with your picture between the two candles. Place the heart on top of your picture. Light the candles and allow them to burn for five minutes. Move the two candles a little closer together then put them out.

Thank divinity and the angels for helping you.

The next evening at the same time, repeat this procedure, and every night thereafter until the seventh day. On the seventh day make sure both candle holders are touching the picture and the heart. Let the candles burn until there is nothing left. Take the heart and your picture (keep them together) and put them in a safe, undisturbed place. When what you have called comes to you, be sure to go back to your altar and thank both divinity and the angels for your good fortune. You may keep the heart and picture together as long as you like.

LOVE ARABIAN STYLE

BY MARGUERITE ELSBETH

Once upon a time, the Sultan Schahriar was disappointed in love. Vowing he would never be deceived again, he took a new wife to his bed every evening and had her strangled the following morning. Then Schahriar took Scheherazade, the beautiful, intelligent, cultured daughter of his Grand Vizier, to wife. She regaled him with exciting stories for a thousand and one nights, thus remaining alive far beyond the eve of their wedding feast, as well as saving other women from an evil fate.

Today, Arabia remains an exotic land steeped in mystery; the sensual magic of Arabic love concealed behind veils of dark, shadowy secrets. In Saudi Arabia, the shroud which covers women is quite literal, for a woman may not be seen in public without a black, full-length outer garment to cover her clothes, and a veil made of black fabric to cover her face. Often the Saudi woman is confined to her home and may travel only when accompanied by a man who is her father, husband, brother, or uncle. Therefore, unlike the days of Scheherazade, it is more common for a woman to "speak" to her lover in symbolic gestures, rather than in words:

❧ Should a man receive a gift of salt and charcoal, it means that his lover believes his only concerns are money and the pretty lies he tells.

❧ If a man receives a die-cut bone or a child's play stick for a present, his lover may feel that although his body is present his heart is absent or yearning for another.

❧ If a woman serves a man a date with the pit still inside, she is telling him that her passionate heart will not sleep and that she greatly desires his company.

❧ To gift a man with carob beans means that he must be patient, even though the lovers can hardly wait for love.

Mock Goose and
Other Irish Delights

By D. J. Conway

If you have ever had the good fortune to sit down at an Irish dinner table, you know the meaning of a hearty meal. One recurring ingredient is the potato, for the Irish have long used potatoes as a staple part of their diet. However, there are other interesting Irish dishes as well.

Mock Goose

Beef and potatoes were regular parts of Irish meals, so the cooks knew a number of ways to use these ingredients. The measurements listed here are as they were handed down to me, so cooks must adjust them to suit themselves.

- 1 large piece of thick beef steak

  Dried sage to taste

  Mashed potatoes
- 1 bunch green onions or 1 small yellow onion

  Salt and pepper to taste

Preheat oven to 350°F. Take the piece of thick beef steak. If this is a cheaper cut of meat, you might want to trim off all the fat and tenderize it by pounding with a steak hammer or the edge of a plate. Just be sure you don't make holes in it. If you don't have one large steak, make individual smaller steaks in the same manner. Sprinkle the meat lightly with dried sage. Spread mashed potatoes over the raw steak, leaving a bare edge all around. Chop 1 bunch of green onions or 1 small yellow onion and sprinkle this over the potatoes. Season with salt and pepper to taste. Roll up the steak with the ingredients on the inside. Tie tightly with a string so it stays together. Roast uncovered at 350°F until the steak is done, but not dry. If you don't want to use an oven, brown the steak in a skillet with a spray of oil. Then place it in a baking dish, cover, and microwave at the equivalent of 350°F for 25–30 minutes, depending on

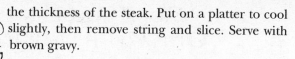

the thickness of the steak. Put on a platter to cool slightly, then remove string and slice. Serve with brown gravy.

PRATIE SALMON

I am not a fan of fish in any form, but this I will eat. This recipe is also a good way to stretch expensive salmon. You can use fresh salmon that has been baked, or use canned. This Irish dish probably originated from a desire to find a new way for leftovers using the ever-familiar potato.

1 cup salmon, cooked, cooled, de-boned, and flaked
4 cups mashed potatoes
1 small onion, finely chopped
 Milk, if needed
 Oil for frying
 Salt and pepper to taste

Stir together salmon and potatoes. Add onion. Stir until blended. Form into flat patties. If too dry, mix in a little milk. Heat a small amount of oil in a skillet. Place the pratie salmon cakes into the oil. Salt and pepper them to taste. Fry lightly on each side. Serve with a white gravy. Delicious! If you don't have salmon, make the praties with just the onion. Cook in the same way.

BREAD AND BUTTER PUDDING

This was always a special treat which my grandmother served with her own hard-sauce. Hard-sauce is very sweet, but oh so scrumptious on the hot pudding.

8 slices white bread
 Butter
1 cup raisins
½ teaspoon nutmeg, divided, plus extra for sprinkling
½ cup sugar, plus extra for sprinkling
2 eggs
1 cup heavy cream
2 cups milk
4 drops vanilla
½ cup sugar

Preheat oven to 350°F. Remove the crusts from bread and butter one side of each slice. Put 4 slices, buttered side down, in a small baking dish. Sprinkle raisins over the bread; sprinkle with ¼ teaspoon nutmeg and sprinkling sugar. Place the remaining four slices of bread on top, buttered side down, and sprinkle with remaining ¼ teaspoon nutmeg and sprinkling sugar. Lightly beat eggs until lemon-colored. Add heavy cream, milk, vanilla, and the ½ cup white sugar. Mix well. Pour this over the layered bread and add a sprinkle of nutmeg on the top. Bake in the oven for one hour, or until the liquid is all absorbed and the mixture is golden brown. Serve with hard sauce (below), whipped cream, or a scoop of vanilla ice cream. I have never found a recipe for hard-sauce elsewhere, so it may well have been from my grandmother's family.

HARD SAUCE

½   cup margarine, softened
     (not melted!)
1½ cups powdered sugar
½   teaspoon vanilla

Blend together margarine and powdered sugar. If the mixture is too soft, keep adding powdered sugar until it just holds together. Blend in vanilla. Serve as is with the hot pudding.

33

Magical Meals

By Rachel Raymond

The evening meal has traditionally been an occasion for familial bonding. Supper was a time to come together, to break bread, to share in the day's events, and to give thanks to Mother Earth for Her bounteous blessings.

You can perform powerful magic by preparing and consuming your food with magical intent. The most important elements of a magical meal are the ingredients, the way those ingredients are prepared, and the way the meal is presented.

There are foods which are appropriate to each sabbat and esbat in the wheel of the year. When preparing the menu for your magical meal, you may wish to incorporate a seasonal theme, or focus on a specific personal or group goal, such as prosperity or healing.

Organize a magical feast with your friends, or for a magically nurturing gift, prepare a bewitching meal for a loved one (with their consent of course: it's no fair feeding magic to the unwary or unwilling). The following is a brief guide to the magical qualities of food.

Flesh

Since ancient times people have ingested the flesh of animals in order to absorb qualities of the animal which they wanted to emulate. During an important festival the animal would have been blessed and sacrificed. Its entrails would have been used to divine portents for the community, and the meat would have been roasted and shared by all present. When consuming flesh for magical purposes, be aware that it is a very powerful act. The energies of what you consume become part of you. Beef, pork, lamb, seafood, or fowl of any kind are all flesh, as are eggs. Eggs symbolize the force of creation itself as well as the manifested physical world.

Dairy

Milk is one of the four sacred fluids. Dairy products are good for imparting energies of love, nurturing, and acceptance.

GRAINS, LEGUMES, AND NUTS

All grains impart energies of fertility and prosperity. Beans enhance psychic powers, increase divinitory skills, and assist you in contacting those who have crossed over. Each type of nut has a rich esoteric lore of its own. All contain energies which impart wisdom, magical abilities, and sexual potency.

VEGETABLES AND FRUITS

Cruciferous vegetables such as cabbage and broccoli are governed by the Moon and have protective energies. Greens attract wealth. Onions and garlic are for protection and healing. Squashes and potatoes create energies of love and abundance. Citrus fruits are purifying. All fruits enhance love, fertility and prosperity.

HERBS

There are many magical herbs which double as cooking herbs. Basil is used for protection, prosperity, and communicating with dragons. Rosemary is for purification; and sage is for psychic cleansing.

BREAD, CAKES, AND COOKIES

Bread is the original magical food. The act of making bread with your hands is both soothing and satisfying. Magical loaves can be made for any purpose. Sesame seed bread is good for fertility and prosperity; dill bread is good for protection. Once your loaf is ready to bake, you can inscribe magical symbols on it. Bread still plays a central role in many religious rites. Christmas cookies are full of pagan symbolism as are danish pastries and birthday cakes.

BEVERAGES

Spring water is an all-purpose powerful magical beverage. Juices take on the qualities of the plant from which they are made. Red wine was often used as a magical substitute for blood in ancient rituals. Beer takes on the qualities of the grains from which it is made. All beers are sacred to the Goddess.

INTENT

As with any magical process, intent is everything. Throughout the entire preparation be sure to keep your goal in mind. Reinforce your magical workings by inscribing magical symbols into the food.

Once the food is ready to eat, set your table as though it were an altar. There will most likely be nothing arcane in the appearance of your magical dining table. Candles, flowers, special tokens of the season—these are common objects to find on an altar or a table's centerpiece. This is because in ancient times the dining table was the household altar.

Next ground, center and cast a circle. Hold your hands over the table and invoke the energy (love, peace, prosperity, etc.) you want to work with. Take some time to integrate and harmonize all the energies contained in the food and in your table setting. Visualize your goal and direct all your energy into the meal in front of you.

A Magical Meal

The following is an example of a magical meal for prosperity. Remember this is only a suggested meal plan. Be sure to tailor it to your own needs and tastes.

Pita Bread

Hummus

Tahini (sesame seed butter)

Cornbread

Millet flavored with basil, honey, pine nuts, and salted to taste

Spinach with lemon

Fresh vine-ripened tomatoes with basil, grapes and figs

Ginger Tea

Chocolate anything for dessert

Centerpiece

Your centerpiece may include a green and/or gold tablecloth, money, gold trinkets, jewelry, nuts, dried corn ears, cornucopias, dried squash, agates, jade, and green and/or gold candles.

If you are hoping to enhance your prosperity in your chosen career, be sure to include symbols of that in your altar. An artist might choose a paint brush; a computer programmer could use a floppy disc; a car mechanic might use a wrench. Spray your chosen object gold and decorate it with faux gems. After the meal place it on your personal altar or hang it prominently at your workplace.

Last but not least, eat your magical meal and enjoy it to the utmost. Now is the time to surrender to your gastronomic bewitchery and enjoy the fruits of your magical labors.

Once you have tasted your first magical meal, you will be sure to want to repeat the experience so eat, drink, and bewitch, and may all your meals be magical ones.

SUGGESTED READING

Beyerl, Paul. *The Master Book of Herbalism.* Washington: Phoenix Publications, 1984.

Cunningham, Scott. *The Magic in Food.* St. Paul, MN: Llewellyn Publications, 1990.

Cunningham, Scott. *Cunningham's Encyclopedia of Magical Herbs.* St. Paul, MN: Llewellyn Publications, 1985.

How to Communicate with Your Pet

By Marguerite Elsbeth

The animal companions we choose as pets have much to teach us, and we have a lot to learn, especially in the way of communication. I knew of a family who had a pot-bellied pig named Taylor. Usually Taylor was well-behaved, but every time Grandpa Jones came for a visit, Taylor would do something nasty on the living room rug. Close communication revealed that Taylor resented Grandpa referring to him as "Porkchop." In fact, the pig knew exactly what Grandpa had in mind, because Grandpa visualized juicy, succulent porkchops every time he called Taylor by that name. Obviously Taylor was threatened and angered by Grandpa's rude mental imagery.

Pet Talk

Animals are psychic. Because they are primarily feeling creatures and spend so much time dreaming, they are accustomed to think in pictures. Therefore, in order to communicate with your pet, you must learn to increase your ability to transmit and receive mental images, so that you can fulfill your pet's wants and needs as well as your own.

First, "bone" up on your own innate super-sensory abilities. Gaze at a candle flame. Hold an image in your mind, such as a cube or circle. Now, watch for certain telling signs that your pet needs to talk. For example, if Hairball, your beloved cat, takes to sitting on your head every time your friends come over, she may be jealous, cold, lonely, or simply letting you know that her glorious pelt is far more attractive than your new hair-do. Or, should Puddles the Pooch not respond when you call his name, he may a) want a bribe, or b) want a new name.

Finally, once you have determined that something unusual is happening with your pet, try the following: Catch your pet's attention. Look into his or her eyes. Leave your mind blank to receive an image. Fashion a response image and send it to your pet

Trust me. With a lot of patience and a little practice, you and your pet will be communicating beyond words in no time!

Tails Out of the Flame:
Cats in Ritual

By Cerridwen Iris Shea

I share my home with four cats: Olivia, Felicia, Maude, and Elsa. They are not pets; they are cohabitants, and they participate in ritual with me. However, they are cats, and once in awhile they will get distracted by something fascinating and nearly get us all in trouble. My apologies to dog lovers out there—I too, love dogs. I don't happen to live with them, however, so I am concentrating on cats here.

The distinct personalities of each cat play a large part in how they work in ritual, so please indulge me for a moment while I introduce them. Olivia, at age nine and all black, is queen cat. She is a Taurus, and is therefore very home and hearth oriented. Most of the time, she is placid and easygoing, but when she puts her paw down, the others pay attention. Felicia, age seven, is black and white. A Gemini, she is very quick-witted and intelligent. I had to get rid of my microwave because she figured out how to run it. She liked to watch the carousel turn inside. Felicia can also negotiate all cabinets (even child safety ones), the fax machine, and those dry food machines that supposedly ration out the food for seven days. Maude, four, and also all black, is an Aries. She loves attention, but, because she was abused before I got her, is suspicious of all other humans. She hisses at unknowns, and is afraid every meal is her last. She will literally go through fire if she thinks there's food on the other side. Elsa is an orange and black tortoiseshell. She looks like a black cat who fell into a pumpkin pie and never quite got cleaned off. She is a true Leo, and believes life is wonderful and that everyone is her friend.

Olivia, Felicia, Maude, and Elsa have each been in ritual with me ever since they joined the household. I keep my quarter candles in jars, which means the cats are less likely to catch their tails in the flame or knock a candle over and start a fire. The cats are quite good at leaving my altars alone, although Elsa does like to curl up on the copper pentacle on my primary altar and nap. If they start playing with something they shouldn't, I tell them firmly, "no" and remove them. I give them other toys to distract them. The only time I raise my voice is if I am doing work with free-standing candles and one of them could get hurt.

They are familiar with all of my tools. I let them sniff each new object as I bring it into the household, and then they know what it is and leave it alone. I did wake up once in the middle of the night to find Elsa playing hockey up and down the hallway with my crystal ball, but she seems to have gotten over that stage. I find that if I don't make my items "forbidden" they are easily accepted, and it doesn't become a game of let's-explore-them-when-she's-not-looking.

In a cast circle, my cats are beautifully behaved. I was the most concerned about Elsa, as, at the time of this writing, she is only four months old and firmly believes that everything was put on this Earth to either be eaten or to serve as a cat toy. The first time I cast a circle with Elsa in the room she was fascinated, but watched the others to see what they did. Because they were calm, and I was calm, she was calm.

Each has a preferred spot within the circle. Usually, after a few minutes, Olivia will curl up and go to sleep. Felicia is partial to tarot cards; Olivia and Maude to runes. Elsa, needless to say, likes crystal ball and mirror work. Once in awhile, someone will sneak a drink from my cauldron or the chalice, but I can live with that. If I am seated, Maude and/or Elsa will be in my lap. Maude is especially sensitive to chakras, and will lie on whichever chakra is the most vulnerable at the time. Usually, all of them are purring, which can lead to some interesting images in deep meditation.

Once or twice a year, I cast a special circle just for the cats, dedicated to either Bast or to the Irish goddess Flidais, in which I bless each one of them individually for the love, joy, and companionship they bring to my life, and ask for their continued happiness and good health. The cats enjoy it and I enjoy it.

I have found these tips most helpful when working with cats:

- Remain calm. If you get tense, they get tense. Animals pick up your vibrations and emotions. If they do something they are not supposed to, say "no" calmly and firmly. Remove the object from them, or remove them from the object. If necessary, take a spray bottle or a bottle of apple bitters into the circle with you. You can spray the cats with water and you can spray objects with apple bitters.

- Don't leave candles unattended. This is a general rule anyway, but even more important when animals are around. Even the best behaved animal can be frightened or startled by an unexpected noise, or get curious about something just beyond the flame.

- Include instead of exclude. Try to keep the cat with you in meditation, however, and create a calming ritual for the cat. The cat will enjoy the attention. If you cat is especially rambunctious, however, you may need to put him or her in another room. The ritual work should not become competition with the cat for your attention, but something you can do together. If the cat is frightened or upset during ritual, pay attention. There might be negative energies around that could be detrimental to the work. Take the extra few minutes to hone in on those energies and cleanse the space again, if need be. I have learned a great deal about serenity, intuition, and play from having my cats with me in ritual. After all, what better connection with both nature and spirit than an animal?

Aztec Animal Soul Magic

By Marguerite Elsbeth

The Nahuat Indians of central Mexico believe that every person has an animal soul, or nagual, born on the same day and at the same moment that the person is born. We share our fate with this creature; whatever happens to it also happens to us.

The nagual can be any kind of critter one can imagine. The naguals are kept by the Lord of Animals in great corrals in Talocan, the Aztec underworld. He cares for them and safeguards them, helping those who help him to protect his spirit animals. So, in this way, we are protected also. The Nahuat also say that a person can have more than one nagual.

Would you like to learn which animal is your nagual, your protective guardian spirit? First, create an Aztec-style altar as follows.

CREATING AN AZTEC ALTAR

- Arrange pictures of your living relatives, friends and acquaintances, and even your pets, on the altar table. This area represents the Earth.

- Dress the altar daily with a vase of fresh white flowers, five little glasses of water, some fresh tortillas or bread, and a small plate of just-cooked food. Also keep a pack of strong, dark tobacco cigarettes as well as a bottle of good liquor on the altar, as the spirits of the underworld like to smoke and drink.

- Hang pictures of your favorite deities and saints on the wall above and behind your altar. This area represents the sky.

- Place a box or trunk containing relics and mementos of your deceased ancestors, such as articles of clothing or cherished books or jewelry, underneath your altar. This area represents Talocan, the region of the underworld.

🔸 Keep a small votive candle burning at all times, or as often as is safe.

FIND YOUR NAGUAL

🔸 Now, dream in the Aztec underworld, where animal soul magic happens.

🔸 Prepare a sleeping place in front of your altar. Every night, after the house is quiet and you are ready for bed, light five white candles on the altar.

🔸 Sit and pray to the powers that be, to the underworld spirits and the Lord of the Animals in Talocan, that your nagual, your animal soul, will appear to you in a dream. Now go to sleep.

🔸 Write down your dreams in a journal, making sure to note any animals that are prominent. The one that shows itself most often is your nagual.

🔸 Try to make contact with the animal in real life.

🔸 Acquire some part of the animal, such as some hair or fur, a claw or tooth, and keep it in a box below your altar.

🔸 "Feed" your nagual regularly by making food offerings of the things it likes to eat in life.

BIBLIOGRAPHY

Knab, Timothy J. *A War of Witches: A Journey into the Underworld of the Contemporary Aztecs.* San Francisco: Harper Collins Publishers, 1995.

KIHA: THE KING OF HAWAII

BY BERNYCE BARLOW

In Hawaiian lore there are many rich and colorful legends which give the interested voyeur a peek at a culture that runs deep among the island chain. The story of Kiha, the king of Hawaii, is one of those legends, handed down carefully through generations of royal bloodline Hawaiians, whose primary responsibility was to recite intact the original accounts of their families' genealogy and holy history. The epic of Kiha and the kiha-pu is indeed magical, and a favorite among the islanders.

First, I will tell you of Kiha, a king of Hawaii. In his family was a mystical shell charm, a war-clarion that could be heard for many miles when sounded. The sacred shell had been in Kiha's family for generations, and had been passed on to him accordingly. Kiha called upon all the magical qualities of this shell in a way that had never before been achieved. In his hands, the kiha-pu (as the shell is called) became all powerful. Stories about the king's battle victories were directly related to his ability to summon up the supernatural with the kiha-pu when in need of assistance. This strategy worked so well that Kiha's reign was relatively a quiet one, but when the kiha-pu was stolen from its altar and replaced by a grotesque carved stone face, the strategy worked against him. Had the king lost his power? The secret was out!

Not to let this secret undermine his authority, Kiha announced to his people the clarion had been misplaced and was again found. The truth of the matter is that it was missing for eight long years, stolen by a band of rag-tag misfits whose leader's name was Ika. With the prestige of the kiha-pu to boost his importance, Ika became boastful and cruel, which led his companions to eventually compromise his position by having a sympathetic priest secretly place a tabu cross, or pea mark, on the shell, voiding it of its powers.

When Ika next blew the kiha-pu its sound was ordinary. Its magic was gone and he knew it, yet he continued to keep the shell

44

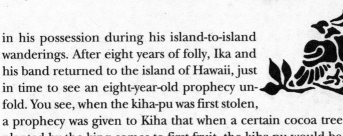

in his possession during his island-to-island wanderings. After eight years of folly, Ika and his band returned to the island of Hawaii, just in time to see an eight-year-old prophecy unfold. You see, when the kiha-pu was first stolen, a prophecy was given to Kiha that when a certain cocoa tree planted by the king comes to first fruit, the kiha-pu would be retrieved. With the tree grown and its fruit ready to eat, Kiha prepared to take revenge on those who had stolen his most precious possession.

The exact day the fruit of the cocoa was offered and eaten by the king, he heard from his spies of a band of wild men, marauders, who had taken up residence in the mountains near Waipio. Around the same time, Kiha's men had dragged a prisoner and his dog to where the king was meeting with his counsel. The man had been accused of stealing from the royal estate, a crime punishable by death. The thief was old and tattered, and around his neck he wore an ivory charm of a dog's foot. He appeared savage to the court. The intruder's dog was also a sight, with its blue-black unkempt coat, one glaring green eye, and one white eye. Its tail was scraggly and its ears almost human. It was a demon-dog if the king had ever seen one! The prisoner confided that the dog was a spirit thief with the intelligence of a kahuna, a magical cur driven by supernatural instincts. He then offered the services of the dog in exchange for favor.

Meanwhile, Kiha's spies had located the kiha-pu in Ika's camp, so a plan was put into action. The diabolic dog would steal back the magical shell! Under the cover of night, Kiha met with the owner of the dog to explain what needed to be done. The old man understood and assured the king the dog understood as well.

No one knows what form the dog took to enter the camp or how the dog knew of the hiding place of the shell. Legend only tells us the dog captured the kiha-pu by some magical means. With the clarion in his mouth, the dog descended the steep ravines below Ika's encampment at breakneck speed to avoid detection. During this descent, the war-trumpet was dropped, chipping off the pea mark on its rim. Once the tabu cross was removed, the power of the kiha-pu was restored. Picking up the sacred charm, the dog continued his journey, racing through the jungles like the wind. Upon the dog's return, the outer gate of the heiau was opened by the prisoner, the dog dashed forward, dropped the shell at the feet of the king, and died.

The king then raised the kiha-pu to his lips and the trumpet sounded a glorious wail full of might and mystery. Overjoyed, the king allowed the dog's grieving owner to be fed from the royal table from that day on, then set into tale the account of the green-eyed demon dog and the kiha-pu. As for Ika and his band, most were killed in combat with the king's warriors, except for Ika and two others who were taken alive for the altar sacrifice at the sacred temple of Paakalani. With the king's confidence and power restored, and the magical trumpet blasting throughout the valleys, Kiha settled in for a successful, peaceful reign.

Magic Business Cards

By Silver RavenWolf

In generations past, it was appropriate for one to leave his or her card when making a call on an individual of importance. Since that time, business cards have moved from the social drawing room to the corporate arena. You're nobody in today's competitive world unless you carry a business card and can produce it on demand at both business and social functions. Since magical people deal with a wide variety of customers, clientele, and acquaintances, however, it is not always wise to proclaim your occult affiliations on your card.

Once you have chosen the design for your card and have that fresh box of thousands in your hand, it is time to cleanse, consecrate and empower this important tool. Cleanse the box by sprinkling it with holy water, running it through purifying incense, slipping a candle flame (quickly, very quickly) under the box, then dabbing the box with salt.

Hold the box up to the sky, asking the Mother and Father to bless your work and to send harmonious energy into the cards. Ask that the cards go forth into the world, bringing you prosperity, peace and happiness. You may also ask that all negative energies that could work their way toward you be dispelled.

As you take the cards out of the box to fill your wallet or purse, hold them tightly, affirming your positive intentions and visualizing abundance. As your cards leave your hand during the networking process, again affirm your positive feelings and the desire for abundance. Ask that the right people get, and keep, your card.

Cards can hold magic from thirty to ninety days. After that, you will need to rework the magic. If, for some reason, you choose to destroy the cards and purchase new ones, remember to de-activate the cards before trashing them.

A Magical Glossary of Hawaiian Words

By Bernyce Barlow

Aha: a tabu prayer.

Aka: a shadow.

Aku: a mythical bird of the kahunas.

Akua: a spirit or a god.

Anu: a container in the temple from which oracles came.

Anuenue: praying someone to death.

Aumakua: a dead ancestor.

Haiao: a day sacrifice.

Haipo: a night sacrifice.

Haili: a ghost.

Heiau: a sacred temple.

Iku-pan: priestly bloodline.

Iu: a sacred place.

Kahoaka: a living spirit or aura seen by priests.

Kahuna: class of priest, medicine man, or sorcerer.

Kaike: a ceremonial drum.

Kapu: a tabu.

Kapua: wizard.

Kaula: prophet.

Kaula-wahine: prophetess.

La: sun.

Lani: heavens.

Lenalena: yellow, a sacred color.

Lua: ancient practice of breaking bones to kill.

Luakina: place of sacrifice within a heiau.

Mahini: Moon.

Mahini-hou: New Moon.

Mahini-peopeo: Full Moon.

Mu: person who found human sacrifices.

Ohia-apane: a sacred wood used to make gods out of.

Oi-e: name for the Hawaiian godhead.

Opelu: a sacred fish to the kahunas.

Palaoa: ivory charm worn around the neck by royalty.

Pea: a sacred cross.

Pule: prayer.

Puloulou: a tabu staff.

Ulaula: red, a sacred color.

Unauna: a tabu mark.

Unihipili: spirit of the dead.

MIDDLE EASTERN FOLK MAGIC

BY MARGUERITE ELSBETH

Witch shops and sorcerers abound in the medinas or old cities of the Middle East, trading in potions and spells to rid tired wives of unwanted husbands or make mischief among neighbors and rivals. So the Arabic people are always very careful to protect themselves by a variety of magical means.

- Doors and window frames are painted blue in Islamic cultures to keep evil spirits from entering into the house.

- Throughout the Middle East, one can see the image of a large, five-fingered blue hand painted in the windows of most homes. The Berbers believe the hand signifies protection, support, authority, power, and strength. Islamic people often wear the hand as an amulet. Sometimes it appears with other symbols, such as a star, dove, bird, fan, zigzag, or circle. A hand with an eye in the center of the palm indicates clairvoyance.

- Arabs wear jewels such as jacinth, chrysolite, and pearl, or carry perfume balls of musk, ambergris, and saffron to attract and maintain wealth.

- Wealthy Moroccan Moors keep wild boars in their stables to attract the jinn away from the horses.

- Arabs lead camels through the villages to absorb sickness or evil spirits; then the camel is sacrificed in a sacred place, ridding the town of trouble.

- Turks and Armenians never throw away nail parings, but hide them in the wall cracks, floor boards, house pillars or tree hollows to keep safe from harm and sorcery.

- Moroccans consider iron a great protection against demons. A knife or dagger made of the metal is often placed under a sick person's pillow.

- Moroccan shamans give tired patients ants to swallow; fearful folk are prescribed a dinner of lion's flesh; and chicken hearts are not eaten lest one be rendered timid and shy. Also, the Turks give children who are late in learning to speak the tongues of certain birds to eat.

- Turkish shamans burn tree branches, ring bells, beat on tambourines, make snorting noises, and fall into frenzied trance when performing purification ceremonies to exorcise harmful spirits. Sometimes they will run their patients through fire to complete the purification process.

- Berbers, Arabs, and other Moroccans kindle bonfires in courtyards, at crossroads, and in the fields on Midsummer Eve. The burning plants, including fennel, chervilseed, thyme, rue, chamomile, geranium, and pennyroyal, give out a thick, magical smoke that removes misfortune from people, animals, crops, and homes. Leaping through the flames seven times increases fertility. A paste made of the ashes is rubbed on the hair to keep it from falling out, or on the body for good health.

- The new year and the autumnal equinox are gift-giving times in Arab cultures. This makes all safe and secure for the coming year.

51

BIRTH

BY JEN BESEMER

*no older than before, i wait
hands sticky with longing
and potential. i have begun again.
there is a name for me now
though i have forgotten it. i wait.*

*my face is young, my words unformed.
embrace me, Earth, i am your daughter
come home once more. whisper to me
so that when my voice comes i shall sing
of you.*

GIFTED

BY JEN BESEMER

in the heat of the city,
hidden from the children
like some trauma or scandal, i sit
before this altar, casting a spell
with my sweat, my hands,
the blood seeping from me
like water from a slow, buried spring.
my empty stomach mumbles murder,
my feet itch in their boots,
my knee laughs through the hole
in my husband's jeans—
this is where I want to spend my life,
right here , in the sweat and the hunger
bleeding out my words
pounding the keys like a drum.
this spell is for you, Mother,
this offering of change,
this blood:
a gift.

FEATHER POWER

BY MARGUERITE ELSBETH

Feathers are a gift from the Great Spirit and a spirit offering from the bird, who releases part of its body to us. Native Americans and other traditional peoples have long recognized the curative powers in feathers; they see the feather as a tool for focusing power into the person to be cured, or for bringing good spirit energy to a situation. The medicines carried by our winged friends may be remembered by watching their flighty ways.

- Blue jay feathers bring sunlight and the daytime sky into dark places.

- Crow feathers are used for mourning. The Lakota Sioux pray with crow feathers for four days when someone has died, then keep the feathers in a sacred place.

- Eagle feathers symbolize the sacredness of all birds. They represent peace, and are used by the medicine person to fan people off when doctoring, thus blowing harmful energies away on the wind. The eagle feather fan wafts our thoughts and prayers to the Great Spirit, and catches the spirit songs sung by shamans out of the air.

- Flicker feathers are used for protection and to maintain good health.

- Hummingbird feathers are popular among the Southwest Indian tribes for bringing beauty, joy and happiness to any situation.

- Hawk feathers are very powerful medicine for diagnosing illnesses in the body because the hawk is a strong hunter and brings understanding.

- Macaw feathers, when available, are used for dances and ceremonies. These feathers represent communication, because a macaw can learn to talk in any language. A fan made of macaw feathers is considered a translator by various Indian tribes. The red, blue and green colors re-create the rainbow.

- Magpie feathers are for doctoring any sickness. This bird is a natural scavenger; just as the magpie cleans up the environment, his feathers will cleanse and purify a sick body. In Lakota culture, the black and white feathers at the edge of the wing represent an Indian maiden, with black hair and a white buckskin dress.

- Nightingale feathers can teach ritual and the use of sacred things.

- Robins are the first birds to return from migration in spring. Their feathers bring renewal and may be used to induce fertility. A robin feather found on the ground can sometimes bring news.

- Roadrunner feathers embody the trickster energy of Coyote and may help to increase magical ability of an instinctual nature.

- Scissortail feathers are used to honor the mothers of all Indian Nations. Sometimes these feathers stand for the Sun and the four directions.

- Swan feathers represent grace, beauty and goodness. In the Creek Indian Nation they are a symbol for union and marriage.

- Water birds are all-powerful symbols in American Indian culture, especially in the Native American Church. Like the eagle, water bird feathers carry our prayers to the spirit above us.

- Woodpecker feathers are used to cure gallstones, because they are thought to dissolve rock in the human body.

- Yellowhammer feathers represent the family because this bird makes a fine nest of weeds.

DION FORTUNE

BY deTRACI REGULA

A single photograph is all that we have to stare at for insight into one of the more enigmatical magical figures of the twentieth century. Hair cut short, a firm jaw turned to the side, eyes seemingly half-closed, offering a further veil, a leopard print vest calling up the sacerdotal garb of ancient Egyptian priests, she seems either about to speak or slide away, out of the frame.

Like quicksilver in the palm of the hand, she is hard to grasp, eluding understanding even after the publication of three biographies and her own extensive writings. Ceremonial magicians claim her as one of their own; Wiccans of almost all varieties see in her a great revealer and guide; mystical Christians believe she is safe in the embrace of the Christian Mystery tradition; Norse pagans trust that she came home to that aspect of her genetic history; and modern practitioners of Egyptian worship acknowledge her contribution to the understanding of their mysteries. Though known for her extensive magical writings, Dion Fortune was also captivated by the mysteries contained in the hard sciences. She realized the impact of our individual genetics on our spiritual natures, and understood that the physical tides caused by the Moon could have a spiritual effect on the human mind and spirit. Science and magic were, to her, two complementary sides of the same coin. A paper she wrote on the possible beneficial uses of soy bean protein predated the "tofu boom" by several decades.

Born Violet Mary Firth on December 6th, 1890, in Llandudno, Wales, Dion Fortune turned to occult studies in self-defense after a nervous breakdown she had was followed by a devastating psychic attack. Although the precise

circumstances of this attack were long veiled in mystery, the research of Janine Chapman in her recent book *Quest for Dion Fortune* definitively places the site and date of this key incident at Studley Agricultural College in Warwickshire during the years 1911-1913.

Dion Fortune died in 1947 of leukemia and blood poisoning brought on by a bad tooth. Her magical efforts during World War II may have exhausted her, or perhaps her role, for the time being, had ended. We are fortunate that in the past few years new information on her life and work has begun to surface. The magical fraternity she founded, The Society of the Inner Light, went through rough waters after her passing, and at one time acted to "exorcise" any remaining influence her spirit had over the group. This led to the suppression of much information about Dion Fortune which did not fit with the later goals of the group. Recent years have seen the release of more materials, including the series of instructional "letters" she wrote during World War II, guiding relatively inexperienced members through the techniques they needed to become a potent magical force for the Allied cause.

In ancient times in many cultures, the body of a divine sacrifice was cut into pieces and buried in different parts of the land. In a sense, this is what has happened to the memory of Dion Fortune, whose influence is pervasive, yet often unacknowledged, by so many groups and individuals.

Further Reading

Chapman, Janine. *Quest for Dion Fortune.*

Fortune, Dion. *The Magical Battle of Britain.* Edited by Gareth Knight.

Grant, Kenneth. *The Magical Revival.*

Richardson, Alan. *Priestess.*

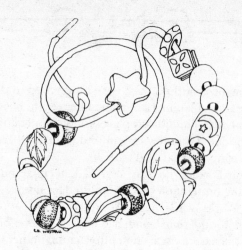

THE STORY NECKLACE

BY D. J. CONWAY

One of my most precious memories was being allowed to string buttons at my grandmother's house. She kept a can of old buttons of every shape, color, and kind just for this purpose. Later my daughter remarked that she also had enjoyed the privilege of stringing buttons at Grandmother's house. Then I remembered my children stringing the buttons and telling a story as they went.

This activity can be beneficial to opening the creativity in young minds, but can also be used in a therapeutic manner for both adults and children. Those who have been through a traumatic experience and are having difficulty expressing their feelings about it can use the story necklace in a non-threatening way to bring out all they are feeling. This can be very helpful when dealing with very small children who have experienced abuse or personal loss and don't have the full vocabulary needed to tell about it.

Since it is not advisable to give a sharp needle and thread to small children, use a shoelace, or child's lacing yarn that is wrapped at one end. Get a number of large colored beads of all shapes and sizes. Hobby stores carry some quite unique ones, often in animal or human shapes. Have several beads of the same color. Put the beads in a pretty container, and have them available for "talking times."

Perhaps the child has just experienced the death of a pet or a person and isn't quite sure how to express or deal with the pain he or she feels. Start off by talking about all the good and humorous times the child spent with the deceased. Have him or her chose a bead or button that expresses that time. Next, of course, you must come to the stressful time of losing the pet or person to death. Allow the child to chose a button which symbolizes to him or her this experience. Discuss this transformation into another realm of existence and follow this by having the child choose a bead which symbolizes the new "birthday" into the spiritual realm. Tie the ends of the string or yarn together and let the child keep this story necklace as long as he or she has a need.

The same idea can be used to encourage children to tell you about their day or an outing. Adults often forget to ask children how their days went. By sitting down and talking while the child strings beads and tells you what they mean, you establish a greater rapport.

The story necklace can be used to encourage children to use their creative minds in story telling. Begin a fanciful story and put a bead on the yarn to symbolize that point, then pass the necklace to one of the children. Have him or her continue the story and string a bead or beads. The necklace makes the rounds of the children involved until the story comes to an end. Never interrupt the child adding to the story or comment on what he or she is saying. Let the story progress in its wild, fanciful twists and turns, and enjoy the creative ideas being shared.

Sometimes adults are as reticent as children about voicing their anger and sorrow over things in their lives. When you, or someone you are talking with, have difficulty voicing feelings about a loss or traumatic event, telling a story with the beads is often a good method to break down the mental and emotional barriers. Choose a bead that symbolizes the beginning of the problem; string it on the lace, and tell something about it, even if it is just a few words. Then choose a bead that represents your feelings about it. Continue to the next thing that arose out of the situation, then your feelings about that, until you come to the end of the event.

If you are helping someone else, you might have to ask simple questions, such as "What happened first? How did you feel about it? What happened next? How did you feel about that?" When the person has come to the end of choosing beads to express their feelings, don't let the conversation grind to a stop. Ask a few more questions. Center the person's attention on positive activity for the future. In a time when psychologists can cost you a year's wages in less than a year, you will find you can work out many of your own and your family's problems through use of the story necklace.

TEEN WITCH :
HOW DO I TELL MY PARENTS?

BY SILVER RAVENWOLF

Teen Witches are more prevalent than you might suppose. Groups of two and three fifteen- to eighteen-year-old witches meet all over the country, trying desperately to find their own religious path in an unfamiliar world. These brave young adults seek to know their destinies, learn how to enhance their lives, and raise their spiritual consciousness.

Some of these teen Witches, however, have a handicap—the spiritual mindset of the adults around them. If the environment encircling the teen becomes barren or stagnated, his or her spiritual growth wanes. Some teens truly follow the old ways, practicing in secret for several years, until they reach adulthood and can move to an environment suitable to practice their belief system.

Serious teen Witches of non-Craft parents know that if they try to assert their independence by changing the package they display to their parents, life will be harder, not easier.

Adult Witches rarely give credit to our youthful counterparts. We have an excuse, you see— our rule not to train non-Craft children until they are twenty-one. Although we have a good reason for the rule, this dictate does not assist the aspiring teen Witch. How do these resourceful young ones find their spirituality? Mostly by reading. How do I know the answer to this question? By the hundreds of letters I receive from teens who are seeking the Craft of the Wise.

The most asked question is, "How do I tell my parents I am a Witch?" It isn't only teens who ask this question. Many individuals in their twenties have written me with the same tone of despair on the issue. This query is a tough one, full of ramifications. Each situation is different, and there is no single appropriate answer to be tossed into the mind of the teen or young adult. However, here are some ideas, should you be facing the monumental decision of "breaking the news" to your parents.

DO NOT DO A ONE-EIGHTY ON YOUR PARENTS. You will give them heart failure if you have been Rebecca of Sunnybrook Farm for fifteen (or fifty) years, and suddenly turn into a pseudo-vampire complete with leather collar and pointy spikes. Real Witches don't dress like that anyway (we hope). Be creative, but don't be off-the-wall. Forget the hair color that changes your naturally blonde tresses to the fine sheen of a raven's wing. Let the fingernail polish that makes your fingers look as if you've dipped them in graveyard dirt alone. Radical changes in behavior or dress signal the parent that you are in over your head, and are barreling straight into serious, mental trouble.

ACT WITH HONOR AND INTEGRITY AT ALL TIMES. If your behavior reflects good values and principles, then your parents won't rush to the Ritalin cabinet. Being a teen is difficult as it is. Don't make fun of your peers, for any reason. Be honest in money dealings. Be kind to those who are less fortunate than you. Don't run with the pack of those who think that they are better than the rest. Don't allow your mood swings to get out of hand. Learn to control your environment without hatred or weapons; you are not as helpless as you may think. Seek individuals who bring harmony into your life, rather than those who bring chaos.

INVESTIGATE SEVERAL RELIGIONS AND TALK TO THE PARENT WHO IS MOST OPEN on the concepts of life about these various belief systems. Have family discussions, telling your parents what you have read, and ask them why or why they do not support this or that religion or belief system. Don't get into an argument, but be firm on your personal beliefs.

TAKE YOUR TIME. If today you are Baptist and tomorrow you are Craft, look for terror in the eyes of your parents. It just isn't fair to do that to them. Leave various articles about the Goddess hanging around the house. Look for material that is historically and archeologically correct. Find reading material that is inspirational and non-threatening, and share this information with your parents. Turn on the Learning Channel where features include investigations of matri-focal religions and various religious aspects of different cultures. Parents have the capability of learning. This mode of behavior does not shut down when they turn thirty. There is still hope. Your parents can learn as much from you as you can from them. Think about it. Are you a kind and gentle teacher?

WALK SOFTLY AND CARRY A BIG STICK. Walk softly means don't rock the proverbial boat. Try to be harmonious in all you do. Your "big stick" is the magic you are learning to do. Work for joy, harmony, and positive influences in your life.

DON'T EXPECT YOUR LIFE TO CHANGE OVERNIGHT. Magic for various ends can be like a beautiful silver or gold chain—you forge one link at a time, until the matter comes full circle. Some magics take only a few days, others, weeks or even months. A few magics will take years. Accept this, and keep your spirit always reaching for divinity.

TERMINALIA

By Edain McCoy

The Roman festival of Terminalia, celebrated on February twenty-third, honors Terminus, the God of boundaries and portals. The festival was believed to have begun around 200 BCE when a Roman emperor declared that all citizens must mark clearly the boundaries of their property for tax purposes. The outraged citizens of Rome responded by outlining their lands with garlands, flowers, plants, coins, and gifts for Terminus.

The festival soon became an annual event which not only honored an ancient deity, but was beautifying to the city, since it became customary on this date to clear out winter's dust and grime to make way for spring. Those who decorated the perimeters of their property as shrines to Terminus believed that he would protect their homes and land in the year to come, and perhaps even cut their tax burden.

Not everyone today has property to be protected or taxed, but wherever we live we have limits to our personal space, boundaries which we may from time to time feel the need to protect. We can honor Terminus at these boundaries, and get a jump on spring cleaning, by making and using a window wash designed to protect the portals of our homes and evoke his blessings.

In a small sauce pan, boil 3 cups water with ¼ cup mugwort, 1 teaspoon sage, and ½ teaspoon lemongrass. Strain the water through a cheesecloth or other strainer and pour into a large, clean wash bucket. Add cool water to fill the bucket.

As you mix the herbal water with the other water, stir the mixture clockwise while consecrating it in the name of Terminus:

> *God of boundary, portal and pass,*
> *Blessed be these panes of glass,*
> *Warded be each entry way,*
> *Terminus, bless them night and day.*

With a sponge, wash each window in your home while visualizing these boundaries and portals being protected by Terminus. Dry them with a squeegee or newspaper until they gleam.

RITUALS FOR HOUSECLEANING

By Cerridwen
Iris Shea

I am a lousy housekeeper. In fact, I suggested this article as a way to force myself to find a way to keep my home cleaner. I am a single urban pagan currently working theater jobs and maintaining a heavy writing schedule. In addition, I work the craft as a solitary and with a coven, teach the craft, and do work for clients including tarot readings, house blessings, healings, and hex breaking. I currently share my apartment with four cats. While I have little trouble tending to the household altars and shrines I use, keeping the rest of the place fit for habitation can be a challenge. There aren't enough hours to do everything, and while I stretch time as much as I can, certain tasks slide until they become monumental instead of simple. While I will never be a candidate for the latest issue of *Better Groves and Sanctuaries*, at least I can invite my mother over with a clear conscience.

GETTING MOTIVATED

While I don't cast a circle except during my twice-yearly major overhaul rituals, I do keep one blue jar candle in each quarter part of the apartment. I light them before I begin cleaning tasks, beginning with the candle in the North. I also burn what I consider "hearth" incense—herbal rather than floral. I usually use rosemary, or sometimes sage. In winter, I keep a pot of water with a cut-up apple and some cinnamon, mace, nutmeg, and cloves simmering on the stove while I am home. It keeps the entire apartment scented. To prevent fire, don't forget to watch the pot and add more water, or turn it off when you leave. I also put on music compatible with my mood of the day, or in harmony with where I'd like my mood to turn.

VACUUMING

Sharing my household with four cats, I need to vacuum once a day, two or three times during shedding season. I vacuum the rooms in the same order, starting in the same place and working my way around the apartment to finish where I began. Sometimes I toss herbs on the floor, such as lavender or rosemary, and let them sit for a few moments before a vacuum them up. Imagine dirt and negativity being sucked away into the vacuum. If possible, change your vacuum bag on each dark of the Moon.

THE FLOOR

I wash my floors twice. The first time, I use the cleaner of my choice and I envision the dirt and any negative energy scrubbed away. Then, I empty the bucket and refill it with hot water. I put in a few drops of one of the following oils: lavender, peppermint, rosemary, sage, or Willow World. I scrub the floors again, visualizing the positive qualities of the oil seeping into the floors of the home, remembering all the wonderful times that have taken place in the home, and imagining all the wonderful times that will continue to take place. I also wipe down windowsills, doorways, doorknobs, metal or ceramic lampshades, faucets, fixtures, the front of the fridge, stove, and dishwasher, etc. with a cloth dipped in hot water mixed with a few drops of the same oil. If you use floor wash and vacuuming herbs, make sure they are the same, or at least complimentary, or there will be a mishmash of scents.

LAUNDRY

Laugo-Edne is the Saami goddess of laundry, and she is the one I ask for help in both stain removal and ironing. I usually light a small candle to her when I'm doing the wash or the ironing as a token of thanks that the clothes will come out clean, I won't have run any colors, I won't scorch the fabrics, and they will come out smoothly ironed. So far, I have not been able to find out

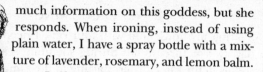

much information on this goddess, but she responds. When ironing, instead of using plain water, I have a spray bottle with a mixture of lavender, rosemary, and lemon balm. I take the herbs and make a tea with boiling water, then let it cool and keep it in the spray bottle. It is a nice way to scent ironed items, especially linens. Shake the bottle before you use it, and be careful using it on whites, because sediment can build up and sometimes it can stain.

KITCHEN AND BATHROOM

Put on a pair of rubber gloves, use your favorite cleaner, and sing at the top of your lungs!

DISHES

I give thanks for the abundance of food and the nourishment of the Earth as I do the dishes. Keeping spicy sachets tucked in the cupboards keeps them smelling fresh and clean.

EQUINOX HOUSECLEANING RITUAL

I do this around the spring equinox and the fall equinox. It takes an entire day each time.

* Get up around dawn. Spend a few moments meditating on the turning of the wheel. Ask for focus, strength, and endurance for the day.

* Have something light but nourishing to eat. Prepare coffee, or any other beverage that you find motivating throughout the day. Gather your gloves, cleaning supplies, trash bags, vacuum cleaner, broom, etc.

* Place one quarter candle and one blue jar candle at each quarter point in your living space. I live in an apartment on one floor, but if you have multiple levels, figure it out so that one point is also all the way at the top, and one all the way at the bottom. Light the candles. Light the incense. Cast your circle, encompassing your entire dwelling. I invoke the goddess

Silkie, the Scottish goddess of housecleaning. In the kitchen, I also invoke Hestia, the goddess of the hearth. I keep an altar to Her in my kitchen and frequently work with Her, so I like Her to reap the benefits of the large housecleaning as well.

❊ Put on music. Work your way through each room of your home. Take items out of the cupboards, wash them if necessary, replace shelf paper, wash shelves, replace and rearrange if appropriate. Wash windows, mop down walls. Take out the silver and polish it. Do laundry. Catch up ironing. Take things out of closets. Set aside piles for cleaning , mending, discarding, or donating to charity. Repot plants. Sort papers so that when you put aside a day to go through and organize all of those annoying slips of paper, you at least have a starting point. Sweep, vacuum, mop.

❊ When you're done with that cleaning and organizing, stack the piles where you can easily take them out. Go into the bathroom and give yourself a nice, relaxing bath or shower.

❊ Go back to your starting point. You can say whatever you wish, but this is what I sometimes use:

Thank you Silkie and Hestia, as the wheel of the year turns, so does the wheel of my life turn, and I thank you for helping me get rid of the old, the worn out, the harmful, to cleanse and purify my own sacred space so that I am renewed and ready for the new challenges and opportunities of this next cycle.

❊ Close your circle. Extinguish the candles. Order in a good meal or take yourself out to a nice restaurant for dinner. Blessed be!

BIBLIOGRAPHY

Monaghan, Patricia. *The Book of Goddesses and Heroines.* St. Paul: Llewellyn Publications, 1993.

Housekeeping for Ritual

By Cerridwen Iris Shea

Altars and ritual items need special care and attention. I find that I have less trouble keeping my altars neat and tended than the rest of my home, but there are still tasks that tend to pile up. Also, in ritual, accidents happen. How do you keep your tools looking well-loved, but not neglected?

Wax

Wax is probably the biggest challenge. To get wax off of candlesticks, I take an aluminum roasting pan, put the candlestick in it, and pour boiling water over it. I wear rubber gloves when I do this, and then, as the wax melts, I can rub it off with the glove. Remove the candle holder from submersion as soon as the wax starts to melt, or the entire candleholder will have a waxy glaze. When the wax is off, run the candleholder under cool water, dry thoroughly, and then polish as usual. Wait until the water is completely cool, and then, preferably, get rid of it outside. Don't pour hot, waxy water down your drain or you will clog it up. When the wax dries, it can be peeled off the gloves and the pan, and both gloves and pan can be stored to use again. For materials that could be hurt with boiling water, I generally scrape off as much wax as I can, then take a scouring pad and gently remove the rest with a little warm water.

Wax can be removed from clothing with a hot iron. Place several layers of paper towels underneath the waxed spot. Place the waxed spot on top. Place a layer of paper towel over the spot. Press with the hot iron. Use the iron somewhat like a blotter. Move to a clean spot or change paper towels frequently, so that you do not get wax buildup on your iron. To get rid of the leftover ring, rub the fabric gently with a baby wipe, let it soak in gentle detergent and warm water for a few minutes, and then wash as you normally would.

Baby Wipes

Baby wipes, in general, will get most stains out, especially cosmetics and food. They can be used on most fabrics. Be careful on very delicate silks and rayons with a silk feel. When in doubt, test the baby wipe on an inside seam first. Jewelry cleaners will take off most stains on non-fabric items, but always read the directions first.

RITUAL TOOLS

Statues and figures can usually be cleansed with mild soap and a little warm water (baby soap is good). Be careful about using soaps containing essential oils. If the oil is strong, it can damage the statue, especially if it's painted.

Tarot cards, runes, etc. should be cleaned every time they are used. In addition, I also try to cleanse them a couple of times a year and then leave them out in the light of the Full Moon to recharge. Stones should be cleaned in salt water once or twice a year and also left under the Full Moon or Sun to recharge.

Wooden wands can be cleansed with the appropriate oil massaged into them, and any crystals with a mild salt solution. Crystal wands can be washed in a mild soap and water solution, dried, then wiped in a mild salt solution, rinsed, and dried.

The care of clothing depends on the type of fabric used. Hand or machine wash when able, but, in the case of delicate silks or velvets, send them to the dry cleaner. When the items return, smudge them with your favorite incense to get rid of the smell of the fluid.

Crystal balls can be washed in a mild soap and water solution, cleaned with a mild salt solution, rinsed off, and rubbed with mugwort.

Athames, cauldrons, chalices, etc. can be cleaned and polished with mild solutions appropriate to the material of which they are made. When in doubt, mild soap and water, gentle rinsing, and thorough drying with a soft, clean cloth rarely go wrong.

When the coven or clients come over, I usually vacuum and then use a floor wash, light a few candles, and either burn incense, or have a pot of something like apples and cinnamon gently simmering on the stove. I wipe down surfaces with warm water and a few drops of the same oil I used in the floor wash. I also check and spot clean all the items to be used in the ritual.

A LITTLE MAGIC IN YOUR LAUNDRY

BY SILVER RAVENWOLF

You can take a boring, mundane task such as laundry, and turn the chore into a fun, magical application. Here are a few tips that our family uses on the dreaded laundry day

- After you have the clothing separated, cleanse each pile by drawing a banishing pentagram over the clothing. This should get rid of any residue you've managed to collect on your clothing. The residue could come from your own negative feelings or from the actions and emotions of others.

- Hold your hand under the running water as the washing machine fills up. Ask the God and Goddess to release any negativity from the water and empower the liquid with the blessings of the Lord and Lady. Of course, if you are using only hot water, be careful that you don't burn your hand.

- Banish, then bless, laundry detergent and fabric softeners. Ask that the chemicals break down safely in the water so as not to harm the environment. Empower the detergent and softener to function as a protective shield in your clothing.

- To give strength to the sick, add a sunflower seed, a pinch of rosemary, and a clove of garlic to the water. (Be sure to take the garlic out of the clothes before you put the load into the dryer, or you'll have yucky smelling clothes.)

🐛 To stop arguments in the home, wash everyone's clothing with a pinch of basil and a rose petal or two.

🐛 For a romantic evening, throw rose petals and rosemary into the wash water.

🐛 For extra protection, add a pinch of angelica to the wash water.

🐛 For extra money, add a pinch of three finger grass to the wash water.

🐛 A teenager or spouse giving you a bad time? Write the person's name on a small piece of paper. Add a pinch of sugar to the wash water, then throw in the paper. This should sweeten them up.

🐛 Want someone to move out? Do their laundry with a bit of nettle and thistle. They'll be gone in no time.

🐛 If you are having a particularly rough patch in your life, add a little holy water to the wash water. Ask that all negativity from your life be banished.

🐛 Nightmares got you down? A bit of lilac and lavender in the wash water should do the trick.

🐛 After you load the wash into the dryer, empower the dryer sheet and put it on top of the clothing. Ask that harmony be released into your clothing as the dryer sheet releases its chemicals into your laundry.

🐛 As you hang or fold each piece of clothing, recite a positive affirmation or two. Because folding laundry is so boring, your mind naturally goes into the alpha state and becomes fertile ground for positive magic.

I'm sure that you can come up with additional magical applications for laundry day. Why not try to add a little magic to your laundry the next time you face this necessary, but irritating task?

How to Perform A House Banishing and Blessing

By Silver RavenWolf

I am often called upon to perform house banishings for magical as well as mundane individuals. I find this task fun and fulfilling, and am always delighted to pack up my magical bag of goodies and trot off to someone's home, hopefully spreading peace and harmony in the lives of another family.

House banishings are very easy to perform and take approximately forty-five minutes to complete. Before you zip off to do your magical thing, here are some things you may wish to pack in your "have magic, will travel" bag: salt (Earth); Holy water (water); a white candle and a lighter (fire); incense of your choice (air); clove oil; a rattle; a small gift tailored after the home owner's personality; and honey and milk.

How to Begin

When you arrive at the home, explain to the owners exactly what you plan to do. Invite them to participate with you. The ceremony will mean more to them if they help and will also squash any fears they may have. Ask them for a family portrait of those individuals who currently reside in the home. Individual pictures are acceptable.

Begin by placing the four items that equate to the elemental directions on a table that is near the center point of the house. Place the picture(s) of the family on the table below your tools. Cleanse, consecrate and empower each item you plan to use in the house banishing. Call upon the ancestors of those living presently in the home as well as the powers of the four directions to aid you in this house blessing ritual. Invoke divine energy into your body for the task at hand. You don't need to cast a circle because you are going to create an entire house of sacred space. If, and only if, there have been nasty manifestations within the home, then you should cast a magic circle before you begin the banishing/blessing ask that the circle move with you as you move throughout the house.

Procedure for Each Room

Beginning in the attic, walk counter-clockwise around the room, sprinkling the salt in the four corners. Follow the same procedure with the incense, candle, and holy water.

Stand in the center of the room and shake the rattle, envisioning that all negativity cowers at the sound of the rattle, and leaves the room. If you feel there is something exceptionally tough in the room, open a window and imagine the negativity escaping outside. If you have come across something really nasty, do the lesser banishing ritual mentioned in my book entitled *HexCraft: Dutch Country Pow-Wow Magick*.

The room should now be clean of all negativity. Assume the Goddess position and raise energy, focusing on white light and the blessings of the Lord and Lady. Fill the room with this energy, permeating every corner, every piece of furniture, from floor to ceiling. Hold this visualization until you feel the entire room centers itself in harmony. Ask the Lord and Lady to bless the room and any who enter into it.

Finally, take the clove oil and seal every door and window in the room by drawing a banishing pentagram either above or below the windows and directly on the doors. Draw the pentagram on the doorknobs as well.

When you are through, go to the center of the room, clap your hands and say: "This room is sealed! No evil or negative energies can abide the breath of divinity that has taken residence in this room."

Go through every room in the house, from attic to basement, following the procedure outlined above.

FINISHING

When you are finished go back to the center table and set your things as you did to begin. Stand in the Goddess position and raise energy, filling every crevice of the house with white light and the energy of the divine. Ask for the blessings of the Lord and Lady upon this home, and request that no negative energies or individuals cross the threshold. (If you did cast a circle, now is the time to take it down.)

Lower your arms and thank the ancestors, the elements, and divinity for their presence in the working and bid them farewell. Gather up your tools and put them away. Leave the gift for the homeowner on the table.

When you leave the home, pour honey and milk onto the ground at the front stoop or porch, asking the devas of the property to welcome and care for the humans who now live upon it. If the homeowner is having trouble with nasty neighbors, sprinkle dill and parsley along the property line, along with a pinch (just a little bit) of pickling salt. Too much salt and you will kill the plants.

Use holy water to draw a large pentacle on the front door of the house. Tap the center of the pentacle three times and say:

This house is sealed and blessed in this world and in the world of the phantasm. The Goddess watches over and the long arm of the God prevents disharmony and unhappiness. So mote it be.

Medicine Plants of the Great Basin

By Bernyce Barlow

When one looks across the vast basin and range complex that makes up the Great Basin in Nevada, one sees dry lake beds turned into salt flats, lonely basalt formations, and hundreds of miles of vacuous desert. Here, the sky and the land meet on equal terms. The ranges, seventy or so, separate the basins, isolating them into districts of solitude. Basin and range, basin and range—they seem to go on forever. Some folks might say there is nothing out there, just vast stretches of barren ground and a few crows picking at road kill. A closer look at this region tells us something different.

As empty as this land appears, it is, without doubt, a medicinal metropolis teeming with life-giving plants. That's correct, many of those scrubby-looking plants that grow in the desert basins are really resident physicians in their own right! Early on, in the 1920s and 1930s, pharmaceutical companies used a lot of what are now called natural or homeopathic remedies. Before synthetic substitutes were found, many Great Basin plants were regularly used for pharmaceutic practice. Of course, long before Eli Lilly & Company set up shop on these northern shores, the Native Americans of the continent had been refining the healing properties of medicine plants.

The tribes of the Desert Culture had a heightened awareness of the specialness of their land. They did not see it as void and barren, but full of life. Their intimacy with the sacred was keen and their knowledge of it acute. Each animal had its own unique spirit and power, as did each plant. In the Great Basin, where life is so sparse, every life form's purpose is precious and necessary. For example, if a wood gatherer received a deep splinter in an arm or finger, the sap of the Piñon tree would be heated to a semi-liquid form, cooled enough to avoid burning the skin,

Prickly poppy

75

then applied as a warm bandage covering the splinter. When the pitch patch had completely hardened it was pulled off, removing the splinter with the patch.

A widely used medicine plant of the Desert Culture was the wild oat, a marvelous plant often referred to as a pesky weed. Not so! The cream-colored liquid that forms in the grain (halfway through seed maturity) contains powerful properties that reduce stress, depression, and spasms. A tincture made from these grains is a surefire remedy for the blues. Cover one part plant completely with two parts Everclear or some other high octane ethanol (i.e. one cup seeds to two cups liquid). Contain the mixture in a bottle and let it set for a week, then squeeze whatever else you can out of the plant, strain, and bottle the tincture. Eye-dropper bottles work well for this.

The Prickly Poppy is not a flower you would pick to put in a bouquet for you sweetheart. Its thistle-like character might cause a sticky situation if you did. It's not a bad idea to wear gloves when harvesting this plant, unless you are immune to pain. What you want to collect and dry are the seed pods and the leaves. Once both are dried, the leaves and the seeds from within the pods can be made into a tea that can be used externally for sunburn or skin abrasions, similar to the Aloe Vera plant. The seeds can be crushed and added to lanolin by melting the lanolin in the hot sun with the crushed seeds mixed in, or using a low, slow burner. The product will thicken as it cools, becoming a soft salve that can also be applied externally for skin disorders. For salve, use one part seeds to one part lanolin (i.e. three ounces seeds to three ounces of lanolin). For tea, add one part leaves to eighteen parts liquid, and slow boil for twenty minutes.

Two other wonderful medicine plants found in the Great Basin are Sage and Sagebrush. Although the two are synonymous in many folks' minds, they actually belong to two different families with unique healing properties. Sagebrush is a curious purifier and

Sage

disinfectant, which has many uses. The leaves can be gathered, dried, then made into an external tea for cleansing, or used as a first aid wash. Powdered leaves can be used in place of talcum, absorbing excess moisture, and preventing rashes. Inhaling sagebrush from incense, smudge sticks, or in steam or sweat baths is the way sagebrush is used internally.

Sage, on the other hand, is a different plant. Like sagebrush, it is also a purifier, but it has an added histamine effect when taken internally. Aromatically, sage is a delight to the senses, and sweeter than its Wormwood cousin. In a tea it can be used as a gargle or as a topical analgesic wash. Sage kills germs. I would not use wild sage at Thanksgiving in the turkey dressing. It's pretty gamy (blech)! Also, do not drink sage tea if you are nursing a child, due to its drying properties.

The agave, or century plant, is found in the southern Great Basin. Its leaves and roots make a tea that is helpful to folks with gas or indigestion. Agave is also a diuretic. The Yucca plant, which is sometimes mistaken for the Agave, can also be found in the southern basin area. Its uses are practical, as an ingredient in soap and shampoo for example, but its medical applications are questionable. Traditionally, the root of the Yucca has been used to help with joint inflammation, but on a long-term basis, the tea does more harm than good by preventing vitamin and mineral absorption.

Despite first impressions, the Great Basin is a medicine chest full of remedies. There are over seventy-five significant healing plants, and others that are effective but not as concentrated in their constituents. Consequently, next time you find yourself driving through the Great Basin, blankly gazing out the window at hundreds of miles of sagebrush and sand, remember that what you are looking at is nature's free clinic with no lines, no papers to fill out, and no ridiculous medical bills.

Agave

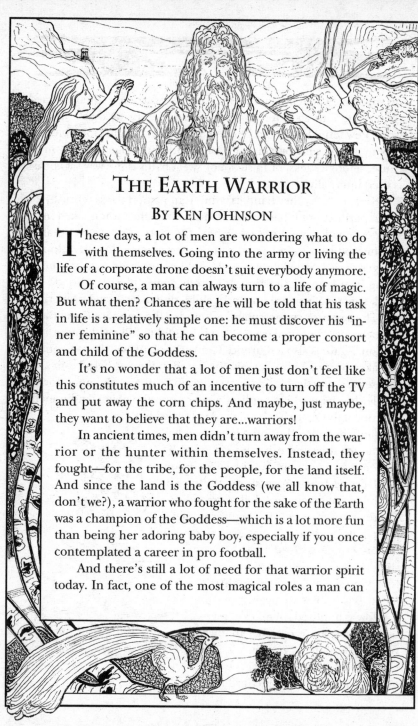

The Earth Warrior

By Ken Johnson

These days, a lot of men are wondering what to do with themselves. Going into the army or living the life of a corporate drone doesn't suit everybody anymore.

Of course, a man can always turn to a life of magic. But what then? Chances are he will be told that his task in life is a relatively simple one: he must discover his "inner feminine" so that he can become a proper consort and child of the Goddess.

It's no wonder that a lot of men just don't feel like this constitutes much of an incentive to turn off the TV and put away the corn chips. And maybe, just maybe, they want to believe that they are...warriors!

In ancient times, men didn't turn away from the warrior or the hunter within themselves. Instead, they fought—for the tribe, for the people, for the land itself. And since the land is the Goddess (we all know that, don't we?), a warrior who fought for the sake of the Earth was a champion of the Goddess—which is a lot more fun than being her adoring baby boy, especially if you once contemplated a career in pro football.

And there's still a lot of need for that warrior spirit today. In fact, one of the most magical roles a man can

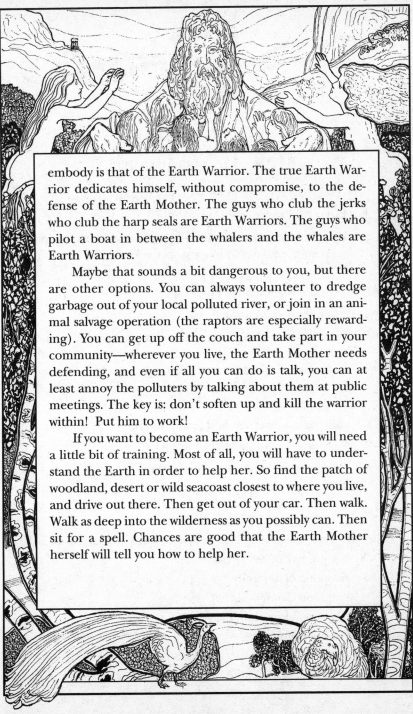

embody is that of the Earth Warrior. The true Earth Warrior dedicates himself, without compromise, to the defense of the Earth Mother. The guys who club the jerks who club the harp seals are Earth Warriors. The guys who pilot a boat in between the whalers and the whales are Earth Warriors.

Maybe that sounds a bit dangerous to you, but there are other options. You can always volunteer to dredge garbage out of your local polluted river, or join in an animal salvage operation (the raptors are especially rewarding). You can get up off the couch and take part in your community—wherever you live, the Earth Mother needs defending, and even if all you can do is talk, you can at least annoy the polluters by talking about them at public meetings. The key is: don't soften up and kill the warrior within! Put him to work!

If you want to become an Earth Warrior, you will need a little bit of training. Most of all, you will have to understand the Earth in order to help her. So find the patch of woodland, desert or wild seacoast closest to where you live, and drive out there. Then get out of your car. Then walk. Walk as deep into the wilderness as you possibly can. Then sit for a spell. Chances are good that the Earth Mother herself will tell you how to help her.

Magical Teas

By Ann Moura (Aoumiel)

Instructions for a Good Pot of Tea

1. Bring cold water to boil in a kettle

2. Place bulk leaves loosely in a china or ceramic teapot and set near the tea kettle to warm as the kettle is brought to a boil.

3. Pour boiling water into the teapot.

4. Steep for 3–5 minutes.

5. Pour tea through a strainer into teacup or warm a second teapot by swirling a bit of the hot water from the kettle in it, discard, then pour tea through a strainer into the fresh pot (this will keep the tea from becoming bitter) and serve.

6. Add milk, sweetener, and lemon to taste.

7. For tea leaf reading, do not strain.

8. Cover teapot with a cozy to keep it warm.

Recipes to Try

Faery Tea

Drink this prior to working with the plant devas and faeries.

3 teaspoons English Breakfast tea

½ teaspoon chamomile

1 teaspoon dandelion root

1½ teaspoon elder flower

1½ teaspoon hops

½ teaspoon mullein

½   teaspoon raspberry leaf

1½ teaspoons rose hips

As you place the ingredients into the pot, chant:

Black for strength, then apple of night, wild grown root, and Lady's blessing. Leap for joy, then between the worlds, tangle of bramble and fairy love knots. Brewed to invite the fair folk to tea, working together, they and me.

DIVINATION TEA

Drink prior to or in conjunction with divinations.

1 tablespoon black tea

1 tablespoon mugwort

2 teaspoons lemon balm

1 teaspoon eyebright

1 tablespoon rose hips

As you place the ingredients into the pot, chant:

Black for power and wards negativity, wort for inspiration in divination, balm for success, bright for the psychic eye, and hips for divination, protection, and love. Herbs of the Lady infuse thy blessings in me as I infuse thee into this tea.

LOVERS' TEA

Share with a loved one or prior to doing love magics (you may want to create a suitable chant).

1 tablespoon China rose

2 teaspoons chamomile

1 teaspoon damiana

1 teaspoon mullein

1 teaspoon raspberry leaf

2 teaspoons rose hips

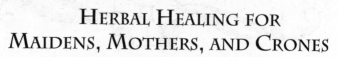

Herbal Healing for Maidens, Mothers, and Crones

By Marguerite Elsbeth

In cultures all over the world there are great stores of folklore regarding plants and the wise women who use them to create healing medicines. Try the following herbal tea preparations for maidens, mothers, and crones. You will need cheesecloth for straining herbs; a fine-meshed, stainless-steel strainer; glass bottles and jars for storage; and a mortar and pestle for grinding herbs. Do not use aluminum or copper pots and utensils.

Maiden Herbs

For newly raging hormones, menstrual discomfort. and skin problems, try astragalus, black haw, burdock root, cinnamon bark, dandelion root, ginger root, licorice root, nettle leaf, seaweed, or valerian root

Moon Maiden Tea

- 1 tablespoon ginger root
- 1 tablespoon black haw
- ½ tablespoon cinnamon bark
- 1 tablespoon valerian root

Moon Maiden Tea is used against menstrual cramps and employs the mystical, wild, enchanted energy of night. Place black haw, ginger and cinnamon in a crystal bowl. Cover with fresh, cold water and set outside under the moonlight. Let stand overnight. In the morning, move container to a warm, shady spot. Add valerian root and infuse for thirty minutes. Strain and drink a little every fifteen minutes.

Mother Herbs

For general health, menstrual problems, fertility, and childbirth, try angelica, black cohash, chaste berry, comfrey, dong quai, motherwort, mugwort, pau d'arco, raspberry, sassafras bark, or yarrow

Mother Sun Power Tea

- 3 tablespoons sassafras bark
- 2 tablespoons dandelion root

1	tablespoon ginger root
½	tablespoon cinnamon
1	tablespoon licorice root
¼	tablespoon orange peel
1	tablespoon pau d'arco
¼	tablespoon dong quai root
1	tablespoon chaste berry
1	tablespoon wild yam

Mother Sun Tea attracts the dynamic, vital energy embodied in solar force. Mix herbs together. Place four to six tablespoons of herbal mixture in a glass jar filled with one quart of cold water. Cover with a tight-fitting lid, and set the jar out of doors in strong, hot, direct sunlight for several hours. Strain. Drink three cups daily.

CRONE HERBS

For menopause and beginning a new cycle of life, try blue cohash, borage, camomile, false unicorn root, ginkgo leaf, ginseng, gota kola leaf, horsetail, oat straw, peppermint, sage, or sarsaparilla.

CRONE ROOT TEA

2	tablespoons wild yam
2	tablespoons licorice
3	tablespoons sarsaparilla
1	tablespoon chaste berry
1	tablespoon ginger
1	tablespoon false unicorn root
2	tablespoons sage
1	tablespoon cinnamon
½	tablespoon black cohash

This tea is believed to help with the challenges of menopause. Empower with the Sun or Moon methods described above. Or place six tablespoons of herbal mixture into one quart of cold water and simmer for twenty minutes. Strain. Drink two cups daily.

Tips On Making Your Own Self-Hypnosis Tapes

By Silver RavenWolf

When you practice self-hypnosis you are a dreamweaver. You become the master creator of an illusion that will manifest into the reality you desire. You are the birth parent of a thoughtform that will materialize on this plane. Heavy stuff.

In order for any self-hypnosis to work, you must have a strong, motivating desire to change or bring toward you your greatest desires. If you are the proverbial doubting Thomas, don't bother with self-hypnosis until you have learned to reprogram your mind to a more positive outlook on life.

Self-hypnosis bypasses the critical, conscious mind and deals with the emotional, subconscious mind. Everything you hear, see, smell, read, touch, taste, or experience is stored in the mind. Your mind doesn't forget and lose information; rather your mind blocks and stores information. (For example, I never forget a face, but I always have trouble remembering a person's name.) Any memory can be accessed through self-hypnosis and used in a positive manner for healing or goal programming purposes.

It is my firm belief that there is not a single, well-adjusted person who cannot use self-hypnosis techniques for positive change. Your body is familiar with the alpha state. You experience this state of mind when you eat, watch a boring television show, or daydream. It's that easy.

To create your own taped self-hypnosis sessions you will need a tape recorder that is in good working order, a ninety-minute tape, and peace and quiet. You may wish to tape music in the background, so do a few tests with your voice and the volume level on your music system. You don't want to drown out your own words.

To listen to your taped sessions I suggest using earphones with your tape recorder, rather than setting the recorder beside you on a desk or table. The earphones will block out any extraneous noises.

When you talk to yourself out loud in a positive manner you aid in the body's mental, physical, and spiritual healing process. By talking in these affirmations, you can create success and well-being for yourself. By listening to personalized tapes for thirty days (yes, I know, bummer on the thirty days) you can produce astounding changes and advancement within your own mind.

The key element to mental and magical success is programming. In fact, did you know that most maladaptive behavior is the result of inappropriate programming, and eighty percent of all illnesses are psychosomatic and can be healed with hypnotherapy, or self-talk? You betcha!

It is suggested that you tape your self-hypnosis induction once or twice to practice before you do your final copy. After a while, you'll be able to tape right away, but for now, a dry run or two is best. No coughing, no dropping the mike, no rustling the pages of a book close to the recorder, no fiddling with the music. It is suggested that you use a musical background, because you must make pauses in the session, and there will be points where you will tape several minutes without speaking. The music helps to drown out daily noises, such as traffic on the road outside, the hum of your fridge, etc. Compact disc music is best because it plays longer, therefore you won't be fiddling with turning a tape during the recording of your session. Don't use a radio station.

Why not just use over-the-counter hypnosis tapes instead of creating your own? It is cheaper to create your own, although they won't be as high of quality. Secondly, you listen to yourself better than you listen to anyone else. Best of all, you can tailor the tape just the way you want to. Sometimes over-the-counter hypnosis and self-hypnosis tapes won't work for you. It could be that you don't like the voice of the narrator, or there is a statement on the tape that you do not agree with, and therefore you resist the suggestions. Finally, you may be one of those people who needs a live body to give you a pre-programmed instruction before you listen to the tape. Remember, unless you listen to your tapes faithfully for thirty days, no tape, whether store-bought, or made by you, will make a significant improvement in your life.

Your tape is working if you experience the following during or after a session:

1. Relaxation of body and mind. You should feel terrific, or at least well rested, after the use of any self-hypnosis tape. If you don't, then there is a suggestion on the tape that is not good for you, or steering you in the right direction. Review the tape, then re-tape to suit your needs.

2. Narrowed focus of attention. During the session you shouldn't be worrying if the cookies in the oven are going to burn or what your kid is up to. Take care of these concerns before you begin to listen to your taped session.

3. Reduced awareness of external environment and everyday concerns. During the session

you should be concentrating on doing the work on the tape. Things of the outside world should drift away. In essence, you probably won't care if the house falls down around you.

You should also notice the effects of your tapes in your conscious, every day life. If this is not happening, re-tape the session and add positive suggestions to make it so.

Your tape should contain at least one relaxation exercise, an induction technique, and the designation of a personal sacred space. From there you can progress into positive affirmations, a vision quest, or a visualization to bring something important into your life (such as a skill you are trying to achieve). The tape is completed with a count-up that brings you back to the Beta state. Where can you get good induction techniques? Of course I'm partial, but the best techniques I've found (and used repeatedly) are from Hewitt's books, put out by Llewellyn Publications. He has a generous selection of reading material on hypnosis and self-hypnosis techniques. If you already have a store-bought tape that works fairly well, try using those same techniques, but tailor the tape to your personal needs.

With all this in mind, you are ready to begin practicing your tape recording. One final reminder while taping: take your time. Read the words slowly, don't rush. Give several pauses. Don't do a dramatic reading. The idea of the tape is to bore your conscious mind, so that your subconscious mind can accept the suggestions. If you start vocalizing like Hamlet, it won't work. Now, get out your tape recorder and begin!

MAGICAL DE-STRESSING

BY EDAIN MCCOY

"The hectic pace of modern living produces stress."

This maxim is easily the greatest understatement of the 90s. Short of shelling out a hundred bucks an hour on the analyst's couch, many people feel there is little they can do to lower their stress levels. The gifts of mother nature, however, stirred together with a little bit of magic, can make all the difference.

Deep breathing, the same in-through-the-nose and out-through-the-mouth technique often used to induce meditation, can work wonders. When you feel that the world is closing in on you, close your eyes and spend two or three minutes focusing on nothing but your breathing. As you exhale, visualize all your pent-up tensions being released from you like poisonous gas.

Another trick is to stop and engage in a few minutes of inner-world frolic. Steady yourself with a few deep breaths, then visualize yourself in a fantasy scene of your choice: be promoted to the job you covet or take those extra bows on the stage at Carnegie Hall. Knowing you have this escape hatch to a better place open to you at any time can make even the most miserably stressful situation more bearable.

Grounding yourself can also help. This is an old magical trick whereby we collect and reconnect our scattered energies with the comforting stability of mother earth. If you are in a place where you can stand still for a few minutes, or where you can place your hands on the ground, do so while visualizing all your stress collecting in the center of your body, then being filtered out through your feet or hands into Mother Earth. If you are not in a position to touch the earth, simply sit still and visualize a beam of calming blue-violet light entering the top of your head, passing down though your body collecting all your tension, and then passing the tension right out through the root chakra at the base of your tailbone and on into Mother Earth.

If you are acquainted with personal spirit guides, or have patron deities, you can mentally call out to them to come to you and siphon off the stress. Ask them to place a hand on your head or stomach, or wherever else you feel is the center of your stress, and then place the other hand on the ground. Allow them to be a conduit for channeling away your tension.

If you are one of those people who tends to bring your stresses home and vent them on your family, try a simple grounding exercise as you walk from your place of employment to your car. With each step you take, mentally send your tension into your legs, and each time your feet hit the ground, allow a bit of the stress to ground out into the Earth. Get into the rhythm of this as you walk along, timing it so that when you reach your car, all your stress is gone. Take a few deep breaths before beginning the drive home.

If you find you have trouble sleeping due to stress, try expanding on any of the above mental exercises. If you find you are still wide awake, you might want to try soaking a washcloth in cool apple cider vinegar and placing this across your forehead. This old folk remedy can work wonders. Combine the compress with a foot or forehead massage for best results.

You may also want to treat yourself to a cup of herbal tea laced with ingredients known to produce relaxing effects on the body. Sitting down with a steamy hot drink seems a simple thing, but when you are stressed out and pressed for time, it can be the greatest of luxuries. Try teas of either catnip, valerian, peppermint, camomile, hops, motherwort, passion flower, or any combination of these to help make you drowsy. Use about one teaspoon total of herbs for each six-ounce cup you brew. Unlike most pills, they are not addictive, they will not harm you if used occasionally, and they will not leave you feeling drugged in the morning. (**EDITOR'S NOTE:** Use only small amounts of valerian at first, until you determine how it affects you.)

Dream Magic

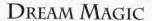

By Silver RavenWolf

Do you ever want to get an important message through to someone, but you just don't know how to do it? Here is what you do:

1. Determine precisely what it is you want them to hear, or perhaps feel. Write down your wish on a piece of paper in simple sentence form.

2. Make a dream pillow using a small square of fabric and a little batting. Throw in a pinch of lavender and rosemary. Put in the piece of paper last, then sew up the end.

3. Put the dream pillow on your altar. Do an altar devotion to center yourself, then create sacred space. Cast a circle and call the quarters if you like, but it isn't necessary.

4. Center yourself, then hold your hands over the dream pillow and say the following:

Holy Mother, Goddess Divine,
I stand before your sacred shrine.
This person won't listen or hear
My words tickle at deafened ear.
Holy Mother, Goddess Divine,
Send a dream, awaken the mind.
Through his/her visions he/she might live
The nightmare/passion/lesson he/she so freely give.
Holy Mother, Goddess Divine
Send them your enchanted design
Clear out the cobwebs, tear down walls
Carry my message through spirit calls.

Feel free to change the incantation to suit your purpose.

DREAM INCUBATION

BY JIM GARRISON

Long ago there were temples that people would visit for the chance to receive a dream or visitation that would heal them, give them answers or direction, or bless them with a bit of prophecy. Most of those temples are ruins these days, but it was never the building that gave the dreams; rather it was a gift from the gods. You can learn much from your dreams through dream incubation.

Prepare for bed as usual, only this time, before lying down, take a Tarot deck—any deck you like will do—and shuffle the cards until you have the deck thoroughly mixed and you feel ready to proceed.

Pick a card through any method you like. Study the card and build an image of it in your mind that you can see even when you close your eyes. Go to bed, and get comfortable.

Close your eyes and visualize the card before you. Let the image of the card fill your mind, and release your hold on the image. Let the card flow through you. Feel the image washing through your consciousness, your relaxed body, and beyond. Let yourself fall to sleep. Stop concentrating if you can't sleep. Upon awakening, write down your impressions in a journal.

Once you've experimented with the tarot cards, consider using other sources for inspiration, such as runes, statues, paintings, or images of god-forms. This technique is also a good way to begin training yourself for astral projection or scrying. You can do this anywhere you would normally fall asleep, and if you have an image in mind, you really need no tools.

A VISIT FROM THE SANDMAN

BY EDAIN MCCOY

M iddle Eastern folklore introduced tales of the mischievous "sleep genie" who tosses magical sand into tired human eyes so that we will begin rubbing them. As we do, our eyelids become weighed down with sleep, and the genie can then do as he pleases, unnoticed by us. When these folktales traveled to Europe, this faery became the gentle night nomad we call the Sandman.

Just why sand is the item used to induce sleep is unclear, but it may have something to do with the annoying sandy residue we often find on our eyelashes upon awakening, or it may be a metaphor for the sparkling substance we see on the astral plane which we often refer to as faery dust. The Sandman was likely once a deity of sleep, now long forgotten. Today he clearly dwells in the faery realms of the astral kingdom and, as such, he can be contacted by the diligent faeryland traveler.

During your next bout of insomnia, close your eyes and allow your thoughts to carry you to the edges of the astral world near the gates of the faery kingdom. Mentally call out to the Sandman to work his magic on you as he sets out on his nightly rounds. Try something like:

Sandman, Sandman, bring me your faery dust,
Sandman, Sandman, your magic powers I trust.

Then return to consciousness and focus on slowing your mind and your breathing, allowing yourself to relax and prepare for sleep. If you are lucky, you may see the soft sparkle of the faery dust behind your eyelids, which is the Sandman's trademark. When this happens, know that you have been showered with the magic of sleep, and allow yourself to peacefully drift off.

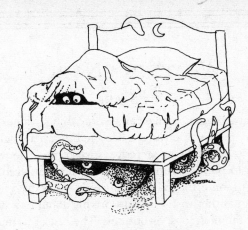

NIGHTMARES

BY SILVER RAVENWOLF

E veryone has experienced a nightmare at one time or another. Statistics relate that about half of all children experience frequent nightmares, but these decrease with age. In general, nightmares are not indicators of a sleep disorder, nor do they relate to physical or mental illnesses. Nightmares most often occur when we are under stress, or following a period of stressful events.

If you or your loved ones have been experiencing nightmares, take a close look at current and immediately past events. For children, nightmares revolve around unrest in the home, tough times at school, before a major exam, a busy holiday season, the death of a family member or school pal, or altercations with friends. For adults, the circumstances giving birth to nightmares can form a complicated matrix, as we willingly and unwillingly carry various responsibilities. Modern magical anti-nightmare applications include:

- Discovering stressful connections and eliminating or reducing them.

- Working magic to bring harmony into your life.

- Meditating every evening before sleep to assist in eliminating stress.

- Invoking a spirit protector before sleep.

- Making a poppet for children to scare dream-boogies.

- Enchanting a toy soldier to guard a bedroom door.

WHAT'S IN A NAME?

BY STARR

If you are a Pagan, names can be everything. Names are the key to whether a person is a "closeted" or open Pagan. The decision to be public or secretive is frustrating. Do we open ourselves to public scrutiny, or do we stay cloistered in our homes? For some, there are no concerns—they may choose to be as open as they wish without worrying about how it will affect their families, jobs, or business. The rest of us must consider the repercussions on every aspect of our lives. Can we afford to lose our jobs because bosses do not understand the differences between Paganism and Satanism? Or the custody of children when a judge refuses to listen to a Pagan parent?

So what's in a name?

A person's name holds the key to his or her security and privacy. Someone who is openly Pagan and uses his or her real name in public may be harassed. A stranger, knowing the name and city of residence of another person, can call directory assistance and obtain listed numbers. This is one reason why many Pagans choose to be known by Craft names, PICs (Pagan Identification Codes), "handles," etc. These are not to be confused with magical names, which are used when a person is performing magic, although the names may be the same.

Pagans usually go by first names, aliases, or legal names. By using an assumed name, people are protecting themselves and their families from possible harassment. Even though using a pseudonym insures some security, it places limitations upon a person. A "closet" Pagan must be careful with his or her choice of words and aware of who is within earshot. A kind of code appears, like referring to magic and ritual as "arts and crafts." When a housemate, neighbor, parent, or other potentially ominous "watcher" is nearby, the feeling of caution looms during ritual. This kind of continual guardedness is tiring, and it can make the lifestyle of an open Pagan look very appealing.

Due to job, family, or other restrictions, if it isn't possible to be open, a middle ground has to be found. This is where pseudonyms come in. The use of assumed names can allow someone, who otherwise found it impossible, to be active within the Pagan community. Assumed names also allow people to choose to what degree they wish to be public.

Unfortunately, taking precautions to maintain privacy doesn't guarantee results. In some situations, coming out of the broom closet is forced upon a person if a relative discovers books or someone either knowingly or unknowingly reveals a Pagan's true identity.

At times, trying to correct others' mistakes can expose Pagans as well. In one case, a Pagan, whom we will call Ranya, submitted an editorial correcting a newspaper's article equating Witchcraft with Satanism. Despite requests that her real name not be published, the newspaper printed her article with her identity and town of residence. The teacher of the dojo where Ranya studied martial arts dismissed her from the class, stating that he "didn't want her kind there." She lost her job. Someone called directory assistance, found her telephone number, and left a bomb threat on the answering machine. While in later articles the paper made clear distinctions between Wicca and Satanism, Ranya's life was changed forever.

Each group and each person has a different philosophy about names. In some groups, no one uses given names, in others everyone does, while other groups lie in between. Each person needs to decide how open he or she wishes to be, and to find a comfortable spot, either solitary or within a group. If we respect each other's choices to be public or private, and take the responsibility to introduce ourselves the way we wish to be known, then all of us can live and enjoy our religions with everyone's wishes regarding privacy intact.

How Planetary Hours Work

By Estelle Daniels

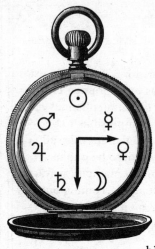

Planetary Hours are a very old system of planetary hour and day correspondences, where each "hour" of the day is attributed to (or ruled by) one of the seven visible planets. The days of the week were named after the planetary hours. Planetary hours have nothing to do with where the planets are in the sky, what aspects they may make, or anything to do with your personal birthchart. Planetary hours are, however, helpful when you are in a hurry, or need to do a working today and want certain influences but the planets in the sky aren't cooperating.

The way they work is that each day of the week is given a planetary correspondence: Sunday = Sun; Monday = Moon; Tuesday = Mars; Wednesday = Mercury; Thursday = Jupiter; Friday = Venus; and Saturday = Saturn. This planet rules the first planetary hour of the day, followed by other rulers in an order called the Chaldean order (after the Chaldeans, the first astrologers). It goes: Saturn, Jupiter, Mars, Sun, Venus, Mercury, Moon. This list shows the seven visible planets in ascending order of average daily speed. This order becomes very important, and if you work with planetary hours frequently, you will probably memorize it over time.

The "day" of planetary hours is different from our standard civil day, which begins at midnight. With planetary hours, each day begins at dawn and lasts until the following dawn. Think of the TV listings, which start each day at 6:00 AM, and you have the idea. There can be confusion here, because 2:00 AM Tuesday is really still Monday with planetary hours. You have to pay attention, because this is the most common mistake made with this system.

Symbol Key

Sun ☉	Saturn ♄	Venus ♀
Mercury ☿	Mars ♂	Moon ☽

The first "hour" after dawn is the same planetary correspondence as the planet of the day, so the first Friday hour, starting at dawn, is a Venus hour. The hours then keep the Chaldean order all around the clock, looping back from Moon to Saturn. So the order for Friday goes, Venus, Mercury, Moon, Saturn, Jupiter, Mars Sun, Venus and so on to the twenty-fourth hour, ruled by the Moon. Then the next hour, which is the first Saturday hour, is attributed to Saturn, the second to Jupiter, the third to Mars, the fourth to the Sun, etc. The Chaldean order is constant, and the first hour always corresponds to the planet of the day. This is how the planetary correspondences of the days were determined, and the days of the week were named.

Each planet has three or four hours in each day. You shouldn't have to wait for more than ten clock hours or so for a certain planetary hour. The length of the planetary hours differs from day to night, and from day to day, month to month throughout the year. In summer, in the Northern Hemisphere, the daylight hours can last eighty minutes or more. Conversely, the nighttime hours are only forty minutes or less. In winter, it is reversed. At the equinoxes the day and night hours are all roughly sixty minutes each. When working with planetary hours it is best to allow a bit of slop in the times of the hour changes, roughly five minutes each way. So if the hour changes at 11:44 AM, best to either start before 11:39 or after 11:49 to ensure you are in the correct hour.

When using planetary hours, the hour designation is much more important than the planet of the day. The planet of the hour is the primary correspondence, and the planet of the day is a lesser, secondary influence. In High Magic, both the day and hour are important.

Simply Scent

By Gwydion O'Hara

Eras past may evoke visions of the perfumer who was part scientist, part sorcerer, part chemist, and part artist. Those who dabble in blending essential oils today may consider themselves alchemists, aroma therapists, or, as appeared in one writing on the subject, olfactory engineers.

So what is the truth about aromatherapy? Is it magic or art; science or cosmetology? In fact, there are hints of all of these noble ventures within aromatherapy. The history of scents and their creators is the history of civilization. From the ritual incenses offered to the gods in ancient Egyptian temples to the essential oils and perfumes that beckon today's consumer with product names that seem to promise health, love, or success, aromas have had a significant place in changing cultures.

One of the more fascinating aspects of the field of aromatherapy is not so much that the scents function, but how they function. While we might choose our wardrobes or paint the walls in a room with colors that appeal to our aesthetic sensitivities, aromas have the ability to function on a far more subtle level. With the visual stimulus of color, we fairly submerge our sensitivities in a given hue. Scentual influences, on the other hand, affect us in significant capacity while they exist only as trace components of our surroundings. They can operate strongly as almost indistinguishable, subconscious influences.

It is because of this subtlety that fragrance may be considered the homeopathic remedy of the healing and magical arts. Homeopathic remedies function at their greatest strength as trace elements. Their presence does not necessarily alter physiological conditions, like medicines or herbal mixtures might be employed to clear a skin disorder or to settle a stomach. Instead, at least a part of their functioning is in the subtle effects they have on the psyche. Just as a homeopathic remedy can spur on the immune system to address a particular ill, the presence of different fragrances can enlist the vast resources of the unconscious mind to aid in the recuperative process. This is true whether the ailment is of a physical nature, like a winter cold or migraine headache, or is an ailment of life that needs curing, like depression or lost love.

This level is not the only one on which scent can provide desired effects. It is simply the one that is too often overlooked. However, in addition to their command of the subtle realms, aromas may be utilized in a way not unlike herbal treatments. While herbal mixtures are most often administered by ingestion or by external application (depending on the ailment), aromas are employed by inhalation or by external application, or often a combination of the two. While a bruise oil, for example, is generally applied externally to the affected area, the effect of inhaling the healing fragrance of the applied oil blend should not be understated. Just as vitamin E can be utilized to heal burns and abrasions from the inside out through ingestion, or from the outside in through treatment of the skin, oils may function on more than one level to speed along the desired effects.

There are many approaches to the blending of essential oils to produce the desired end fragrance. There are those who work through astrological associations, considering what properties each planet has, and which body parts it rules. The resulting blends are reflective of a particular astrological influence, and capture the essence of the healing properties of each. On a religious or magical level, these blends may be considered a tribute to different planetary or zodiac influences, and so sacred to the gods and goddesses who rule them. Some work in accordance with elemental influences. They might utilize patchouli or oakmoss, for example, for the element of earth, cinnamon as a fire oil, violet as air, and cypress to represent water.

This is the bottom line on using aromatic blends: Does the blend create the desired effect? If it does, it is self validating. So no matter whether we recognize ourselves as chemists, magicians, healers, aromatherapists, perfumer alchemist or olfactory engineers, in truth the magic is one that has accompanied humankind throughout the rise and fall of successive civilizations. In its most natural unadorned glory, it is simply scent.

WATER BABIES

BY BERNYCE BARLOW

The legend of the Water Babies has been a part of western lore for thousands of years. The story connects two sacred lakes, Pyramid and Tahoe, together in spirit, although they lie ninety miles apart. Lake Tahoe, which straddles the High Sierras of the California/Nevada border, was the first of two lakes to be formed in that area roughly sixty thousand years ago. The Tahoe of today is a relatively new lake, having been in its present form for only about ten thousand years. The last time the fires were lit over Lake Tahoe, the ground uplifted eight hundred feet and shook so hard that the water broached the rim to the east, and formed what is called the Little Truckee river. Little Truckee river drained into a basin and created Pyramid Lake.

The "spirit of place" is different at each lake. Pyramid has a more serious character, simply by its nature. A great deal of Native American legend that encompasses a number of tribes in the region surrounds these two lakes, but the story of the Water Babies seems to cross all boundaries. Even today folks will warn you about the Water Babies.

It seems that for thousands of years, the people indigenous to this region noticed that if a body was lost in Lake Tahoe, it was rarely recovered. The same went for the shallower Pyramid Lake. The other odd observance was that bodies drowned in Lake Tahoe occasionally turned up in Pyramid Lake, albeit, not in good condition. Legends were spun from these incidences and handed down through time. The story of the Water Babies is one of the stories explaining the mystery.

Water Babies are spirits that live beneath the springs, streams, and lakes. They can take physical form whenever they choose, or remain as spirits. Their name is a warning about the tactics they use to lure unsuspecting folks to their demise. Although their name may be endearing, they will lure you to your death if you let them by pulling you under water and drowning you. The Water Babies keep their victims in underwater caves and lava tubes. They keep their victims' spirits there as well, for company. That is why bodies are rarely found at Pyramid Lake or Lake Tahoe.

Sometimes you can tell where the Water Babies are. Hot springs are a sign that the Babies are submerged somewhere below, keeping warm. Their fires heat up the water. Water Babies not only live beneath the springs, but in the depths of the lakes and along the rivers and streams. It is these spirits which are perhaps the most deadly, for one must discern which ones are real and which ones are of the imagination. A lonely Water Baby may lure you to a babbling brook by giggling and cooing. Those who would follow this sound might find themselves captured for eternity. As for the Water Babies that live in the lakes, one must be extremely careful, indeed! There are many ways to be captured by them. They have been known to call on the winds to sink a boat, or to capsize one themselves. Their mischievousness can cause a reed raft to leak, or a cramp in the leg while swimming.

So, how do the bodies lost in Lake Tahoe turn up in Pyramid Lake? Well, some say they spill into the Little Truckee river, then make their way some ninety miles downstream. Others say underground rivers or lava tubes filled with fresh water transport the bodies via some ancient subterranean canal. Then, there are those that have knowledge of the Water Babies and how they can cause such things to happen.

If you happen to find yourself near a body of water that seems to call your name, beware. It may be that the spirit of place is just embracing your presence, but it could also be a Water Baby testing your discernment.

HOW TO MAKE YOUR OWN
WOMAN STONE

BY SILVER RAVENWOLF

S everal years ago a friend of mine went to a women's festival in New York and brought me back a very special gift—a woman stone. At the time I didn't know the importance of this stone, or how it would change my life in a positive manner. I played with the stone for a while, rubbing its smooth surface in my palm, and felt the serenity of the Earth and our Mother. To this day, I do not know the artist who painted the woman's figure on the stone, but I feel connected to her every time I hold my precious gift.

The stone is very easy to design. First, you must find a smooth, oblong stone that is no longer and no thicker than your index finger. A glossy creek stone is best. Cleanse and consecrate it in the name of the Lady.

The next step requires artistic ingenuousness on your part. Take out a piece of paper and begin designing a woman's figure to fit the shape of the stone. The figure need not be a masterpiece. Mine is very primitive, showing a woman wrapped in a cloak that fits the contours of the stone. Her face is hard and coarse; the lines depicting her nose and eyes are extraordinarily simple.

After you have worked out the design, you will need red, white, and black acrylic paints and two brushes—numbers 00 and 03 point. Begin by outlining your figure with a pencil. Don't worry if you mess up, you can always paint over your lines. After you have a rudimentary drawing on the stone, begin to paint it. My stone has a white face, one white hand (the other is hidden by the cloak) and a red cape. The detail of the face is done in black, as well as the folds in her cloak.

Let the stone dry overnight, then paint on a gloss sealer to protect your work. Because you use the woman stone, the paint will eventually wear away. About once every two years I renew the paint, then re-gloss.

Empower the stone in the name of the four elements and the Lady. Call forth peace, harmony and strength to imbue the piece. Place it under your pillow the first night to meld your energy with that of the woman stone.

My woman stone has helped me through many trials and tribulations. I hold it during meditation and when I work with hypnotherapy clients. At times you will find her on my altar, and she is always on the table when I read the runes and the tarot cards. My woman stone has gone with me to booksignings, festivals, camping trips, gatherings, circles, seminars, and when things are tough at work. Sometimes she perches on my computer, watching me while I write, helping me to fulfill my destiny and say the right thing to you. To me, she represents the support of the earth and the love of a friend, but she also represents my oath of service to humankind. She even entered into my first fictional book, *Beneath A Mountain Moon,* and plays an important part in the story.

The woman stone is a natural gift to a special friend for birthdays and holy days. This is one gift that you do cleanse, consecrate and empower before the gift is given, linking the stone's energies to divinity and to that special someone. Be sure to put a card with the stone indicating that it carries magic, so your friend knows not to banish and cleanse the stone. I sincerely hope that you enjoy working with your woman stone as much as I have enjoyed working with mine.

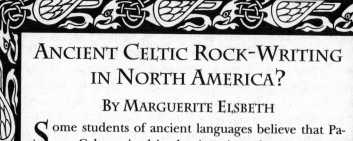

Ancient Celtic Rock-Writing in North America?

By Marguerite Elsbeth

Some students of ancient languages believe that Pagan Celts arrived in the Americas about two thousand years ago, long before the Vikings or Columbus ever set foot here in Indian Country. They left their tracks literally etched in stone, in the ancient Celtic alphabet called Ogham. Rock-writing was one of the earliest forms of communication, and carries great spiritual significance to ancient European and Native American peoples as well as those of us following the shamanic or Pagan traditions of our ancestors.

One known Ogham site in southwest New Mexico is less than three miles from a Mimbres Amerindian site; others are in Apache territory. Another Ogham site may contain a Celtic burial, and three have rock-writing along with the chiseled image of a Pagan Celtic water goddess identifying heretofore unknown water sources. A prayer mask and Sun symbol, Ogham instructions in Gaelic, and several stone notches reveal a winter solstice observatory belonging to a Celtic holy man or shaman. Nearby are several Ogham tracts using the Gaelic language to speak of farming, water, refuge, planting and harvest times, and again, the winter solstice. The "telephone dial," yet another Ogham petroglyph, shows Earth or the Sun surrounded by ten planets. (How did the ancient Celts know there were ten planets, including the Sun, when we did not know until this century?) Other Ogham petroglyphs include a Celtic cross, a sailing ship, a pre-Spanish mounted horseman dated 1500 AD, a man in a leather chest piece brandishing a cross bow and short sword (weapons developed by the Celts), and the image of Tanith, the Carthaginian sailors' goddess of protection.

Some American Indian oral histories and traditions speak of these ancient travelers, and there is evidence to show that many Celts stayed and were absorbed into Native cultures, while others returned to their homelands. For example, some Maliseet Indians believe that they are descendants of Irish Culdee Christians, and that their native speech is related to Gaelic. Scholars who agree that the Celts founded colonies in North America think that the Gaelic word *pooka* shares a common linguistic origin with the Algonquin word *puk,* a reference to woodland faeries and elves called puk-wud-jies or little people.

All of these findings may explain why Euro-American people currently strive to make a cultural cross-over connection with the ancestral spirits and indigenous people of North America, even as we continue to revive our own magical Pagan roots. Do the voices of our Celtic ancestors call us to honor the Great Spirit and Mother Earth along with the Horned God and the Lady? Only the mysterious Ogham-traced stones know for sure.

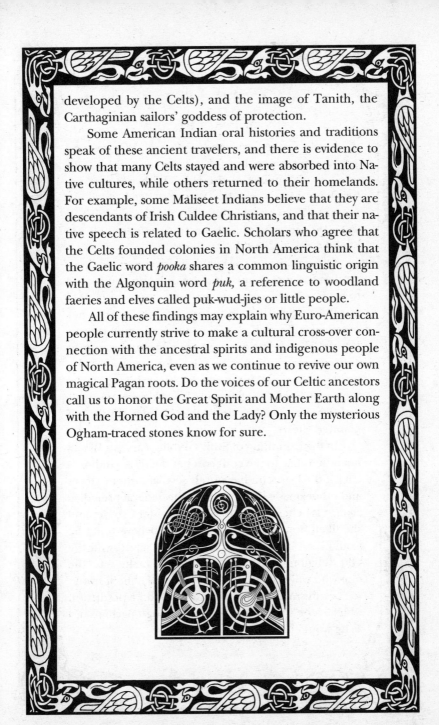

Sybil Leek

By deTraci Regula

S he may make some modern Pagans, Witches, and Wiccans wince, but for a generation, Sybil Leek was a true "opener of the way." With her ground-breaking autobiography *Diary of a Witch*, Sybil announced in her own inimitable style that witchcraft was not dead, never had been, and was definitely not likely to curl up and die on her shift.

Often criticized for her ability to attract media attention for almost anything she did, and considered to be a "sell out" when she became a popular tabloid astrologer, Sybil had little need to profit from her practice of the craft. A canny businesswoman with an IQ of 164, her various non-craft business ventures and extensive writing for television programs supported her family. Intensely psychic, Sybil was a prototype of later "ghostbusters," working extensively with Dr. Hans Holzer and others in explorations of haunted sites.

In the beginning of Sybil's public years as a Witch, her adherence to the craft cost her dearly as landlords cut off the leases on her purely secular antique stores and others made her a target of the general prejudice against Witches. Her family knew Aleister Crowley and she liked him, though she privately believed that he would have been better off if he had stayed with the Old Religion. He told her parents that she was "the one who will take up where I leave off...She'll live to see occultism almost being understood," a prediction which came true in many ways, although perhaps not as he would have expected.

Consistently ahead of her time, in the 1960s Sybil was already pointing out that those who followed the religion of witchcraft should be active in efforts to save the environment as a way of honoring the nature deities. A master astrologer, Sybil wrote *The Astrological Guide to Love and Sex,* where she presented the then-controversial view that being gay was not a sickness but simply one more aspect of the personality which could be charted astrologically. She predicted twenty-five years ago that gay activism and acceptance of gay sexuality would naturally increase as we moved into the influences of the Aquarian Age. Among the more than fifty books she wrote were several election-year works judging the astrological chances of presidential candidates. In 1968, she predicted that the then relatively unknown Ronald Reagan would have close involvement with and impact the destiny of the United States.

When Sybil died in 1982, at an age she was careful not to reveal, she had lived to see the establishment of Wicca as a recognized religion and the fulfillment of many of her predictions about the beginning of the Age of Aquarius. She was an optimist, believing that humans would somehow conquer their mistakes and bring about a new age of peace and fulfillment. We can only hope that this prediction, like her others, also comes true.

FURTHER READING:

Leek, Sybil. *Diary of a Witch.*

——, *A Shop in the High Street.*

——, *The Complete Art of Witchcraft.*

STAR WOMAN

By Marguerite Elsbeth

The legend of Star Woman is a creation myth belonging to various Native American tribes. The Tsalagi or Cherokee people tell this version of the story:

One day, the most beautiful and beloved daughter of Asga Ya Galunlati, the father of all, was walking in her father's favorite garden, when she heard the sound of drumming coming from under a little tree. Curious, she started digging beneath its roots until she created a hole and fell into it. Round and round she spun through the sky, falling from heaven to Earth. It was a long way down.

The creatures that lived on the Earth at that time were very sensitive beings, but they lacked the spark of fire that enabled them to reason. Having no logic, only feelings, these creatures simply floated around without a care on the waters that covered the world. When Asga Ya Galunlati saw his daughter spiraling through the sky, he called upon the winds and the creatures of Earth to help her land safely. At once, the impressionable creatures looked up and saw something bright falling toward them. It was the maiden, shining like a star. The creatures sensed she was a gift from the heavens and knew instinctively that they must do something to protect her. They did not know that she carried clear quartz, ruby, topaz, jasper, emerald, rubillite, amethyst, pearl, fire opal, tourmaline, azurite, and aconite within her womb, crystals that symbolized the potential qualities of humankind.

Turtle was the first to react, offering his back to cushion the Star Maiden's fall. Many of the other creatures dove deep into the great ocean to gather soft, wet sand to support her fall against Turtle's

hard shell. Both Water Spider and Muskrat claimed the honor of bringing up the protective firmament from the bottom of the sea, but whichever of the two put it there, the offshore loam was placed on Turtle's back, where it grew and grew, even as the Star Maiden continued to spiral down and down slowly through the sky, wafted by gentle winds. With the help of Buzzard, the dark, rich Earth grew into rolling hills, snow-capped mountains and verdant green valleys.

At last Star Woman landed on the solid Earth that rose up from the sea, which some Indian people now call Turtle Island. And as the soil was fertile, Star Woman's ample breasts gave forth squash and beans and corn, and her tears forged mighty rivers and placid, blue-mirrored lakes filled with fresh water.

Some Cherokees believe that all humans may trace their ancestry back to Star Woman, and that because she is the mother of all, we are all related. Indeed all people have received her blessing—the spirit of the sacred fire that ignites the mind to wonder, and inspires humankind to see the magical relationship between all creatures and things.

BIBLIOGRAPHY

Ywahoo, Dhyani. *Voices of Our Ancestors: Cherokee Teachings from the Wisdom Fire.* Boston: Shambhala Publications, 1987.

Divination From Eastern Europe

By Ken Johnson

The traditions of Slavic Europe are not as well-known as those of more westerly lands, but they are rich in the lore of the natural world. Here are some Pagan Slavic techniques for divining the future.

Let the women go to the woods early on the morning of the summer solstice. Pick flowers and make wreaths. Choose someone to represent the Summer Maid, and take her into the forest, dancing and singing all the way. Blindfold her and deck her with the garlands, then let everyone dance around her. She must take all the wreaths and distribute them to the others without looking. Those who receive fresh wreaths will be fortunate in marriage; but those whose flowers are withered will not. When everyone receives a garland, all must run away from the Summer Maid, for whoever she touches will never find a lover that year.

Meet your sweetheart near a river on the summer solstice and bathe in the river together till twilight. When the midsummer fire is kindled, join hands with your sweetheart and jump together over the flames. If you can jump without loosening your hands, or if a spark follows you out of the flame, you will someday marry.

Here is a ritual that was performed on Whitsuntide, when the rusalki, or tree nymphs, leave their winter homes in lakes and rivers and come forth to romp among the trees: Let the women weave garlands of birch branches and throw them into a river. If a garland floats, its maker will find a lover in the direction toward which it flows; if it sinks, she will have bad luck in relationships

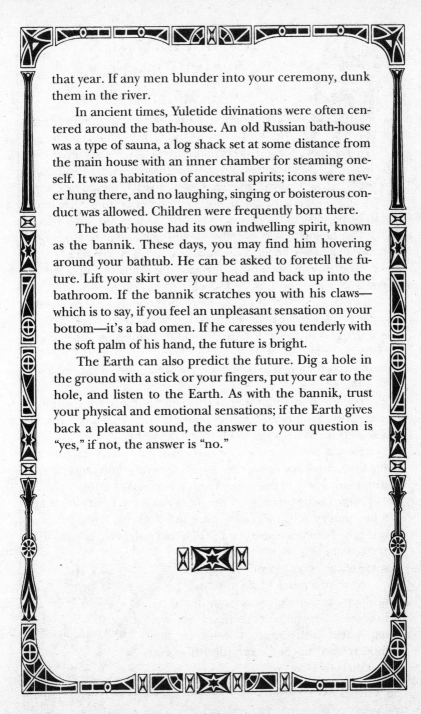

that year. If any men blunder into your ceremony, dunk them in the river.

In ancient times, Yuletide divinations were often centered around the bath-house. An old Russian bath-house was a type of sauna, a log shack set at some distance from the main house with an inner chamber for steaming oneself. It was a habitation of ancestral spirits; icons were never hung there, and no laughing, singing or boisterous conduct was allowed. Children were frequently born there.

The bath house had its own indwelling spirit, known as the bannik. These days, you may find him hovering around your bathtub. He can be asked to foretell the future. Lift your skirt over your head and back up into the bathroom. If the bannik scratches you with his claws—which is to say, if you feel an unpleasant sensation on your bottom—it's a bad omen. If he caresses you tenderly with the soft palm of his hand, the future is bright.

The Earth can also predict the future. Dig a hole in the ground with a stick or your fingers, put your ear to the hole, and listen to the Earth. As with the bannik, trust your physical and emotional sensations; if the Earth gives back a pleasant sound, the answer to your question is "yes," if not, the answer is "no."

MAKE A BRAZILLIAN
SPRIRT OFFERING

BY MARGUERITE ELSBETH

The African-based Yoruba Tradition, which evolved into the Candomble religion in Brazil, offers solutions for all sorts of human difficulties. Business transactions, political concerns, financial woes, marital difficulties, love affairs, illness, and many other personal problems can be brought to the orixas, the Yoruba deities, for resolution.

Candomble is very popular among rich and poor alike. Evidence of a strong belief in the Yoruba spirits is everywhere on the streets of Brazil. Sometimes the moonlit sands of Copacabana Beach are aglow with tablecloths lined with candles and spread with food, a gift to Yemoja, the mermaid goddess. One can easily come across a circle of burning red candles with an image of Xango, the god of thunder and lightning, standing in the center, right in the middle of the sidewalk. These are spirit offerings, or despachos, designed to propitiate the orixas when one is in need of a special favor.

Is there something special that you want; someone to love, prosperity, good health, or the power to overcome a bad habit? Ask an orixa to help you by making a despacho.

First, choose a sympathetic orixa to grant your favor. Some of the most important orixas are listed at the end of this article, each with his or her own color, power, number, and offering:

Next, obtain an image of the orixa you are to propitiate from a botanica or religious goods store in your area. While you are there, buy candles in the orixa's color and number. Then make a pit stop at the grocery to pick up some of the orixa's favorite food.

Now, find a safe place in or out of doors, and circle the orixa with the candles. Offer the orixa the food by placing it next to the image. (Do not eat the food offered to the orixa. Allow it to rot and throw it away.)

Pray to the orixa for what you want. Then, write your desire on a piece of paper, fold it up, and put it under the image.

Light the candles and walk away, leaving your despacho to do its work. Your favor will be granted when the candles burn out. (This may take several days, depending on the size of the candles.) Once the ritual is done and your wish has come true, keep the image of the orixa on a shelf or altar in your room. Show your gratitude to the orixa by feeding him or her regularly.

NAME	COLOR	POWER	NUMBER	OFFERING
Esu	black	messages	3	toys, candy
Orunmila	yellow	divination	16	yams, kola nuts
Ogum	green	employment	7	rum, cigars
Xango	red	power, passion	4, 6	apples, bananas
Oia-Iansa	white	protection	9	eggplant
Oxum	yellow	love, marriage	5	cakes, honey
Yemoja	blue	fertility	7	sugar cane syrup
Sonponno	tan	health	17	beans, corn
Oxala	white	peace	8	cotton, coconut

The Botanica

By Marguerite Elsbeth

I first came across a botanica back in 1979, as I was walking along the street in Spanish Harlem. The botanica is a spirit supply shop, and all manner of magical goods are sold within. I can still remember the pungent aroma that wafted out through the open door.

Once inside, I discovered an infinite variety of dried herbs, leaves, flower petals, cactus thorns, petrified apples, candied citrus fruit peels, bats' wings, parrot feathers, small animal skins and furs, animal jaw bones, pickled snakes, and even dried cockroaches!

There were statues of Christian saints and the Virgin Mary next to images of the devil. All the orishas, or deities of Santeria, the Cuban version of the African-based Yoruba tradition, were represented also: Eshu, Obatala, Orunla, Chango, Oggun, Ochosi, Babalu-Aye, Yemaya, Oshun and Oya, as well as two small men in medieval clothing standing next to an altar, a man in a white loincloth stuck full of arrows, a man on a stallion spearing a serpent, an unattractive toad, and an American Indian in full war paint.

There were boxes of beads in every color under the Sun, alongside trays full of medals stamped with a variety of designs, from axes to lightning bolts. I found out that these were meant to be worn with the beads as a way of propitiating the orisha under whom one was born.

A multitude of fragrant incenses and soaps were available to help smoke and wash away troubles. I was told by the large, jovial proprietor that a riego, an herbal preparation for cleansing the home of bad vibrations, could be concocted on the spot. And let's not forget the perfumes to wear and the rainbow assortment of candles to burn for that special purpose, like "Luck in Love," "Safe Trip," "Amazing Wealth," and "Protection."

Tarot cards, and books on mediumship and Santeria, were accessible, in case one required advice on divination and magic. Of course, I gravitated to that area of the store, curious to learn more about Santeria because there was something about the religion that seemed familiar to me, almost like deja vu. (I later realized that the articles and practices associated with my own Italian Strege roots are similar to those of Santeria, especially the interchange between Pagan deities and Christian saints.)

My browsing ended with me receiving the caracoles, or seashell divination. The shopkeeper's priestess wife, a santera, threw down some cowrie shells and read only the ones that had fallen right side up. The news was startlingly accurate and mostly good, and the remedy easy to apply.

Finally, I left the botanica armed with the Santeria weapons for obtaining love—a yellow candle, a statue of Oshun, and a freshly made despojo in which to bathe—and rushed straight home to engage this newfound magic while waiting for my happily willing victim to arrive.

HUMMINGBIRD HEART

BY JANE CALLARD

Gem jungles glow in eyes
Of malachite, topaz, obsidian while
Purring wings, in endless flight
Carry the vibrant heart to where it
Can sup from sacred flowers,
Don masks of fur, of feathers
Tread the shaman's path
To inner jungles,
Slip the concealing mask over
Your face, cease to exist
In mundane realities,
Dance the Moonpaths
Lotus edged, as heart
Light guides you;
Travel in skins not your own
Yet knowledge makes them
Yours for future questioning;
Ocelot spirit, hummingbird heart
Mind like a river
Walk beneath the trees,
Lianas caress, falling leaves
Dapple skinpelt in sunlight
Like water droplets falling
Through the emerald canopy,
Kneel, touch the Mother
With gentleness, walk her
Breast, light footed,
Learn how to have your
Heart Center light filled.
Know Oneness
Contemplate peace
Experience life
Be still ...

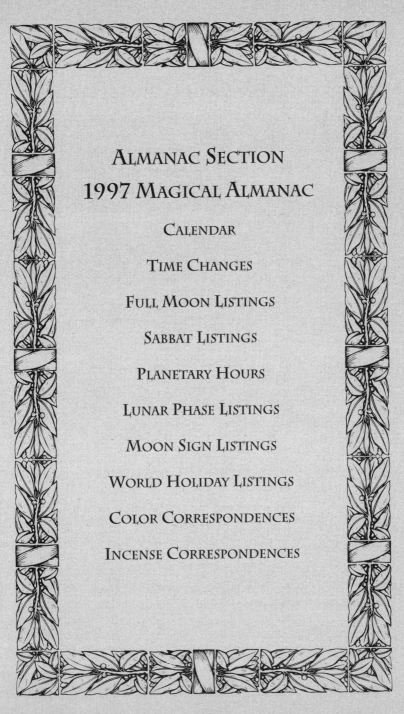

ALMANAC SECTION
1997 MAGICAL ALMANAC

CALENDAR

TIME CHANGES

FULL MOON LISTINGS

SABBAT LISTINGS

PLANETARY HOURS

LUNAR PHASE LISTINGS

MOON SIGN LISTINGS

WORLD HOLIDAY LISTINGS

COLOR CORRESPONDENCES

INCENSE CORRESPONDENCES

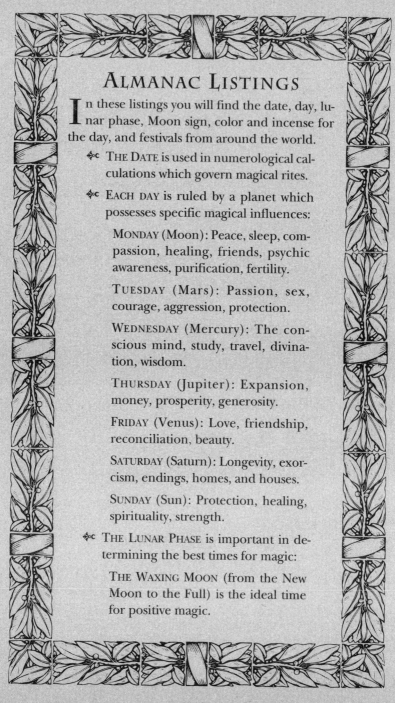

ALMANAC LISTINGS

In these listings you will find the date, day, lunar phase, Moon sign, color and incense for the day, and festivals from around the world.

❖ THE DATE is used in numerological calculations which govern magical rites.

❖ EACH DAY is ruled by a planet which possesses specific magical influences:

MONDAY (Moon): Peace, sleep, compassion, healing, friends, psychic awareness, purification, fertility.

TUESDAY (Mars): Passion, sex, courage, aggression, protection.

WEDNESDAY (Mercury): The conscious mind, study, travel, divination, wisdom.

THURSDAY (Jupiter): Expansion, money, prosperity, generosity.

FRIDAY (Venus): Love, friendship, reconciliation, beauty.

SATURDAY (Saturn): Longevity, exorcism, endings, homes, and houses.

SUNDAY (Sun): Protection, healing, spirituality, strength.

❖ THE LUNAR PHASE is important in determining the best times for magic:

THE WAXING MOON (from the New Moon to the Full) is the ideal time for positive magic.

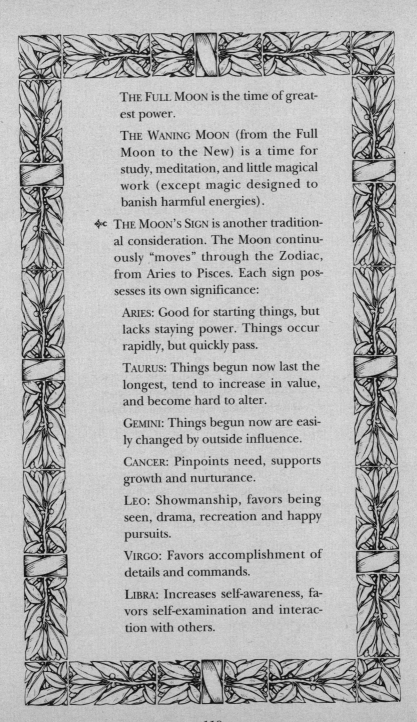

THE FULL MOON is the time of greatest power.

THE WANING MOON (from the Full Moon to the New) is a time for study, meditation, and little magical work (except magic designed to banish harmful energies).

THE MOON'S SIGN is another traditional consideration. The Moon continuously "moves" through the Zodiac, from Aries to Pisces. Each sign possesses its own significance:

ARIES: Good for starting things, but lacks staying power. Things occur rapidly, but quickly pass.

TAURUS: Things begun now last the longest, tend to increase in value, and become hard to alter.

GEMINI: Things begun now are easily changed by outside influence.

CANCER: Pinpoints need, supports growth and nurturance.

LEO: Showmanship, favors being seen, drama, recreation and happy pursuits.

VIRGO: Favors accomplishment of details and commands.

LIBRA: Increases self-awareness, favors self-examination and interaction with others.

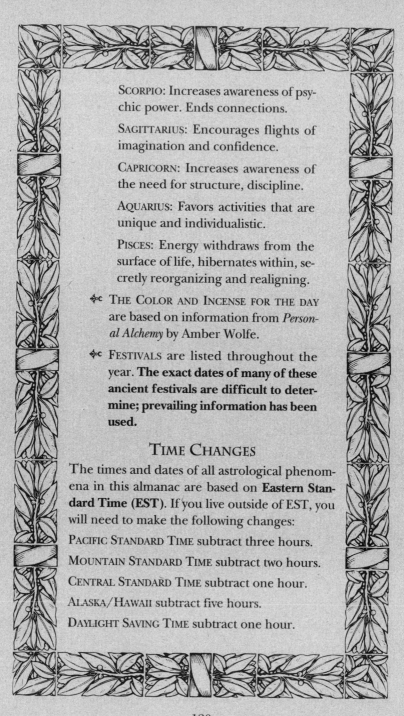

SCORPIO: Increases awareness of psychic power. Ends connections.

SAGITTARIUS: Encourages flights of imagination and confidence.

CAPRICORN: Increases awareness of the need for structure, discipline.

AQUARIUS: Favors activities that are unique and individualistic.

PISCES: Energy withdraws from the surface of life, hibernates within, secretly reorganizing and realigning.

❖c THE COLOR AND INCENSE FOR THE DAY are based on information from *Personal Alchemy* by Amber Wolfe.

❖c FESTIVALS are listed throughout the year. **The exact dates of many of these ancient festivals are difficult to determine; prevailing information has been used.**

TIME CHANGES

The times and dates of all astrological phenomena in this almanac are based on **Eastern Standard Time (EST)**. If you live outside of EST, you will need to make the following changes:

PACIFIC STANDARD TIME subtract three hours.

MOUNTAIN STANDARD TIME subtract two hours.

CENTRAL STANDARD TIME subtract one hour.

ALASKA/HAWAII subtract five hours.

DAYLIGHT SAVING TIME subtract one hour.

120

1997 Sabbats and Full Moons

January 23	Full Moon 10:12 AM
February 2	Imbolc
February 22	Full Moon 5:27 AM
March 20	Ostara (Spring Equinox)
March 23	Full Moon 11:45 PM
April 22	Full Moon 3:34 PM
May 1	Beltane
May 22	Full Moon 4:14 AM
June 20	Full Moon 2:09 PM
June 21	Litha (Summer Solstice)
July 19	Full Moon 10:21 PM
August 1	Lammas
August 18	Full Moon 5:56 AM
September 16	Full Moon 1:51 PM
September 22	Mabon (Fall Equinox)
October 15	Full Moon 10:46 PM
October 31	Samhain
November 14	Full Moon 9:13 AM
December 13	Full Moon 9:38 PM
December 21	Yule (Winter Solstice)

THE PLANETARY HOURS

The selection of an auspicious time for starting any affair is an important matter. When a thing is once commenced, its existence tends to be of a nature corresponding to the conditions under which it was begun. Not only should you select the appropriate date, but when possible you should also start the affair under an appropriate planetary hour.

Each hour of the day is ruled by a planet, and so the nature of any time during the day corresponds to the nature of the planet ruling it. The nature of the planetary hours is the same as the description of each of the planets, except that you will not need to refer to the descriptions for Uranus, Neptune, and Pluto, as they are considered here as higher octaves of Mercury, Venus, and Mars, respectively. If something is ruled by Uranus, you can use the hour of Mercury.

The only other factor you need to know to use the Planetary Hours is the time of your local Sunrise and Sunset for any given day. This is given in the chart following.

EXAMPLE

Determine planetary hours for January 2, 1997, 10º latitude

1) Find sunrise (table, page 131) and sunset (table, page 132) for January 2, 1997, at 10º latitude by following the 10º latitude column down to the January 2 row. In the case of our example this is the first entry in the upper left-hand corner of both the sunrise and sunset tables. You will see that sunrise for January 2, 1997, at 10º latitude is at 6 hours and 16 minutes (or 6:16 am) and sunset is at 17 hours and 49 minutes (or 5:49 pm).

2) Subtract sunrise time (6 hours 16 minutes) from sunset time (17 hours 49 minutes) to get the number of astrological daylight hours. It is easier to do this if you convert the hours into minutes. For example, 6 hours and 16 minutes = 376 minutes (6 hours x 60 minutes each = 360 minutes + 16 minutes = 376 minutes). 17 hours and 49 minutes = 1069

minutes (17 hours x 60 minutes = 1020 minutes + 49 minutes = 1069 minutes). Now subtract: 1069 minutes - 376 minutes = 693 minutes. If we then convert this back to hours by dividing by 60, we have 11 hours and 33 minutes of Daylight Planetary Hours. However, it is easier to calculate the next step if you leave the number in minutes.

3) Next you should determine how many minutes are in a daylight planetary hour for that particular day (January 2, 1997, 10° latitude). To do this divide 693 minutes by 12 (the number of hours of daylight at the equinoxes). The answer is 58, rounded off. Therefore, a daylight planetary hour for January 2, 1997 at 10° latitude has 58 minutes. Remember that except on equinoxes, there is not an even amount of daylight and night time, so you will rarely have 60 minutes in a daylight hour.

4) Now you know that each daylight planetary hour is roughly 58 minutes. You also know, from step one, that sunrise is at 6:16 AM. To determine the starting times of each planetary hour, simply add 58 minutes to the sunrise time for the first planetary hour, 58 minutes to that number for the second planetary hour, etc. So the daylight planetary hours for our example are as follows: 1st hour 6:16 AM–7:14 AM; 2nd hour 7:15 AM–8:11 AM; 3rd hour 8:12 AM–9:08 AM; 4th hour 9:09 AM–10:05 AM; 5th hour 10:06 AM–11:02 AM; 6th hour 11:03 AM–11:59 AM; 7th hour 12:00 AM–12:56 PM; 8th hour 12:57 PM–1:53 PM; 9th hour 1:54 PM–2:50 PM; 10th hour 2:51 PM–3:47 PM; 11th hour 3:48 PM–4:44 PM; 12th hour 4:45 PM–5:51 PM. Note that because you rounded up, this isn't exact to the Sunset Table, which says that sunset is at 5:49 PM. This is a good reason to give yourself a little "fudge space" when using planetary hours. For most accurate sunrise or sunset times, consult your local paper.

5) Now, to determine which sign rules which daylight planetary hour, consult your calendar pages to determine which day of the week January 2 falls on. You'll find it's a Thursday. Next, turn to page 133 to find the sunrise planetary hour chart. (It's the one on the top.) If you follow down the column for Thursday, you will see that the first planetary hour of the day is ruled by Jupiter, the second by Mars, the third by the Sun, etc.

6) Now you've determined the daytime (sunrise) planetary hours. You can use the same formula to determine the night time (sunset) planetary hours. You know you have 11 hours and 33 minutes of sunrise planetary hours. Therefore subtract 11 hours and 33 minutes of sunrise hours from the 24 hours in a day to equal the number of sunset hours. 24 hours - 11 hours 13 minutes = 12 hours 47 minutes of sunset time. Now convert this to minutes $(12 \times 60) + 47 = (720) + 47 = 767$ minutes. (This equals 12.783 hours, but remember to leave it in minutes for now.)

7) Now go to step three and repeat the rest of the process for the sunset hours. When you get to step 5, remember to consult the sunset table on page 132 rather than the sunrise one. When you complete these steps you should get the following answers. There are (roughly) 63 minutes in a sunset planetary hour for this example. This means that the times for the sunset planetary hours are (starting from the 17:49 sunset time rather than the 6:16 sunrise time) first hour 5:49 PM; second 6:52 PM; third 7:55 PM; fourth 8:58 PM; fifth 10:01 PM; sixth 11:04 PM; seventh 12:07 AM; eighth 1:10 AM; ninth 2:13 AM; tenth 3:16 AM; eleventh 4:19 AM; twelfth 5:21 AM. You see which signs rule the hours by consulting the sunset chart on page 184. The first sunset hour is ruled by the Moon, the second by Saturn, the third by Jupiter, and so on.

SUNRISE

UNIVERSAL TIME FOR MERIDIAN OF GREENWICH

Latitude		+10°	+20°	+30°	+40°	+42°	+46°	+50°
		h:m	h:m	h:m	h:m	h:m	h:m	h:m
JAN	2	6:16	6:34	6:57	7:21	7:28	7:42	7:59
	14	6:21	6:34	6:55	7:20	7:26	7:39	7:53
	26	6:23	6:37	6:53	7:14	7:19	7:29	7:42
FEB	7	6:22	6:33	6:46	7:03	7:06	7:15	7:24
	19	6:18	6:27	6:36	6:48	6:50	6:56	7:03
	27	6:15	6:21	6:28	6:37	6:38	6:43	6:48
MAR	7	6:11	6:15	6:19	6:24	6:26	6:28	6:31
	19	6:05	6:05	6:05	6:05	6:05	6:05	6:05
	27	6:00	5:58	5:56	5:52	5:52	5:50	5:49
APR	12	5:51	5:44	5:37	5:27	5:25	5:19	5:14
	20	5:47	5:38	5:28	5:15	5:12	5:05	4:57
	28	5:44	5:33	5:20	5:04	5:00	4:52	4:42
MAY	6	5:41	5:28	5:13	4:54	4:50	4:40	4:28
	18	5:38	5:23	5:05	4:42	4:37	4:25	4:10
	26	5:38	5:21	5:01	4:36	4:30	4:17	4:01
JUN	3	5:38	5:20	4:59	4:32	4:26	4:12	3:54
	15	5:39	5:20	4:58	4:30	4:24	4:09	3:50
	23	5:41	5:22	5:00	4:32	4:25	4:10	3:51
JUL	1	5:43	5:24	5:02	4:35	4:28	4:13	3:55
	9	5:45	5:27	5:06	4:39	4:33	4:19	4:01
	17	5:47	5:30	5:10	4:45	4:39	4:26	4:10
	25	5:48	5:33	5:15	4:52	4:46	4:34	4:20
AUG	2	5:50	5:36	5:19	4:59	4:54	4:43	4:31
	10	5:51	5:38	5:24	5:07	5:02	4:53	4:42
	18	5:51	5:41	5:29	5:14	5:11	5:03	4:54
	26	5:51	5:43	5:34	5:22	5:19	5:13	5:06
SEP	3	5:51	5:45	5:38	5:29	5:27	5:23	5:18
	11	5:50	5:46	5:42	5:37	5:36	5:33	5:30
	19	5:49	5:48	5:47	5:45	5:44	5:43	5:42
	27	5:49	5:50	5:51	5:52	5:53	5:53	5:54
OCT	13	5:48	5:54	6:01	6:08	6:10	6:14	6:19
	21	5:49	5:57	6:06	6:17	6:19	6:25	6:31
	29	5:50	6:00	6:12	6:26	6:29	6:36	6:45
NOV	6	5:52	6:04	6:18	6:35	6:39	6:48	6:58
	14	5:54	6:08	6:24	6:44	6:49	6:59	7:11
	22	5:57	6:13	6:31	6:53	6:58	7:10	7:24
	30	6:01	6:18	6:37	7:02	7:07	7:20	7:35
DEC	8	6:05	6:23	6:44	7:09	7:15	7:29	7:45
	16	6:09	6:28	6:49	7:15	7:22	7:36	7:53
	24	6:13	6:32	6:53	7:20	7:26	7:40	7:57
	30	6:17	6:35	6:56	7:22	7:28	7:42	7:59

SUNSET

UNIVERSAL TIME FOR MERIDIAN OF GREENWICH

Latitude		+10°	+20°	+30°	+40°	+42°	+46°	+50°
		h:m	h:m	h:m	h:m	h:m	h:m	h:m
JAN	2	17:49	17:30	17:09	16:43	16:37	16:23	16:06
	14	17:57	17:41	17:22	16:58	16:52	16:40	16:25
	26	18:03	17:48	17:32	17:12	17:07	16:57	16:44
FEB	7	18:07	17:55	17:42	17:26	17:23	17:14	17:05
	19	18:09	18:01	17:52	17:40	17:38	17:32	17:25
	27	18:10	18:04	17:58	17:50	17:48	17:44	17:39
MAR	7	18:11	18:07	18:03	17:58	17:57	17:55	17:52
	19	18:11	18:11	18:11	18:11	18:11	18:11	18:11
	27	18:11	18:13	18:16	18:19	18:20	18:22	18:24
APR	12	18:10	18:17	18:25	18:35	18:38	18:43	18:49
	20	18:11	18:20	18:30	18:43	18:47	18:53	19:02
	28	18:11	18:22	18:35	18:52	18:55	19:04	19:14
MAY	6	18:12	18:25	18:41	19:00	19:04	19:14	19:26
	18	18:14	18:30	18:48	19:11	19:17	19:29	19:43
	26	18:16	18:33	18:53	19:18	19:24	19:38	19:54
JUN	3	18:18	18:37	18:57	19:24	19:30	19:45	20:02
	15	18:22	18:43	19:03	19:30	19:37	19:53	20:11
	23	18:23	18:42	19:05	19:33	19:39	19:55	20:13
JUL	1	18:25	18:43	19:05	19:33	19:39	19:54	20:12
	9	18:25	18:43	19:04	19:31	19:37	19:51	20:09
	17	18:25	18:42	19:02	19:27	19:33	19:46	20:02
	25	18:24	18:42	18:58	19:21	19:26	19:38	19:53
AUG	2	18:23	18:36	18:53	19:13	19:18	19:28	19:41
	10	18:20	18:32	18:46	19:03	19:07	19:17	19:28
	18	18:16	18:27	18:38	18:53	18:56	19:04	19:13
	26	18:12	18:20	18:30	18:41	18:44	18:50	18:57
SEP	3	18:08	18:14	18:20	18:28	18:30	18:35	18:40
	11	18:03	18:06	18:10	18:16	18:17	18:19	18:23
	19	17:58	17:59	18:00	18:02	18:03	18:04	18:05
	27	17:53	17:52	17:50	17:49	17:49	17:48	17:47
OCT	13	17:44	17:38	17:32	17:24	17:22	17:18	17:13
	21	17:40	17:32	17:23	17:12	17:09	17:04	16:57
	29	17:37	17:27	17:16	17:01	16:58	16:51	16:42
NOV	6	17:36	17:23	17:09	16:52	16:48	16:39	16:29
	14	17:35	17:21	17:04	16:45	16:40	16:30	16:17
	22	17:35	17:19	17:01	16:39	16:34	16:22	16:08
	30	17:36	17:19	17:00	16:36	16:30	16:17	16:02
DEC	8	17:39	17:21	17:00	16:35	16:28	16:15	15:58
	16	17:42	17:24	17:02	16:36	16:30	16:15	15:59
	24	17:46	17:27	17:06	16:40	16:33	16:19	16:02
	30	17:50	17:32	17:11	16:45	16:39	16:25	16:09

Sunrise and Sunset Hours Charts

Sunrise

Hour	Sun	Mon	Tue	Wed	Thu	Fr	Sat
1	☉	☽	♂	☿	♃	♀	♄
2	♀	♄	☉	☽	♂	☿	♃
3	☿	♃	♀	♄	☉	☽	♂
4	☽	♂	☿	♃	♀	♄	☉
5	♄	☉	☽	♂	☿	♃	♀
6	♃	♀	♄	☉	☽	♂	☿
7	♂	☿	♃	♀	♄	☉	☽
8	☉	☽	♂	☿	♃	♀	♄
9	♀	♄	☉	☽	♂	☿	♃
10	☿	♃	♀	♄	☉	☽	♂
11	☽	♂	☿	♃	♀	♄	☉
12	♄	☉	☽	♂	☿	♃	♀

Sunset

Hour	Sun	Mon	Tue	Wed	Thu	Fr	Sat
1	♃	♀	♄	☉	☽	♂	☿
2	♂	☿	♃	♀	♄	☉	☽
3	☉	☽	♂	☿	♃	♀	♄
4	♀	♄	☉	☽	♂	☿	♃
5	☿	♃	♀	♄	☉	☽	♂
6	☽	♂	☿	♃	♀	♄	☉
7	♄	☉	☽	♂	☿	♃	♀
8	♃	♀	♄	☉	☽	♂	☿
9	♂	☿	♃	♀	♄	☉	☽
10	☉	☽	♂	☿	♃	♀	♄
11	♀	♄	☉	☽	♂	☿	♃
12	☿	♃	♀	♄	☉	☽	♂

☉ Sun; ☿ Mercury; ♄ Saturn; ♂ Mars; ♀ Venus; ☽ Moon; ♃ Jupiter

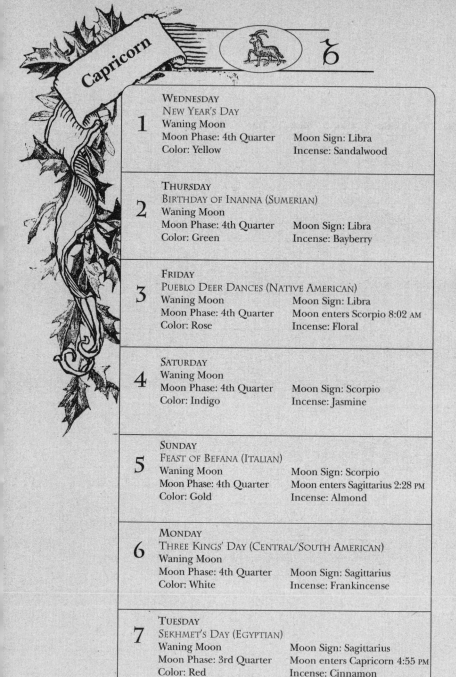

Capricorn ♑

1 WEDNESDAY
NEW YEAR'S DAY
Waning Moon
Moon Phase: 4th Quarter
Color: Yellow
Moon Sign: Libra
Incense: Sandalwood

2 THURSDAY
BIRTHDAY OF INANNA (SUMERIAN)
Waning Moon
Moon Phase: 4th Quarter
Color: Green
Moon Sign: Libra
Incense: Bayberry

3 FRIDAY
PUEBLO DEER DANCES (NATIVE AMERICAN)
Waning Moon
Moon Phase: 4th Quarter
Color: Rose
Moon Sign: Libra
Moon enters Scorpio 8:02 AM
Incense: Floral

4 SATURDAY
Waning Moon
Moon Phase: 4th Quarter
Color: Indigo
Moon Sign: Scorpio
Incense: Jasmine

5 SUNDAY
FEAST OF BEFANA (ITALIAN)
Waning Moon
Moon Phase: 4th Quarter
Color: Gold
Moon Sign: Scorpio
Moon enters Sagittarius 2:28 PM
Incense: Almond

6 MONDAY
THREE KINGS' DAY (CENTRAL/SOUTH AMERICAN)
Waning Moon
Moon Phase: 4th Quarter
Color: White
Moon Sign: Sagittarius
Incense: Frankincense

7 TUESDAY
SEKHMET'S DAY (EGYPTIAN)
Waning Moon
Moon Phase: 3rd Quarter
Color: Red
Moon Sign: Sagittarius
Moon enters Capricorn 4:55 PM
Incense: Cinnamon

8 WEDNESDAY
Waxing Moon
Moon Phase: New 11:26 PM   Moon Sign: Capricorn
Color: Peach   Incense: Fruity

9 THURSDAY
FESTIVAL OF JANUS
Waxing Moon   Moon Sign: Capricorn
Moon Phase: 1st Quarter   Moon enters Aquarius 4:59 PM
Color: Turquose   Incense: Bay Laurel

10 FRIDAY
GERAINT'S DAY (WELSH)
Waxing Moon
Moon Phase: 1st Quarter   Moon Sign: Aquarius
Color: Pink   Incense: Floral

11 SATURDAY
FESTIVAL OF CARMENTALIA (ROMAN)
Waxing Moon   Moon Sign: Aquarius
Moon Phase: 1st Quarter   Moon enters Pisces 4:51 PM
Color: Blue   Incense: Thyme

12 SUNDAY
NEZ PERCE WAR DANCES (NATIVE AMERICAN)
Waxing Moon
Moon Phase: 1st Quarter   Moon Sign: Pisces
Color: Orange   Incense: Ginger

13 MONDAY
MIDVINTERSBLOT (NORSE)
Waxing Moon   Moon Sign: Pisces
Moon Phase: 1st Quarter   Moon enters Aries 6:21 PM
Color: Lavender   Incense: Lavender

14 TUESDAY
MAKAR SANKRATI (HINDU)
Waxing Moon
Moon Phase: 1st Quarter   Moon Sign: Aries
Color: White   Incense: Myrrh

Capricorn ♑

15 WEDNESDAY
BLACK CHRIST FESTIVAL (GUATEMALAN)
Waxing Moon   Moon Sign: Aries
Moon Phase: 2nd Qtr. 3:02 PM   Moon enters Taurus 10:40 PM
Color: White   Incense: Almond

16 THURSDAY
FESTIVAL OF GANISHA (HINDU)
Waxing Moon
Moon Phase: 2nd Quarter   Moon Sign: Taurus
Color: Violet   Incense: Lilac

17 FRIDAY
ST. ANTHONY'S DAY (MEXICAN)
Waxing Moon
Moon Phase: 2nd Quarter   Moon Sign: Taurus
Color: Peach   Incense: Fruity

18 SATURDAY
SURYA (HINDU)
Waxing Moon   Moon Sign: Taurus
Moon Phase: 2nd Quarter   Moon enters Gemini 5:53 AM
Color: Gray   Incense: Patchouli

19 SUNDAY
FESTIVAL OF THOR (NORSE)
Waxing Moon   Moon Sign: Gemini
Moon Phase: 2nd Quarter   Sun enters Aquarius 7:42 PM
Color: Yellow   Incense: Sandalwood

20 MONDAY
FESTIVAL OF THORABLOTTAR (ICELANDIC)
Waxing Moon   Moon Sign: Gemini
Moon Phase: 2nd Quarter   Moon enters Cancer 3:29 PM
Color: Gray   Incense: Sage

21 TUESDAY
SANTA INES' DAY (MEXICAN)
Waxing Moon
Moon Phase: 2nd Quarter   Moon Sign: Cancer
Color: Black   Incense: Cedar

22 WEDNESDAY
ST. VINCENT'S DAY
Waxing Moon   Moon Sign: Cancer
Moon Phase: 2nd Quarter   Moon enters Leo 11:51 PM
Color: Brown   Incense: Evergreen

23 THURSDAY
Waxing Moon
Moon Phase: Full 10:12 AM   Moon Sign: Leo
Color: White   Incense: Frankincense

24 FRIDAY
BLESSING OF THE HAPPY WOMAN'S CANDLE (HUNGARIAN)
Waning Moon
Moon Phase: 3rd Quarter   Moon Sign: Leo
Color: Blue   Incense: Thyme

25 SATURDAY
BURNS' NIGHT (SCOTTISH)
Waning Moon   Moon Sign: Leo
Moon Phase: 3rd Quarter   Moon enters Virgo 3:27 PM
Color: Brown   Incense: Cedar

26 SUNDAY
FESTIVAL OF EKEKO (BOLIVIAN)
Waning Moon
Moon Phase: 3rd Quarter   Moon Sign: Virgo
Color: Peach   Incense: Fruity

27 MONDAY
SEMENTIVAE FERIA (ROMAN)
Waning Moon
Moon Phase: 3rd Quarter   Moon Sign: Virgo
Color: Gold   Incense: Mint

28 TUESDAY
UPELLY-AA (SCOTTISH)
Waning Moon   Moon Sign: Virgo
Moon Phase: 3rd Quarter   Moon enters Libra 4:22 AM
Color: Indigo   Incense: Jasmine

Aquarius

WEDNESDAY
29 MARTYR'S DAY (NEPALESE)
Waning Moon
Moon Phase: 3rd Quarter
Color: Blue

Moon Sign: Libra
Incense: Temple

THURSDAY
30 HOLY DAY OF THE THREE HIERARCHS (EAST. ORTHODOX)
Waning Moon
Moon Phase: 3rd Quarter
Color: Rose

Moon Sign: Libra
Moon enters Scorpio 3:48 PM
Incense: Floral

FRIDAY
31 HECATE'S FEAST (GREEK)
Waning Moon
Moon Phase: 4th Qtr. 2:40 PM
Color: Green

Moon Sign: Scorpio
Incense: Bayberry

JANUARY BIRTHSTONES
Ancient: Garnet
Modern: Garnet

JANUARY FLOWERS
Carnations
Snowdrops

FEBRUARY BIRTHSTONES
Ancient: Amethyst
Modern: Amethyst

FEBRUARY FLOWERS
Violets
Primroses

February

SATURDAY
ST. BRIGHID'S FEAST DAY

1
Waning Moon
Moon Phase: 4th Quarter
Color: White

Moon Sign: Scorpio
Moon enters Sagittarius 11:51 PM
Incense: Vanilla

SUNDAY
IMBOLC

2
Waning Moon
Moon Phase: 4th Quarter
Color: Violet

Moon Sign: Sagittarius
Incense: Lilac

MONDAY
POWAMU FESTIVAL (HOPI)

3
Waning Moon
Moon Phase: 4th Quarter
Color: White

Moon Sign: Sagittarius
Incense: Almond

TUESDAY
KING FROST DAY (ENGLISH)

4
Waning Moon
Moon Phase: 4th Quarter
Color: Red

Moon Sign: Sagittarius
Moon enters Capricorn 3:44 AM
Incense: Clove

WEDNESDAY
FEAST OF ST. AGATHA (SICILIAN)

5
Waning Moon
Moon Phase: 4th Quarter
Color: Yellow

Moon Sign: Capricorn
Incense: Sandalwood

THURSDAY
FESTIVAL OF APHRODITE (GREEK)

6
Waning Moon
Moon Phase: 4th Quarter
Color: Green

Moon Sign: Capricorn
Moon enters Aquarius 4:21 AM
Incense: Bayberry

FRIDAY
SELENE'S DAY (GREEK)

7
Waning Moon
Moon Phase: New 10:06 AM
Color: Indigo

Moon Sign: Aquarius
Incense: Jasmine

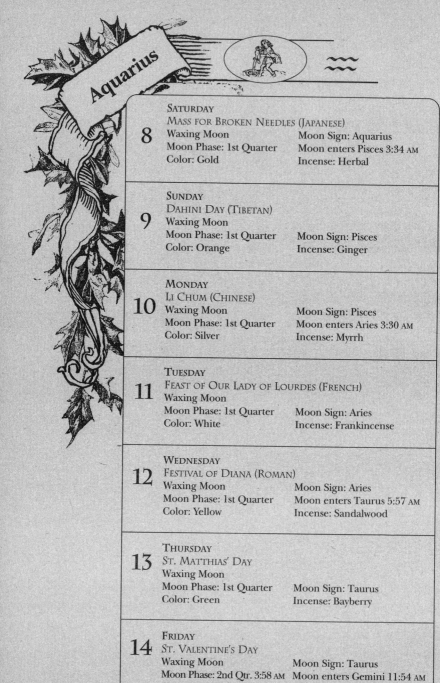

Aquarius

SATURDAY
8
MASS FOR BROKEN NEEDLES (JAPANESE)
Waxing Moon
Moon Phase: 1st Quarter
Color: Gold

Moon Sign: Aquarius
Moon enters Pisces 3:34 AM
Incense: Herbal

SUNDAY
9
DAHINI DAY (TIBETAN)
Waxing Moon
Moon Phase: 1st Quarter
Color: Orange

Moon Sign: Pisces
Incense: Ginger

MONDAY
10
LI CHUM (CHINESE)
Waxing Moon
Moon Phase: 1st Quarter
Color: Silver

Moon Sign: Pisces
Moon enters Aries 3:30 AM
Incense: Myrrh

TUESDAY
11
FEAST OF OUR LADY OF LOURDES (FRENCH)
Waxing Moon
Moon Phase: 1st Quarter
Color: White

Moon Sign: Aries
Incense: Frankincense

WEDNESDAY
12
FESTIVAL OF DIANA (ROMAN)
Waxing Moon
Moon Phase: 1st Quarter
Color: Yellow

Moon Sign: Aries
Moon enters Taurus 5:57 AM
Incense: Sandalwood

THURSDAY
13
ST. MATTHIAS' DAY
Waxing Moon
Moon Phase: 1st Quarter
Color: Green

Moon Sign: Taurus
Incense: Bayberry

FRIDAY
14
ST. VALENTINE'S DAY
Waxing Moon
Moon Phase: 2nd Qtr. 3:58 AM
Color: Blue

Moon Sign: Taurus
Moon enters Gemini 11:54 AM
Incense: Thyme

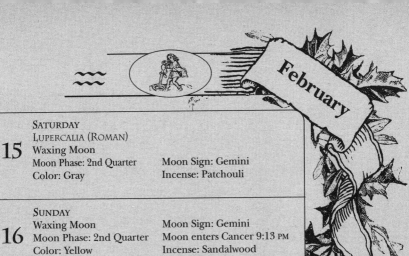

SATURDAY
15
LUPERCALIA (ROMAN)
Waxing Moon
Moon Phase: 2nd Quarter   Moon Sign: Gemini
Color: Gray   Incense: Patchouli

SUNDAY
16
Waxing Moon
Moon Phase: 2nd Quarter   Moon Sign: Gemini
    Moon enters Cancer 9:13 PM
Color: Yellow   Incense: Sandalwood

MONDAY
17
WASHINGTON'S BIRTHDAY (OBSERVED)
Waxing Moon
Moon Phase: 2nd Quarter   Moon Sign: Cancer
Color: Lavender   Incense: Lavender

TUESDAY
18
SPENTA ARMAITI (ZOROASTRIAN)
Waxing Moon
Moon Phase: 2nd Quarter   Moon Sign: Cancer
    Sun enters Pisces 9:51 AM
Color: Black   Incense: Sage

WEDNESDAY
19
MAHASHIVATRI (INDIAN)
Waxing Moon
Moon Phase: 2nd Quarter   Moon Sign: Cancer
    Sun enters Leo 8:53 AM
Color: Brown   Incense: Cedar

THURSDAY
20
DAY OF TACITA (ROMAN)
Waxing Moon
Moon Phase: 2nd Quarter   Moon Sign: Leo
Color: White   Incense: Almond

FRIDAY
21
Waxing Moon
Moon Phase: 2nd Quarter   Moon Sign: Leo
    Moon enters Virgo 9:38 PM
Color: Peach   Incense: Fruity

Pisces ♓

SATURDAY
22 ST. LUCIA'S DAY (ITALIAN)
Waxing Moon
Moon Phase: Full 5:27 AM Moon Sign: Virgo
Color: Blue Incense: Thyme

SUNDAY
23 TERMINALIA (ROMAN)
Waning Moon
Moon Phase: 3rd Quarter Moon Sign: Virgo
Color: Green Incense: Mint

MONDAY
24 Waning Moon
Moon Phase: 3rd Quarter Moon Sign: Virgo
Color: Gold Moon enters Libra 10:23 AM
Incense: Myrrh

TUESDAY
25 DAY OF NUT (EGYPTIAN)
Waning Moon
Moon Phase: 3rd Quarter Moon Sign: Libra
Color: Indigo Incense: Temple

WEDNESDAY
26 HYGEIA'S DAY (NORTH AFRICAN)
Waning Moon Moon Sign: Libra
Moon Phase: 3rd Quarter Moon enters Scorpio 9:56 PM
Color: Violet Incense: Lilac

THURSDAY
27 FEAST OF ESTHER (HEBREW)
Waning Moon
Moon Phase: 3rd Quarter Moon Sign: Scorpio
Color: Rose Incense: Floral

FRIDAY
28 BUDDHA'S CONCEPTION (TIBETAN)
Waning Moon
Moon Phase: 3rd Quarter Moon Sign: Scorpio
Color: Blue Incense: Thyme

1 SATURDAY
MATRONALIA (ROMAN)
Waning Moon
Moon Phase: 3rd Quarter
Color: Yellow

Moon Sign: Scorpio
Moon enters Sagittarius 7:01 AM
Incense: Sandalwood

2 SUNDAY
MOTHER'S MARCH (BULGARIAN)
Waning Moon
Moon Phase: 4th Qtr. 4:38 AM
Color: Gold

Moon Sign: Sagittarius
Incense: Almond

3 MONDAY
DOLL FESTIVAL (JAPANESE)
Waning Moon
Moon Phase: 4th Quarter
Color: White

Moon Sign: Sagittarius
Moon enters Capricorn 12:39 PM
Incense: Frankincense

4 TUESDAY
FEAST OF RHIANNON (WELSH)
Waning Moon
Moon Phase: 4th Quarter
Color: Red

Moon Sign: Capricorn
Incense: Clove

5 WEDNESDAY
CELEBRATION OF ISIS (NORTH AFRICAN)
Waning Moon
Moon Phase: 4th Quarter
Color: Peach

Moon Sign: Capricorn
Moon enters Aquarius 2:55 PM
Incense: Fruity

6 THURSDAY
MARS' DAY (ROMAN)
Waning Moon
Moon Phase: 4th Quarter
Color: Orange

Moon Sign: Aquarius
Incense: Ginger

7 FRIDAY
JUNONALIA (ROMAN)
Waning Moon
Moon Phase: 4th Quarter
Color: Rose

Moon Sign Aquarius
Moon enters Pisces 2:57 PM
Stone: Floral

Pisces

SATURDAY
8
BIRTHDAY OF MOTHER EARTH (CHINESE)
Waning Moon
Moon Phase: New 8:15 PM   Moon Sign: Pisces
Color: Yellow   Incense: Sandalwood

SUNDAY
9
FEAST OF THE 40 MARTYRS (GREEK)
Waxing Moon   Moon Sign: Pisces
Moon Phase: 1st Quarter   Moon enters Aries 2:33 PM
Color: Gold   Incense: Almond

MONDAY
10
HOLI (INDIAN)
Waxing Moon
Moon Phase: 1st Quarter   Moon Sign: Aries
Color: Lavender   Incense: Lilac

TUESDAY
11
HERCULES' DAY (GREEK)
Waxing Moon   Moon Sign: Aries
Moon Phase: 1st Quarter   Moon enters Taurus 3:38 PM
Color: White   Incense: Myrrh

WEDNESDAY
12
FEAST OF MARDUK (MESOPOTAMIAN)
Waxing Moon
Moon Phase: 1st Quarter   Moon Sign: Taurus
Color: Yellow   Incense: Sandalwood

THURSDAY
13
PURIFICATION FEAST (BALINESE)
Waxing Moon   Moon Sign: Taurus
Moon Phase: 1st Quarter   Moon enters Gemini 7:49 PM
Color: Green   Incense: Bayberry

FRIDAY
14
VETURIUS MAMURIUS (ROMAN)
Waxing Moon
Moon Phase: 1st Quarter   Moon Sign: Gemini
Color: Rose   Incense: Floral

SATURDAY
15 IDES OF MARCH (ROMAN)
Waxing Moon
Moon Phase: 2nd Qtr. 7:06 PM Moon Sign: Gemini
Color: Indigo   Incense: Temple

SUNDAY
16 FESTIVAL OF DIONYSUS (GREEK)
Waxing Moon   Moon Sign: Gemini
Moon Phase: 2nd Quarter   Moon enters Cancer 3:51 AM
Color: Yellow   Incense: Sandalwood

MONDAY
17 ST. PATRICK'S DAY (IRISH)
Waxing Moon
Moon Phase: 2nd Quarter   Moon Sign: Cancer
Color: Lavender   Incense: Lilac

TUESDAY
18 SHEELAH'S DAY (ICELANDIC)
Waxing Moon   Moon Sign: Cancer
Moon Phase: 2nd Quarter   Moon enters Leo 3:08 PM
Color: Red   Incense: Cinnamon

WEDNESDAY
19 DAY OF AGANYU (SANTERÍA)
Waxing Moon
Moon Phase: 2nd Quarter   Moon Sign: Leo
Color: White   Incense: Almond

THURSDAY
20 OSTARA (SPRING EQUINOX)
Waxing Moon   Moon Sign: Leo
Moon Phase: 2nd Quarter   Sun enters Aries 8:55 AM
Color: Turquoise   Incense: Bay Laurel

FRIDAY
21 TEA AND TEPHI DAY (IRISH)
Waxing Moon   Moon Sign: Leo
Moon Phase: 2nd Quarter   Moon enters Virgo 3:59 AM
Color: Pink   Incense: Floral

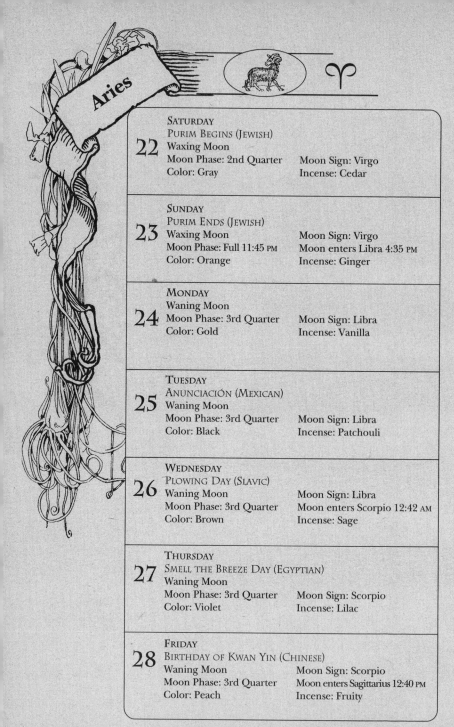

Aries

SATURDAY
22
PURIM BEGINS (JEWISH)
Waxing Moon
Moon Phase: 2nd Quarter · Moon Sign: Virgo
Color: Gray · Incense: Cedar

SUNDAY
23
PURIM ENDS (JEWISH)
Waxing Moon
Moon Sign: Virgo
Moon Phase: Full 11:45 PM · Moon enters Libra 4:35 PM
Color: Orange · Incense: Ginger

MONDAY
24
Waning Moon
Moon Phase: 3rd Quarter · Moon Sign: Libra
Color: Gold · Incense: Vanilla

TUESDAY
25
ANUNCIACIÓN (MEXICAN)
Waning Moon
Moon Phase: 3rd Quarter · Moon Sign: Libra
Color: Black · Incense: Patchouli

WEDNESDAY
26
PLOWING DAY (SLAVIC)
Waning Moon · Moon Sign: Libra
Moon Phase: 3rd Quarter · Moon enters Scorpio 12:42 AM
Color: Brown · Incense: Sage

THURSDAY
27
SMELL THE BREEZE DAY (EGYPTIAN)
Waning Moon
Moon Phase: 3rd Quarter · Moon Sign: Scorpio
Color: Violet · Incense: Lilac

FRIDAY
28
BIRTHDAY OF KWAN YIN (CHINESE)
Waning Moon · Moon Sign: Scorpio
Moon Phase: 3rd Quarter · Moon enters Sagittarius 12:40 PM
Color: Peach · Incense: Fruity

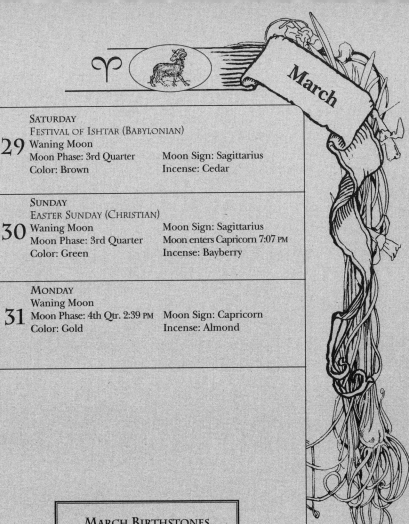

SATURDAY
FESTIVAL OF ISHTAR (BABYLONIAN)
29 Waning Moon
Moon Phase: 3rd Quarter   Moon Sign: Sagittarius
Color: Brown   Incense: Cedar

SUNDAY
EASTER SUNDAY (CHRISTIAN)
30 Waning Moon
Moon Phase: 3rd Quarter   Moon Sign: Sagittarius
                                 Moon enters Capricorn 7:07 PM
Color: Green   Incense: Bayberry

MONDAY
Waning Moon
31 Moon Phase: 4th Qtr. 2:39 PM   Moon Sign: Capricorn
Color: Gold   Incense: Almond

MARCH BIRTHSTONES
Ancient: Jasper
Modern: Bloodstone

MARCH FLOWERS
Daffodils
Jonquils

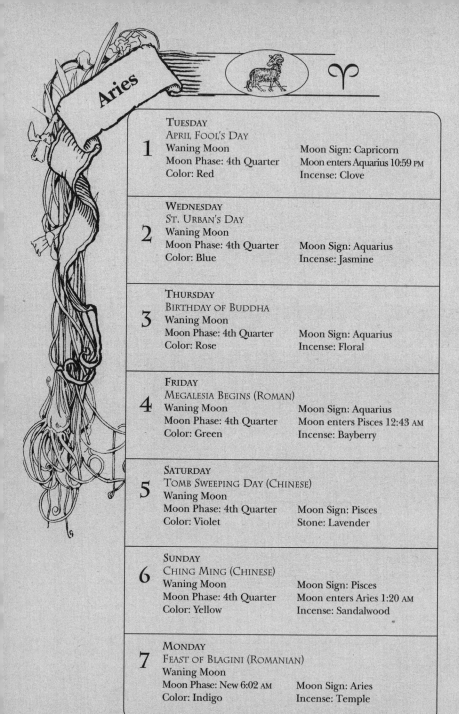

Aries

TUESDAY
1 APRIL FOOL'S DAY
Waning Moon
Moon Phase: 4th Quarter
Color: Red

Moon Sign: Capricorn
Moon enters Aquarius 10:59 PM
Incense: Clove

WEDNESDAY
2 ST. URBAN'S DAY
Waning Moon
Moon Phase: 4th Quarter
Color: Blue

Moon Sign: Aquarius
Incense: Jasmine

THURSDAY
3 BIRTHDAY OF BUDDHA
Waning Moon
Moon Phase: 4th Quarter
Color: Rose

Moon Sign: Aquarius
Incense: Floral

FRIDAY
4 MEGALESIA BEGINS (ROMAN)
Waning Moon
Moon Phase: 4th Quarter
Color: Green

Moon Sign: Aquarius
Moon enters Pisces 12:43 AM
Incense: Bayberry

SATURDAY
5 TOMB SWEEPING DAY (CHINESE)
Waning Moon
Moon Phase: 4th Quarter
Color: Violet

Moon Sign: Pisces
Stone: Lavender

SUNDAY
6 CHING MING (CHINESE)
Waning Moon
Moon Phase: 4th Quarter
Color: Yellow

Moon Sign: Pisces
Moon enters Aries 1:20 AM
Incense: Sandalwood

MONDAY
7 FEAST OF BLAGINI (ROMANIAN)
Waning Moon
Moon Phase: New 6:02 AM
Color: Indigo

Moon Sign: Aries
Incense: Temple

April

TUESDAY
HANA MATSURI (JAPANESE)
8
Waxing Moon
Moon Phase: 1st Quarter
Color: White

Moon Sign: Aries
Moon enters Taurus 2:21 AM
Incense: Frankincense

WEDNESDAY
9
Waxing Moon
Moon Phase: 1st Quarter
Color: Violet

Moon Sign: Taurus
Incense: Lilac

THURSDAY
MEGALESIA ENDS (ROMAN)
10
Waxing Moon
Moon Phase: 1st Quarter
Color: Rose

Moon Sign: Taurus
Moon enters Gemini 5:28 AM
Incense: Floral

FRIDAY
FEAST OF SAN LEO (MEXICAN)
11
Waxing Moon
Moon Phase: 1st Quarter
Color: Blue

Moon Sign: Gemini
Incense: Jasmine

SATURDAY
12
Waxing Moon
Moon Phase: 1st Quarter
Color: White

Moon Sign: Gemini
Moon enters Cancer 12:03 PM
Incense: Myrrh

SUNDAY
BAISAKHI (HINDU)
13
Waxing Moon
Moon Phase: 1st Quarter
Color: Green

Moon Sign: Cancer
Incense: Myrrh

MONDAY
SOMMARSBLÖT (NORSE)
14
Waxing Moon
Moon Phase: 2nd Qtr. 11:59 AM
Color: Yellow

Moon Sign: Cancer
Moon enters Leo 10:22 PM
Incense: Sandalwood

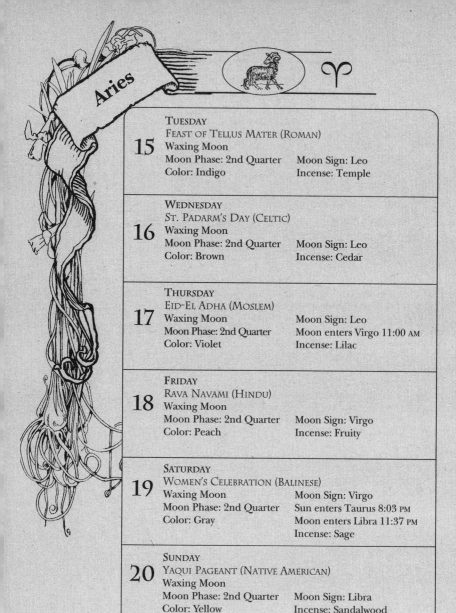

Aries

TUESDAY
15
FEAST OF TELLUS MATER (ROMAN)
Waxing Moon
Moon Phase: 2nd Quarter   Moon Sign: Leo
Color: Indigo   Incense: Temple

WEDNESDAY
16
ST. PADARM'S DAY (CELTIC)
Waxing Moon
Moon Phase: 2nd Quarter   Moon Sign: Leo
Color: Brown   Incense: Cedar

THURSDAY
17
EID-EL ADHA (MOSLEM)
Waxing Moon   Moon Sign: Leo
Moon Phase: 2nd Quarter   Moon enters Virgo 11:00 AM
Color: Violet   Incense: Lilac

FRIDAY
18
RAVA NAVAMI (HINDU)
Waxing Moon
Moon Phase: 2nd Quarter   Moon Sign: Virgo
Color: Peach   Incense: Fruity

SATURDAY
19
WOMEN'S CELEBRATION (BALINESE)
Waxing Moon   Moon Sign: Virgo
Moon Phase: 2nd Quarter   Sun enters Taurus 8:03 PM
Color: Gray   Moon enters Libra 11:37 PM
                              Incense: Sage

SUNDAY
20
YAQUI PAGEANT (NATIVE AMERICAN)
Waxing Moon
Moon Phase: 2nd Quarter   Moon Sign: Libra
Color: Yellow   Incense: Sandalwood

MONDAY
21
PASSOVER BEGINS (JEWISH)
Waxing Moon
Moon Phase: 2nd Quarter   Moon Sign: Libra
Color: Silver   Incense: Myrrh

TUESDAY
EARTH DAY
22
Waxing Moon
Moon Phase: Full 3:34 PM
Color: Black

Moon Sign: Libra
Moon enters Scorpio 10:20 AM
Incense: Patchouli

WEDNESDAY
ST. GEORGE'S DAY (BRITISH)
23
Waning Moon
Moon Phase: 3rd Quarter
Color: White

Moon Sign: Scorpio
Incense: Almond

THURSDAY
CHILDREN'S DAY (ICELANDIC)
24
Waning Moon
Moon Phase: 3rd Quarter
Color: Turquoise

Moon Sign: Scorpio
Moon enters Sagittarius 6:33 PM
Incense: Bay Laurel

FRIDAY
FEAST OF SAN JORGE (MEXICAN)
25
Waning Moon
Moon Phase: 3rd Quarter
Color: Peach

Moon Sign: Sagittarius
Incense: Fruity

SATURDAY
FLOWER PARADES (DUTCH)
26
Waning Moon
Moon Phase: 3rd Quarter
Color: Brown

Moon Sign: Sagittarius
Incense: Cedar

SUNDAY
27
Waning Moon
Moon Phase: 3rd Quarter
Color: Gold

Moon Sign: Sagittarius
Moon enters Capricorn 12:33 AM
Incense: Vanilla

MONDAY
FLORALIA BEGINS (ROMAN)
28
Waning Moon
Moon Phase: 3rd Quarter
Color: Lavender

Moon Sign: Capricorn
Incense: Lavender

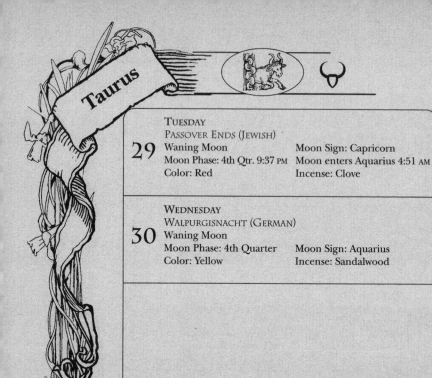

Taurus

29	Tuesday Passover Ends (Jewish) Waning Moon Moon Phase: 4th Qtr. 9:37 pm Color: Red	Moon Sign: Capricorn Moon enters Aquarius 4:51 am Incense: Clove	

30	Wednesday Walpurgisnacht (German) Waning Moon Moon Phase: 4th Quarter Color: Yellow	Moon Sign: Aquarius Incense: Sandalwood	

April Birthstones
Ancient: Sapphire
Modern: Diamond

April Flowers
Daisies
Sweet Peas

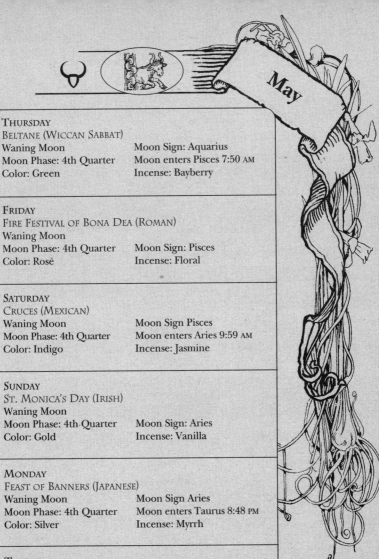

May

1
THURSDAY
BELTANE (WICCAN SABBAT)
Waning Moon
Moon Phase: 4th Quarter
Color: Green

Moon Sign: Aquarius
Moon enters Pisces 7:50 AM
Incense: Bayberry

2
FRIDAY
FIRE FESTIVAL OF BONA DEA (ROMAN)
Waning Moon
Moon Phase: 4th Quarter
Color: Rosé

Moon Sign: Pisces
Incense: Floral

3
SATURDAY
CRUCES (MEXICAN)
Waning Moon
Moon Phase: 4th Quarter
Color: Indigo

Moon Sign Pisces
Moon enters Aries 9:59 AM
Incense: Jasmine

4
SUNDAY
ST. MONICA'S DAY (IRISH)
Waning Moon
Moon Phase: 4th Quarter
Color: Gold

Moon Sign: Aries
Incense: Vanilla

5
MONDAY
FEAST OF BANNERS (JAPANESE)
Waning Moon
Moon Phase: 4th Quarter
Color: Silver

Moon Sign Aries
Moon enters Taurus 8:48 PM
Incense: Myrrh

6
TUESDAY
EYVIND KELVE (NORSE)
Waning Moon
Moon Phase: New 3:47 PM
Color: Red

Moon Sign: Taurus
Incense: Cinnamon

7
WEDNESDAY
Waxing Moon
Moon Phase: 1st Quarter
Color: Peach

Moon Sign: Taurus
Moon enters Gemini 3:21 PM
Incense: Fruity

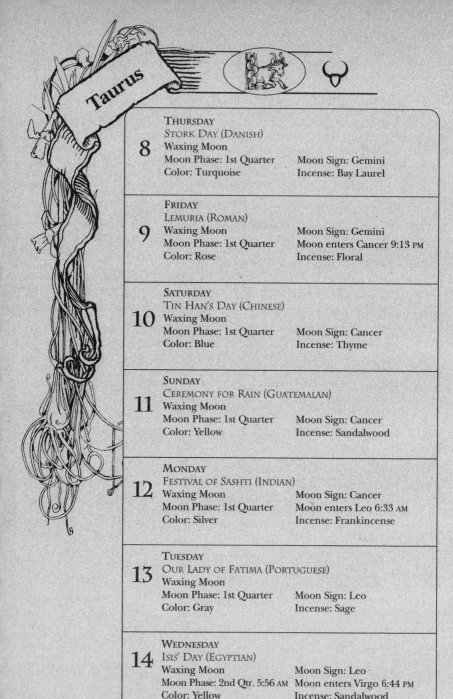

Taurus

THURSDAY
STORK DAY (DANISH)
8 Waxing Moon
Moon Phase: 1st Quarter   Moon Sign: Gemini
Color: Turquoise   Incense: Bay Laurel

FRIDAY
LEMURIA (ROMAN)
9 Waxing Moon
Moon Phase: 1st Quarter   Moon Sign: Gemini
Color: Rose   Moon enters Cancer 9:13 PM
    Incense: Floral

SATURDAY
TIN HAN'S DAY (CHINESE)
10 Waxing Moon
Moon Phase: 1st Quarter   Moon Sign: Cancer
Color: Blue   Incense: Thyme

SUNDAY
CEREMONY FOR RAIN (GUATEMALAN)
11 Waxing Moon
Moon Phase: 1st Quarter   Moon Sign: Cancer
Color: Yellow   Incense: Sandalwood

MONDAY
FESTIVAL OF SASHTI (INDIAN)
12 Waxing Moon
Moon Phase: 1st Quarter   Moon Sign: Cancer
Color: Silver   Moon enters Leo 6:33 AM
    Incense: Frankincense

TUESDAY
OUR LADY OF FATIMA (PORTUGUESE)
13 Waxing Moon
Moon Phase: 1st Quarter   Moon Sign: Leo
Color: Gray   Incense: Sage

WEDNESDAY
ISIS' DAY (EGYPTIAN)
14 Waxing Moon
Moon Phase: 2nd Qtr. 5:56 AM   Moon Sign: Leo
Color: Yellow   Moon enters Virgo 6:44 PM
    Incense: Sandalwood

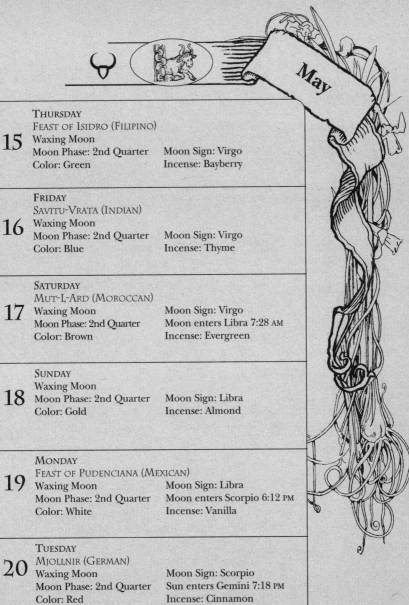

15 THURSDAY
FEAST OF ISIDRO (FILIPINO)
Waxing Moon
Moon Phase: 2nd Quarter Moon Sign: Virgo
Color: Green Incense: Bayberry

16 FRIDAY
SAVITU-VRATA (INDIAN)
Waxing Moon
Moon Phase: 2nd Quarter Moon Sign: Virgo
Color: Blue Incense: Thyme

17 SATURDAY
MUT-L-ARD (MOROCCAN)
Waxing Moon Moon Sign: Virgo
Moon Phase: 2nd Quarter Moon enters Libra 7:28 AM
Color: Brown Incense: Evergreen

18 SUNDAY
Waxing Moon
Moon Phase: 2nd Quarter Moon Sign: Libra
Color: Gold Incense: Almond

19 MONDAY
FEAST OF PUDENCIANA (MEXICAN)
Waxing Moon Moon Sign: Libra
Moon Phase: 2nd Quarter Moon enters Scorpio 6:12 PM
Color: White Incense: Vanilla

20 TUESDAY
MJOLLNIR (GERMAN)
Waxing Moon Moon Sign: Scorpio
Moon Phase: 2nd Quarter Sun enters Gemini 7:18 PM
Color: Red Incense: Cinnamon

21 WEDNESDAY
DAY OF TEFNUT (EGYPTIAN)
Waxing Moon
Moon Phase: 2nd Quarter Moon Sign: Scorpio
Color: Yellow Incense: Sandalwood

Gemini

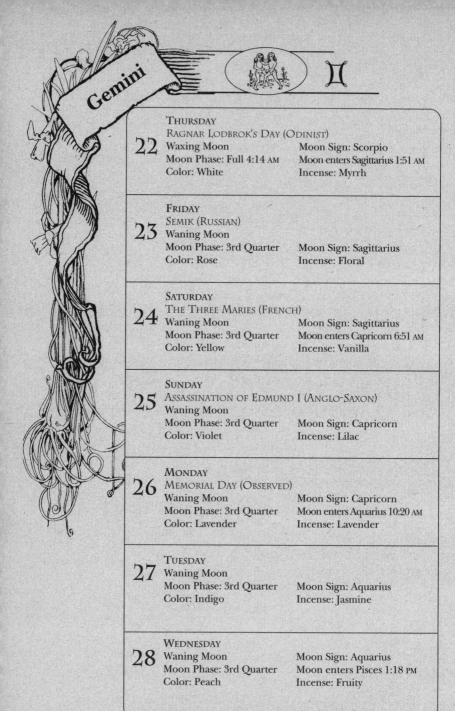

THURSDAY
22 RAGNAR LODBROK'S DAY (ODINIST)
Waxing Moon | Moon Sign: Scorpio
Moon Phase: Full 4:14 AM | Moon enters Sagittarius 1:51 AM
Color: White | Incense: Myrrh

FRIDAY
23 SEMIK (RUSSIAN)
Waning Moon
Moon Phase: 3rd Quarter | Moon Sign: Sagittarius
Color: Rose | Incense: Floral

SATURDAY
24 THE THREE MARIES (FRENCH)
Waning Moon | Moon Sign: Sagittarius
Moon Phase: 3rd Quarter | Moon enters Capricorn 6:51 AM
Color: Yellow | Incense: Vanilla

SUNDAY
25 ASSASSINATION OF EDMUND I (ANGLO-SAXON)
Waning Moon
Moon Phase: 3rd Quarter | Moon Sign: Capricorn
Color: Violet | Incense: Lilac

MONDAY
26 MEMORIAL DAY (OBSERVED)
Waning Moon | Moon Sign: Capricorn
Moon Phase: 3rd Quarter | Moon enters Aquarius 10:20 AM
Color: Lavender | Incense: Lavender

TUESDAY
27 Waning Moon
Moon Phase: 3rd Quarter | Moon Sign: Aquarius
Color: Indigo | Incense: Jasmine

WEDNESDAY
28 Waning Moon | Moon Sign: Aquarius
Moon Phase: 3rd Quarter | Moon enters Pisces 1:18 PM
Color: Peach | Incense: Fruity

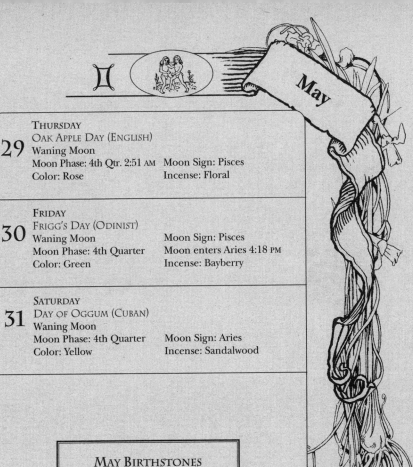

May

29 THURSDAY
OAK APPLE DAY (ENGLISH)
Waning Moon
Moon Phase: 4th Qtr. 2:51 AM   Moon Sign: Pisces
Color: Rose   Incense: Floral

30 FRIDAY
FRIGG'S DAY (ODINIST)
Waning Moon   Moon Sign: Pisces
Moon Phase: 4th Quarter   Moon enters Aries 4:18 PM
Color: Green   Incense: Bayberry

31 SATURDAY
DAY OF OGGUM (CUBAN)
Waning Moon
Moon Phase: 4th Quarter   Moon Sign: Aries
Color: Yellow   Incense: Sandalwood

MAY BIRTHSTONES
Ancient: Agate
Modern: Emerald

MAY FLOWERS
Lilies of the Valley
Hawthorn

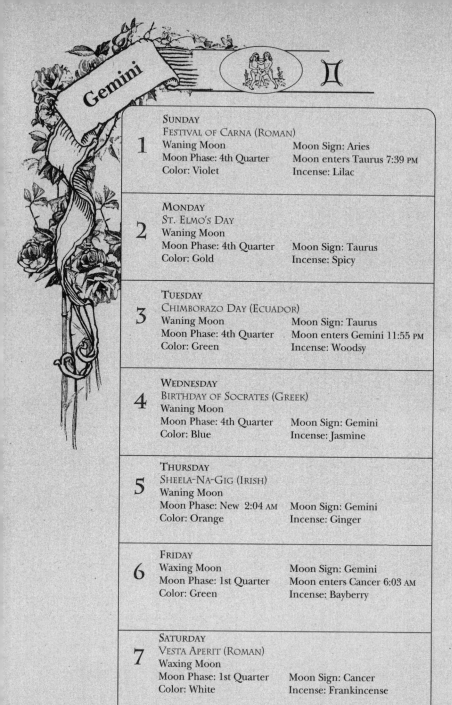

Gemini ♊

SUNDAY
1 FESTIVAL OF CARNA (ROMAN)
Waning Moon
Moon Phase: 4th Quarter
Color: Violet

Moon Sign: Aries
Moon enters Taurus 7:39 PM
Incense: Lilac

MONDAY
2 ST. ELMO'S DAY
Waning Moon
Moon Phase: 4th Quarter
Color: Gold

Moon Sign: Taurus
Incense: Spicy

TUESDAY
3 CHIMBORAZO DAY (ECUADOR)
Waning Moon
Moon Phase: 4th Quarter
Color: Green

Moon Sign: Taurus
Moon enters Gemini 11:55 PM
Incense: Woodsy

WEDNESDAY
4 BIRTHDAY OF SOCRATES (GREEK)
Waning Moon
Moon Phase: 4th Quarter
Color: Blue

Moon Sign: Gemini
Incense: Jasmine

THURSDAY
5 SHEELA-NA-GIG (IRISH)
Waning Moon
Moon Phase: New 2:04 AM
Color: Orange

Moon Sign: Gemini
Incense: Ginger

FRIDAY
6 Waxing Moon
Moon Phase: 1st Quarter
Color: Green

Moon Sign: Gemini
Moon enters Cancer 6:03 AM
Incense: Bayberry

SATURDAY
7 VESTA APERIT (ROMAN)
Waxing Moon
Moon Phase: 1st Quarter
Color: White

Moon Sign: Cancer
Incense: Frankincense

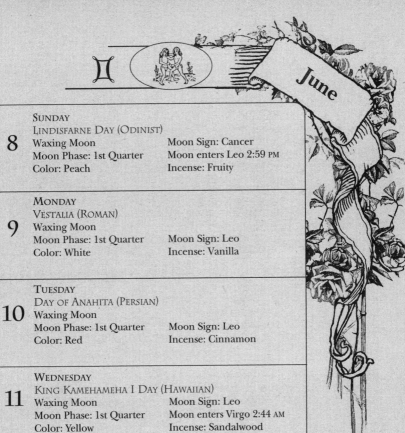

June

8 SUNDAY
LINDISFARNE DAY (ODINIST)
Waxing Moon   Moon Sign: Cancer
Moon Phase: 1st Quarter   Moon enters Leo 2:59 PM
Color: Peach   Incense: Fruity

9 MONDAY
VESTALIA (ROMAN)
Waxing Moon   Moon Sign: Leo
Moon Phase: 1st Quarter
Color: White   Incense: Vanilla

10 TUESDAY
DAY OF ANAHITA (PERSIAN)
Waxing Moon   Moon Sign: Leo
Moon Phase: 1st Quarter   Moon Sign: Leo
Color: Red   Incense: Cinnamon

11 WEDNESDAY
KING KAMEHAMEHA I DAY (HAWAIIAN)
Waxing Moon   Moon Sign: Leo
Moon Phase: 1st Quarter   Moon enters Virgo 2:44 AM
Color: Yellow   Incense: Sandalwood

12 THURSDAY
Waxing Moon
Moon Phase: 2nd Qtr. 11:52 PM Moon Sign: Virgo
Color: Green   Incense: Bayberry

13 FRIDAY
TIBETAN ALL SOULS' DAY
Waxing Moon   Moon Sign: Virgo
Moon Phase: 2nd Quarter   Moon enters Libra 3:36 PM
Color: Rose   Incense: Floral

14 SATURDAY
VIDAR'S DAY (ODINIST)
Waxing Moon
Moon Phase: 2nd Quarter   Moon Sign: Libra
Color: Blue   Incense: Thyme

Gemini ♊

15 SUNDAY
ST. VITUS' DAY
Waxing Moon
Moon Phase: 2nd Quarter   Moon Sign: Libra
Color: Gold   Incense: Spicy

16 MONDAY
NIGHT OF THE DROP (EGYPTIAN)
Waxing Moon   Moon Sign: Libra
Moon Phase: 2nd Quarter   Moon enters Scorpio 2:51 AM
Color: Lavender   Incense: Lilac

17 TUESDAY
LUDI PISCATARI (ROMAN)
Waxing Moon
Moon Phase: 2nd Quarter   Moon Sign: Scorpio
Color: White   Incense: Frankincense

18 WEDNESDAY
Waxing Moon   Moon Sign: Scorpio
Moon Phase: 2nd Quarter   Moon enters Sagittarius 10:39 AM
Color: Peach   Incense: Fruity

19 THURSDAY
WAA-LAA BEGINS (NATIVE AMERICAN)
Waxing Moon
Moon Phase: 2nd Quarter   Moon Sign: Sagittarius
Color: Turquoise   Incense: Bay Laurel

20 FRIDAY
DAY OF IX CHEL (MAYAN)
Waxing Moon   Moon Sign: Sagittarius
Moon Phase: Full 2:09 PM   Sun enters Capricorn 3:02 PM
Color: Pink   Incense: Floral

21 SATURDAY
LITHA (SUMMER SOLSTICE)
Waning Moon   Moon Sign: Capricorn
Moon Phase: 3rd Quarter   Sun enters Cancer 3:20 AM
Color: Blue   Incense: Floral

SUNDAY
FEAST OF SAN ALOISIO (MEXICAN)
22
Waning Moon
Moon Phase: 3rd Quarter
Color: Orange

Moon Sign: Capricorn
Moon enters Aquarius 5:21 PM
Incense: Ginger

MONDAY
23
Waning Moon
Moon Phase: 3rd Quarter
Color: Silver

Moon Sign: Aquarius
Incense: Spicy

TUESDAY
AZTEC FEAST OF THE SUN
24
Waning Moon
Moon Phase: 3rd Quarter
Color: Gray

Moon Sign: Aquarius
Moon enters Pisces 7:09 PM
Incense: Sage

WEDNESDAY
WELL-DRESSING FESTIVAL (BRITISH)
25
Waning Moon
Moon Phase: 3rd Quarter
Color: White

Moon Sign: Pisces
Incense: Myrrh

THURSDAY
IROQUOIS GREEN CORN FESTIVAL (NATIVE AMERICAN)
26
Waning Moon
Moon Phase: 3rd Quarter
Color: Violet

Moon Sign: Pisces
Moon enters Aries 9:39 PM
Incense: Lavender

FRIDAY)
27
Waning Moon
Moon Phase: 4th Qtr. 7:43 AM
Color: White

Moon Sign: Aries
Incense: Vanilla

SATURDAY
FESTIVAL OF THE TARASQUE (FRENCH)
28
Waning Moon
Moon Phase: 4th Quarter
Color: Gray

Moon Sign: Aries
Incense: Sage

Cancer ♋

SUNDAY
FEAST OF OGUN (SANTERIA)

29 Waning Moon
Moon Phase: 4th Quarter
Color: Yellow

Moon Sign: Aries
Moon enters Taurus 1:24 am
Incense: Sandalwood

MONDAY

30 Waning Moon
Moon Phase: 4th Quarter
Color: Gray

Moon Sign: Taurus
Incense: Sage

JUNE BIRTHSTONES
Ancient: Emerald
Modern: Agate

JUNE FLOWERS
Roses
Honeysuckle

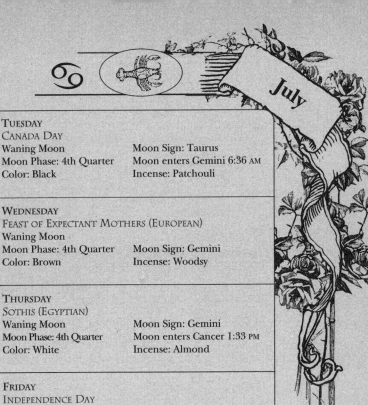

July

1
TUESDAY
CANADA DAY
Waning Moon
Moon Phase: 4th Quarter
Color: Black

Moon Sign: Taurus
Moon enters Gemini 6:36 AM
Incense: Patchouli

2
WEDNESDAY
FEAST OF EXPECTANT MOTHERS (EUROPEAN)
Waning Moon
Moon Phase: 4th Quarter
Color: Brown

Moon Sign: Gemini
Incense: Woodsy

3
THURSDAY
SOTHIS (EGYPTIAN)
Waning Moon
Moon Phase: 4th Quarter
Color: White

Moon Sign: Gemini
Moon enters Cancer 1:33 PM
Incense: Almond

4
FRIDAY
INDEPENDENCE DAY
Waning Moon
Moon Phase: New 1:40 PM
Color: Peach

Moon Sign: Cancer
Incense: Fruity

5
SATURDAY
OLD MIDSUMMER'S DAY
Waxing Moon
Moon Phase: 1st Quarter
Color: Brown

Moon Sign: Cancer
Moon enters Leo 10:45 PM
Incense: Cedar

6
SUNDAY
Waxing Moon
Moon Phase: 1st Quarter
Color: Peach

Moon Sign: Leo
Incense: Fruity

7
MONDAY
TANABATA (JAPANESE)
Waxing Moon
Moon Phase: 1st Quarter
Color: Gold

Moon Sign: Leo
Incense: Spicy

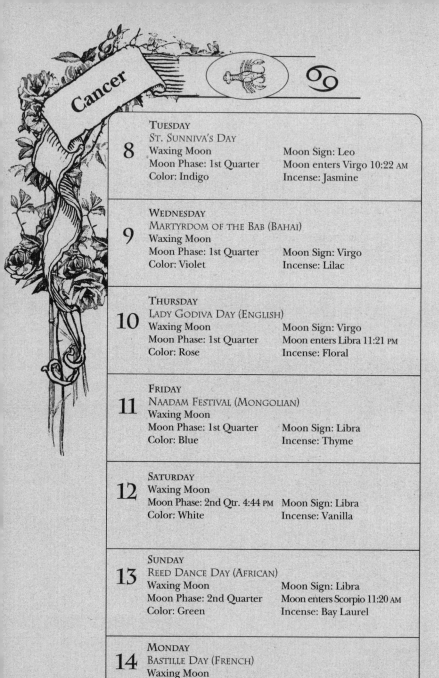

Cancer ♋

8 TUESDAY
ST. SUNNIVA'S DAY
Waxing Moon
Moon Phase: 1st Quarter
Color: Indigo

Moon Sign: Leo
Moon enters Virgo 10:22 AM
Incense: Jasmine

9 WEDNESDAY
MARTYRDOM OF THE BAB (BAHAI)
Waxing Moon
Moon Phase: 1st Quarter
Color: Violet

Moon Sign: Virgo
Incense: Lilac

10 THURSDAY
LADY GODIVA DAY (ENGLISH)
Waxing Moon
Moon Phase: 1st Quarter
Color: Rose

Moon Sign: Virgo
Moon enters Libra 11:21 PM
Incense: Floral

11 FRIDAY
NAADAM FESTIVAL (MONGOLIAN)
Waxing Moon
Moon Phase: 1st Quarter
Color: Blue

Moon Sign: Libra
Incense: Thyme

12 SATURDAY
Waxing Moon
Moon Phase: 2nd Qtr. 4:44 PM
Color: White

Moon Sign: Libra
Incense: Vanilla

13 SUNDAY
REED DANCE DAY (AFRICAN)
Waxing Moon
Moon Phase: 2nd Quarter
Color: Green

Moon Sign: Libra
Moon enters Scorpio 11:20 AM
Incense: Bay Laurel

14 MONDAY
BASTILLE DAY (FRENCH)
Waxing Moon
Moon Phase: 2nd Quarter
Color: Yellow

Moon Sign: Scorpio
Incense: Sandalwood

July

15 TUESDAY
DAY OF RAUNI (FINNISH)
Waxing Moon
Moon Phase: 2nd Quarter
Color: Green

Moon Sign: Scorpio
Moon enters Sagittarius 8:03 PM
Incense: Bayberry

16 WEDNESDAY
ROSA MUNDI (PALESTINIAN)
Waxing Moon
Moon Phase: 2nd Quarter
Color: Blue

Moon Sign: Sagittarius
Incense: Thyme

17 THURSDAY
FESTIVAL OF AMA-TERASU-O-MI-KAMI (JAPANESE)
Waxing Moon
Moon Phase: 2nd Quarter
Color: Orange

Moon Sign: Sagittarius
Incense: Ginger

18 FRIDAY
BIRTHDAY OF NEPHTHYS (EGYPTIAN)
Waxing Moon
Moon Phase: 2nd Quarter
Color: Green

Moon Sign: Sagittarius
Moon enters Capricorn 12:46 AM
Incense: Babyberry

19 SATURDAY
WEDDING OF ADONIS AND APHRODITE (GREEK)
Waxing Moon
Moon Phase: Full 10:21 PM
Color: Yellow

Moon Sign: Capricorn
Incense: Sandalwood

20 SUNDAY
BINDING OF THE WREATHS (LITHUANIAN)
Waning Moon
Moon Phase: 3rd Quarter
Color: Violet

Moon Sign: Capricorn
Moon enters Aquarius 2:29 AM
Incense: Lavender

21 MONDAY
DAMO'S DAY (GREEK)
Waning Moon
Moon Phase: 3rd Quarter
Color: White

Moon Sign: Aquarius
Incense: Myrrh

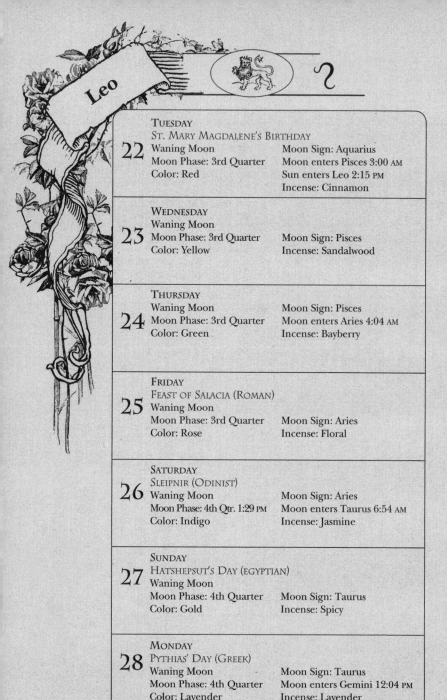

Leo

TUESDAY
ST. MARY MAGDALENE'S BIRTHDAY

22
Waning Moon
Moon Phase: 3rd Quarter
Color: Red

Moon Sign: Aquarius
Moon enters Pisces 3:00 AM
Sun enters Leo 2:15 PM
Incense: Cinnamon

WEDNESDAY

23
Waning Moon
Moon Phase: 3rd Quarter
Color: Yellow

Moon Sign: Pisces
Incense: Sandalwood

THURSDAY

24
Waning Moon
Moon Phase: 3rd Quarter
Color: Green

Moon Sign: Pisces
Moon enters Aries 4:04 AM
Incense: Bayberry

FRIDAY
FEAST OF SALACIA (ROMAN)

25
Waning Moon
Moon Phase: 3rd Quarter
Color: Rose

Moon Sign: Aries
Incense: Floral

SATURDAY
SLEIPNIR (ODINIST)

26
Waning Moon
Moon Phase: 4th Qtr. 1:29 PM
Color: Indigo

Moon Sign: Aries
Moon enters Taurus 6:54 AM
Incense: Jasmine

SUNDAY
HATSHEPSUT'S DAY (EGYPTIAN)

27
Waning Moon
Moon Phase: 4th Quarter
Color: Gold

Moon Sign: Taurus
Incense: Spicy

MONDAY
PYTHIAS' DAY (GREEK)

28
Waning Moon
Moon Phase: 4th Quarter
Color: Lavender

Moon Sign: Taurus
Moon enters Gemini 12:04 PM
Incense: Lavender

160

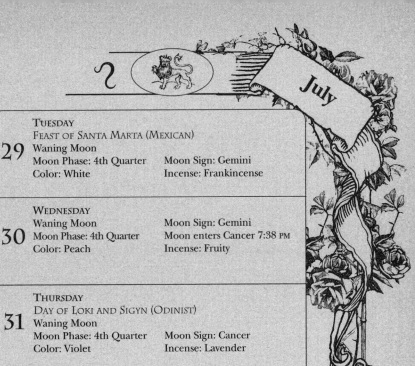

July

TUESDAY
FEAST OF SANTA MARTA (MEXICAN)

29 Waning Moon
Moon Phase: 4th Quarter   Moon Sign: Gemini
Color: White   Incense: Frankincense

WEDNESDAY
Waning Moon   Moon Sign: Gemini

30 Moon Phase: 4th Quarter   Moon enters Cancer 7:38 PM
Color: Peach   Incense: Fruity

THURSDAY
DAY OF LOKI AND SIGYN (ODINIST)

31 Waning Moon
Moon Phase: 4th Quarter   Moon Sign: Cancer
Color: Violet   Incense: Lavender

JULY BIRTHSTONES
Ancient: Onyx
Modern: Ruby

JULY FLOWERS
Water Lilies
Larkspur

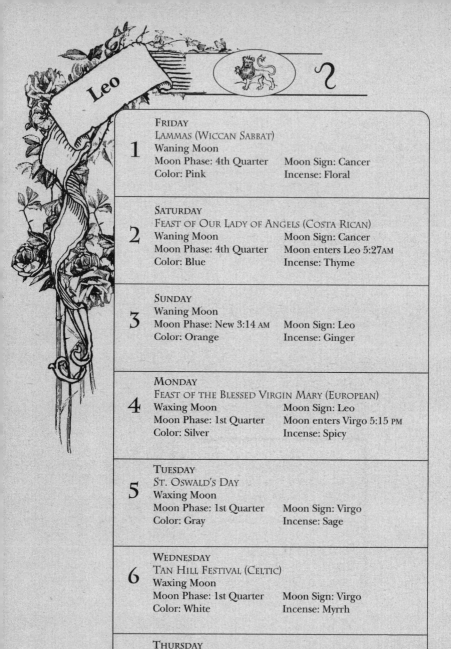

Leo

FRIDAY
LAMMAS (WICCAN SABBAT)
1
Waning Moon
Moon Phase: 4th Quarter   Moon Sign: Cancer
Color: Pink   Incense: Floral

SATURDAY
FEAST OF OUR LADY OF ANGELS (COSTA RICAN)
2
Waning Moon   Moon Sign: Cancer
Moon Phase: 4th Quarter   Moon enters Leo 5:27AM
Color: Blue   Incense: Thyme

SUNDAY
3
Waning Moon
Moon Phase: New 3:14 AM   Moon Sign: Leo
Color: Orange   Incense: Ginger

MONDAY
FEAST OF THE BLESSED VIRGIN MARY (EUROPEAN)
4
Waxing Moon   Moon Sign: Leo
Moon Phase: 1st Quarter   Moon enters Virgo 5:15 PM
Color: Silver   Incense: Spicy

TUESDAY
ST. OSWALD'S DAY
5
Waxing Moon
Moon Phase: 1st Quarter   Moon Sign: Virgo
Color: Gray   Incense: Sage

WEDNESDAY
TAN HILL FESTIVAL (CELTIC)
6
Waxing Moon
Moon Phase: 1st Quarter   Moon Sign: Virgo
Color: White   Incense: Myrrh

THURSDAY
BREAKING OF THE NILE (EGYPTIAN)
7
Waxing Moon   Moon Sign: Virgo
Moon Phase: 1st Quarter   Moon enters Libra 6:17 AM
Color: Violet   Incense: Lilac

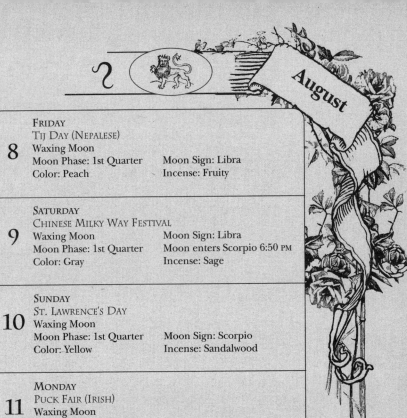

8 FRIDAY
TIJ DAY (NEPALESE)
Waxing Moon
Moon Phase: 1st Quarter
Color: Peach

Moon Sign: Libra
Incense: Fruity

9 SATURDAY
CHINESE MILKY WAY FESTIVAL
Waxing Moon
Moon Phase: 1st Quarter
Color: Gray

Moon Sign: Libra
Moon enters Scorpio 6:50 PM
Incense: Sage

10 SUNDAY
ST. LAWRENCE'S DAY
Waxing Moon
Moon Phase: 1st Quarter
Color: Yellow

Moon Sign: Scorpio
Incense: Sandalwood

11 MONDAY
PUCK FAIR (IRISH)
Waxing Moon
Moon Phase: 2nd Qtr. 7:43 AM
Color: Gray

Moon Sign: Scorpio
Incense: Sage

12 TUESDAY
LIGHTS OF ISIS (EGYPTIAN)
Waxing Moon
Moon Phase: 2nd Quarter
Color: Black

Moon Sign: Scorpio
Moon enters Sagittarius 4:46 AM
Incense: Patchouli

13 WEDNESDAY
HECATE'S DAY (GREEK)
Waxing Moon
Moon Phase: 2nd Quarter
Color: Brown

Moon Sign: Sagittarius
Incense: Cedar

14 THURSDAY
FIESCHI'S CAKE DAY (ITALIAN)
Waxing Moon
Moon Phase: 2nd Quarter
Color: Rose

Moon Sign: Sagittarius
Moon enters Capricorn 10:43 PM
Incense: Floral

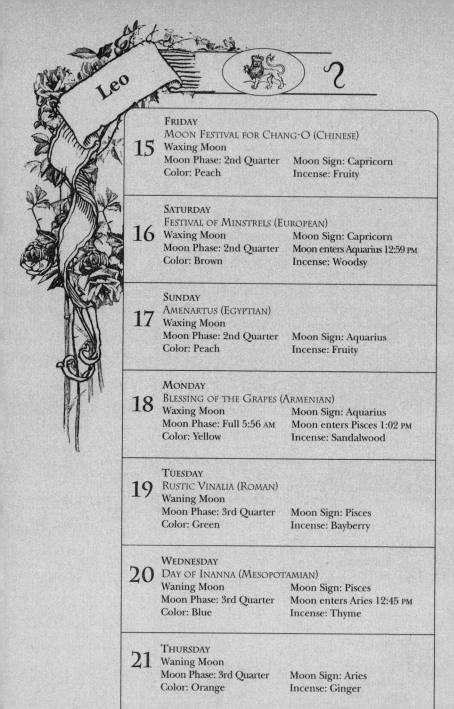

Leo ♌

FRIDAY
MOON FESTIVAL FOR CHANG-O (CHINESE)
15
Waxing Moon
Moon Phase: 2nd Quarter | Moon Sign: Capricorn
Color: Peach | Incense: Fruity

SATURDAY
FESTIVAL OF MINSTRELS (EUROPEAN)
16
Waxing Moon | Moon Sign: Capricorn
Moon Phase: 2nd Quarter | Moon enters Aquarius 12:59 PM
Color: Brown | Incense: Woodsy

SUNDAY
AMENARTUS (EGYPTIAN)
17
Waxing Moon
Moon Phase: 2nd Quarter | Moon Sign: Aquarius
Color: Peach | Incense: Fruity

MONDAY
BLESSING OF THE GRAPES (ARMENIAN)
18
Waxing Moon | Moon Sign: Aquarius
Moon Phase: Full 5:56 AM | Moon enters Pisces 1:02 PM
Color: Yellow | Incense: Sandalwood

TUESDAY
RUSTIC VINALIA (ROMAN)
19
Waning Moon
Moon Phase: 3rd Quarter | Moon Sign: Pisces
Color: Green | Incense: Bayberry

WEDNESDAY
DAY OF INANNA (MESOPOTAMIAN)
20
Waning Moon | Moon Sign: Pisces
Moon Phase: 3rd Quarter | Moon enters Aries 12:45 PM
Color: Blue | Incense: Thyme

THURSDAY
21
Waning Moon
Moon Phase: 3rd Quarter | Moon Sign: Aries
Color: Orange | Incense: Ginger

FRIDAY
22
AEDESIA'S DAY (GREEK)
Waning Moon
Moon Phase: 3rd Quarter
Color: Green

Moon Sign: Aries
Moon enters Taurus 1:57 PM
Sun enters Virgo 9:19 PM
Incense: Bayberry

SATURDAY
23
DAY OF MOIRA (GREEK)
Waning Moon
Moon Phase: 3rd Quarter
Color: Yellow

Moon Sign: Taurus
Incense: Sandalwood

SUNDAY
24
ST. BARTHOLOMEW'S DAY
Waning Moon
Moon Phase: 4th Qtr. 9:24 PM
Color: Violet

Moon Sign: Taurus
Moon enters Gemini 5:56 PM
Incense: Lilac

MONDAY
25
PARYUSHANA PARVA (HINDU)
Waning Moon
Moon Phase: 4th Quarter
Color: White

Moon Sign: Gemini
Incense: Almond

TUESDAY
26
FEAST DAY OF ILMATAR (FINNISH)
Waning Moon
Moon Phase: 4th Quarter
Color: Gray

Moon Sign: Gemini
Incense: Sage

WEDNESDAY
27
WORSHIP OF MOTHER GODDESS DEVAKI (EAST INDIAN)
Waning Moon
Moon Phase: 4th Quarter
Color: Brown

Moon Sign: Gemini
Moon enters Cancer 1:10 AM
Incense: Cedar

THURSDAY
28
Waning Moon
Moon Phase: 4th Quarter
Color: Turquoise

Moon Sign: Cancer
Moon enters Leo 11:19 AM
Incense: Bay Laurel

Virgo ♍

FRIDAY
29 HATHOR'S DAY (EGYPTIAN)
Waning Moon
Moon Phase: 4th Quarter
Color: Blue

Moon Sign: Cancer
Moon enters Leo 11:19 AM
Incense: Floral

SATURDAY
30 ST. ROSE OF LIMA DAY (PERUVIAN)
Waning Moon
Moon Phase: 4th Quarter
Color: Brown

Moon Sign: Leo
Incense: Evergreen

SUNDAY
31 Waning Moon
Moon Phase: 4th Quarter
Color: Yellow

Moon Sign: Leo
Moon enters Virgo 11:27 PM
Incense: Sandalwood

AUGUST BIRTHSTONES
Ancient: Carnelian
Modern: Topaz

AUGUST FLOWERS
Gladiolus
Poppies

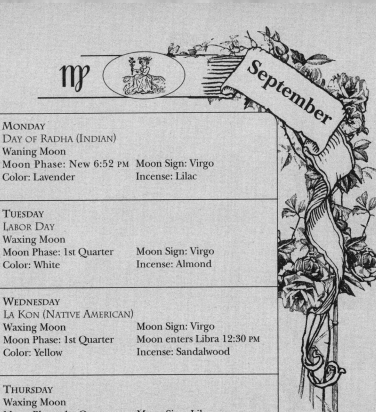

MONDAY
DAY OF RADHA (INDIAN)
1 Waning Moon
Moon Phase: New 6:52 PM   Moon Sign: Virgo
Color: Lavender   Incense: Lilac

TUESDAY
LABOR DAY
2 Waxing Moon
Moon Phase: 1st Quarter   Moon Sign: Virgo
Color: White   Incense: Almond

WEDNESDAY
LA KON (NATIVE AMERICAN)
3 Waxing Moon   Moon Sign: Virgo
Moon Phase: 1st Quarter   Moon enters Libra 12:30 PM
Color: Yellow   Incense: Sandalwood

THURSDAY
4 Waxing Moon
Moon Phase: 1st Quarter   Moon Sign: Libra
Color: Green   Incense: Bayberry

FRIDAY
DAY OF NANDA DEVI (EAST INDIAN)
5 Waxing Moon
Moon Phase: 1st Quarter   Moon Sign: Libra
Color: White   Incense: Vanilla

SATURDAY
6 Waxing Moon   Moon Sign: Libra
Moon Phase: 1st Quarter   Moon enters Scorpio 1:10 AM
Color: Brown   Incense: Cedar

SUNDAY
FESTIVAL OF DURGA (BENGALESE)
7 Waxing Moon
Moon Phase: 1st Quarter   Moon Sign: Scorpio
Color: Green   Incense: Bayberry

Virgo ♍

8
MONDAY
PINNHUT FESTIVAL (NATIVE AMERICAN)
Waxing Moon   Moon Sign: Scorpio
Moon Phase: 1st Quarter   Moon enters Sagittarius 11:55 AM
Color: Yellow   Incense: Sandalwood

9
TUESDAY
HORNED DANCE AT ABBOTS BROMLEY (ENGLISH)
Waxing Moon
Moon Phase: 2nd Qtr. 8:32 PM   Moon Sign: Sagittarius
Color: Indigo   Incense: Jasmine

10
WEDNESDAY
Waxing Moon   Moon Sign: Sagittarius
Moon Phase: 2nd Quarter   Moon enters Capricorn 7:24 PM
Color: Brown   Incense: Cedar

11
THURSDAY
EGYPTIAN DAY OF QUEENS
Waxing Moon
Moon Phase: 2nd Quarter   Moon Sign: Capricorn
Color: Turquoise   Incense: Bay Laurel

12
FRIDAY
ASTRAEA'S DAY (GREEK)
Waxing Moon   Moon Sign: Capricorn
Moon Phase: 2nd Quarter   Moon enters Aquarius 11:10 PM
Color: Pink   Incense: Floral

13
SATURDAY
LECTISTERNIA (ROMAN)
Waxing Moon
Moon Phase: 2nd Quarter   Moon Sign: Aquarius
Color: Indigo   Incense: Jasmine

14
SUNDAY
FEAST OF LIGHTS (EGYPTIAN)
Waxing Moon   Moon Sign: Aquarius
Moon Phase: 2nd Quarter   Moon enters Pisces 11:59 PM
Color: Gold   Incense: Spicy

15 MONDAY
ACORN FESTIVAL (NATIVE AMERICAN)
Waxing Moon
Moon Phase: 2nd Quarter   Moon Sign: Pisces
Color: Silver   Incense: Myrrh

16 TUESDAY
ST. NINIAN'S DAY
Waxing Moon   Moon Sign: Pisces
Moon Phase: Full 1:51 PM   Moon enters Aries 11:25 PM
Color: Red   Incense: Clove

17 WEDNESDAY
HILDEGARD OF BINGEN'S DAY (GERMAN)
Waning Moon
Moon Phase: 3rd Quarter   Moon Sign: Aries
Color: Peach   Incense: Fruity

18 THURSDAY
Waning Moon   Moon Sign: Aries
Moon Phase: 3rd Quarter   Moon enters Taurus 11:21 AM
Color: White   Incense: Vanilla

19 FRIDAY
FAST OF THOTH (EGYPTIAN)
Waning Moon
Moon Phase: 3rd Quarter   Moon Sign: Taurus
Color: Blue   Incense: Floral

20 SATURDAY
BIRTHDAY OF QUETZALCOATL (AZTEC)
Waning Moon
Moon Phase: 3rd Quarter   Moon Sign: Taurus
Color: White   Incense: Frankincense

21 SUNDAY
RAUD THE STRONG'S MARTYRDOM (NORWEGIAN)
Waning Moon   Moon Sign: Taurus
Moon Phase: 3rd Quarter   Moon enters Gemini 1:38 AM
Color: Violet   Incense: Lavender

Libra

Monday
Mabon (Fall Equinox)

22
Waning Moon
Moon Phase: 3rd Quarter
Color: Gold

Moon Sign: Gemini
Sun enters Libra 6:56 PM
Incense: Almond

Tuesday
Day of Mielikki (Finnish)

23
Waning Moon
Moon Phase: 4th Qtr. 8:35 AM
Color: Indigo

Moon Sign: Gemini
Moon enters Cancer 7:33 AM
Incense: Temple

Wednesday
Feast of Obatala (Santeria)

24
Waning Moon
Moon Phase: 4th Quarter
Color: Brown

Moon Sign: Cancer
Incense: Evergreen

Thursday

25
Waning Moon
Moon Phase: 4th Quarter
Color: White

Moon Sign: Cancer
Moon enters Leo 5:13 PM
Incense: Myrrh

Friday
Feast of Santa Justina (Mexican)

26
Waning Moon
Moon Phase: 4th Quarter
Color: Pink

Moon Sign: Leo
Incense: Floral

Saturday
Day of Willows (Mesopotamian)

27
Waning Moon
Moon Phase: 4th Quarter
Color: Gray

Moon Sign: Leo
Incense: Sage

Sunday
Confucious' Birthday

28
Waning Moon
Moon Phase: 4th Quarter
Color: Peach

Moon Sign: Leo
Moon enters Virgo 5:28 AM
Incense: Fruity

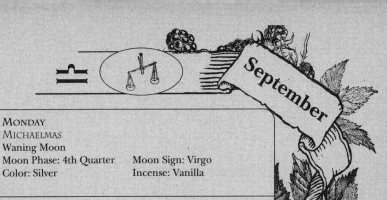

September

MONDAY
MICHAELMAS
29 Waning Moon
Moon Phase: 4th Quarter   Moon Sign: Virgo
Color: Silver   Incense: Vanilla

TUESDAY
MEDETRINALIA (ROMAN)
30 Waning Moon   Moon Sign: Virgo
Moon Phase: 4th Quarter   Moon enters Libra 6:33 PM
Color: Red   Incense: Clove

SEPTEMBER BIRTHSTONES
Ancient: Chrysolite
Modern: Beryl

SEPTEMBER FLOWERS
Morning Glories
Asters

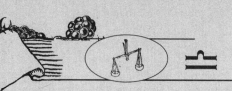

Libra

WEDNESDAY
1 ROSH HASHANAH BEGINS (JEWISH)
Waning Moon
Moon Phase: New 11:53 AM   Moon Sign: Libra
Color: Brown   Incense: Cedar

THURSDAY
2 OLD MAN'S DAY (ENGLISH)
Waxing Moon
Moon Phase: 1st Quarter   Moon Sign: Libra
Color: White   Incense: Myrrh

FRIDAY
3 ROSH HASANAH ENDS (JEWISH)
Waxing Moon   Moon Sign: Libra
Moon Phase: 1st Quarter   Moon enters Scorpio 6:58 AM
Color: Pink   Incense: Floral

SATURDAY
4 ELK FESTIVAL (NATIVE AMERICAN)
Waxing Moon
Moon Phase: 1st Quarter   Moon Sign: Scorpio
Color: Blue   Incense: Thyme

SUNDAY
5 ROMANIAN WINE FESTIVAL
Waxing Moon   Moon Sign: Scorpio
Moon Phase: 1st Quarter   Moon enters Sagittarius 5:43 PM
Color: Orange   Incense: Ginger

MONDAY
6 WATER FESTIVAL (PERUVIAN)
Waxing Moon
Moon Phase: 1st Quarter   Moon Sign: Sagittarius
Color: Yellow   Incense: Sandalwood

TUESDAY
7 PALLAS ATHENA'S DAY (ROMAN)
Waxing Moon
Moon Phase: 1st Quarter   Moon Sign: Sagittarius
Color: Green   Incense: Bayberry

WEDNESDAY

8

Waxing Moon
Moon Phase: 1st Quarter
Color: Peach

Moon Sign: Sagittarius
Moon enters Capricorn 2:04 AM
Incense: Fruity

THURSDAY

9

ST. DENIS' DAY
Waxing Moon
Moon Phase: 2nd Qtr. 7:22 AM
Color: Rose

Moon Sign: Capricorn
Incense: Floral

FRIDAY

10

YOM KIPPUR BEGINS (JEWISH)
Waxing Moon
Moon Phase: 2nd Quarter
Color: Blue

Moon Sign: Capricorn
Moon enters Aquarius 7:29 AM
Incense: Thyme

SATURDAY

11

YOM KIPPUR ENDS (JEWISH)
Waxing Moon
Moon Phase: 2nd Quarter
Color: White

Moon Sign: Aquarius
Incense: Frankincense

SUNDAY

12

FOURTH GAHAMBAR (ZOROASTRIAN)
Waxing Moon
Moon Phase: 2nd Quarter
Color: Orange

Moon Sign: Aquarius
Moon enters Pisces 9:59 AM
Incense: Ginger

MONDAY

13

COLUMBUS DAY (OBSERVED)
Waxing Moon
Moon Phase: 2nd Quarter
Color: Yellow

Moon Sign: Pisces
Incense: Sandalwood

TUESDAY

14

Waxing Moon
Moon Phase: 2nd Quarter
Color: Green

Moon Sign: Pisces
Moon enters Aries 10:25 AM
Incense: Bayberry

Libra

WEDNESDAY
15
SUKKOT BEGINS (JEWISH)
Waxing Moon
Moon Phase: Full 10:46 pm   Moon Sign: Aries
Color: Blue   Incense: Floral

THURSDAY
16
FESTIVAL OF PANDROSUS (GREEK)
Waning Moon   Moon Sign: Aries
Moon Phase: 3rd Quarter   Moon enters Taurus 10:16 AM
Color: Orange   Incense: Ginger

FRIDAY
17
SUKKOT ENDS (JEWISH)
Waning Moon
Moon Phase: 3rd Quarter   Moon Sign: Taurus
Color: Green   Incense: Pine

SATURDAY
18
FESTIVAL OF HERNE (CELTIC)
Waning Moon   Moon Sign: Taurus
Moon Phase: 3rd Quarter   Moon enters Gemini 11:27 AM
Color: Yellow   Incense: Musk

SUNDAY
19
Waning Moon
Moon Phase: 3rd Quarter   Moon Sign: Gemini
Color: Violet   Incense: Lilac

MONDAY
20
FESTIVAL OF ANCESTORS (CHINESE)
Waning Moon   Moon Sign: Gemini
Moon Phase: 3rd Quarter   Moon enters Cancer 3:46 PM
Color: White   Incense: Vanilla

TUESDAY
21
FESTIVAL OF ISHHARA (MESOPOTAMIAN)
Waning Moon
Moon Phase: 3rd Quarter   Moon Sign: Cancer
Color: Red   Incense: Cinnamon

m ⟨scorpio symbol⟩ **October**

22
WEDNESDAY
Waning Moon
Moon Phase: 4th Qtr. 11:49 PM   Moon Sign: Cancer
Color: Yellow   Incense: Sandalwood

23
THURSDAY
SWALLOWS OF SAN JUAN CAPISTRANO DAY (MEXICAN)
Waning Moon   Moon Sign: Cancer
Moon Phase: 4th Quarter   Moon enters Leo 12:11 AM
Color: Green   Sun enters Scorpio 4:15 AM
    Incense: Pine

24
FRIDAY
UNITED NATIONS DAY
Waning Moon
Moon Phase: 4th Quarter   Moon Sign: Leo
Color: Rose   Incense: Floral

25
SATURDAY
ST. CRISPIN'S DAY
Waning Moon   Moon Sign: Leo
Moon Phase: 4th Quarter   Moon enters Virgo 12:00 PM
Color: Indigo   Incense: Jasmine

26
SUNDAY
ABAN JASHAN (JAPANESE)
Waning Moon
Moon Phase: 4th Quarter   Moon Sign: Virgo
Color: Gold   Incense: Frankincense

27
MONDAY
OWAGIT (NATIVE AMERICAN)
Waning Moon
Moon Phase: 4th Quarter   Moon Sign: Virgo
Color: Lavender   Incense: Lilac

28
TUESDAY
FYRIBOD (CELTIC)
Waning Moon   Moon Sign: Virgo
Moon Phase: 4th Quarter   Moon enters Libra 1:05 AM
Color: White   Incense: Myrrh

Scorpio ♏

WEDNESDAY
29 IROQUOIS FEAST OF THE DEAD (NATIVE AMERICAN)
Waning Moon
Moon Phase: 4th Quarter   Moon Sign: Libra
Color: Peach   Incense: Fruity

THURSDAY
30 LOS ANGELITOS (MEXICAN)
Waning Moon   Moon Sign: Libra
Moon Phase: 4th Quarter   Moon enters Scorpio 1:16 PM
Color: Turquoise   Incense: Bay Laurel

FRIDAY
31 SAMHAIN (WICCAN SABBAT)
Waning Moon
Moon Phase: New 5:01 AM   Moon Sign: Scorpio
Color: Pink   Incense: Floral

OCTOBER BIRTHSTONES
Ancient: Aquamarine
Modern: Pearl

OCTOBER FLOWERS
Calendula
Cosmos

1
SATURDAY
ALL SAINTS' DAY
Waxing Moon
Moon Phase: 1st Quarter
Color: Blue

Moon Sign: Scorpio
Moon enters Sagittarius 11:27 PM
Incense: Thyme

2
SUNDAY
ANIMAS (MEXICAN)
Waxing Moon
Moon Phase: 1st Quarter
Color: Orange

Moon Sign: Sagittarius
Incense: Ginger

3
MONDAY
FESTIVAL FOR THE NEW YEAR (GAELIC)
Waxing Moon
Moon Phase: 1st Quarter
Color: Silver

Moon Sign: Sagittarius
Incense: Musk

4
TUESDAY
Waxing Moon
Moon Phase: 1st Quarter
Color: Black

Moon Sign: Sagittarius
Moon enters Capricorn 7:31 AM
Incense: Patchouli

5
WEDNESDAY
GUY FAWKES' NIGHT (BRITISH)
Waxing Moon
Moon Phase: 1st Quarter
Color: Brown

Moon Sign: Capricorn
Incense: Evergreen

6
THURSDAY
BIRTHDAY OF TIAMAT (BABYLONIAN)
Waxing Moon
Moon Phase: 1st Quarter
Color: Violet

Moon Sign: Capricorn
Moon enters Aquarius 1:33 PM
Incense: Lilac

7
FRIDAY
MAKAHIKI FESTIVAL (HAWAIIAN)
Waxing Moon
Moon Phase: 2nd Qtr. 4:44 PM Moon Sign: Aquarius
Color: Peach
Incense: Fruity

Scorpio

SATURDAY

8
FESTIVAL OF KAMI OF THE HEARTH (JAPANESE)
Waxing Moon   Moon Sign: Aquarius
Moon Phase: 2nd Quarter   Moon enters Pisces 5:35 PM
Color: Brown   Incense: Cedar

SUNDAY

9
Waxing Moon   Moon Sign: Pisces
Moon Phase: 2nd Quarter   Incense: Fruity
Color: Peach

MONDAY

10
FESTIVAL OF THE GODDESS OF REASON (FRENCH)
Waxing Moon   Moon Sign: Pisces
Moon Phase: 2nd Quarter   Moon enters Aries 7:44 PM
Color: Gray   Incense: Sage

TUESDAY

11
GURU NANAK'S BIRTHDAY (SIKH)
Waxing Moon   Moon Sign: Aries
Moon Phase: 2nd Quarter   Incense: Temple
Color: Indigo

WEDNESDAY

12
BIRTHDAY OF BAHA'U'LLAH (BAHA'I)
Waxing Moon   Moon Sign: Aries
Moon Phase: 2nd Quarter   Moon enters Taurus 8:46 PM
Color: Violet   Incense: Lilac

THURSDAY

13
FESTIVAL OF JUPITER (ROMAN)
Waxing Moon   Moon Sign: Taurus
Moon Phase: 2nd Quarter   Incense: Floral
Color: Rose

FRIDAY

14
MOCCAS' DAY (CELTIC)
Waxing Moon   Moon Sign: Taurus
Moon Phase: Full 9:13 AM   Moon enters Gemini 10:05 PM
Color: Blue   Incense: Thyme

15
SATURDAY
SEVEN-FIVE-THREE FESTIVAL (JAPANESE)
Waning Moon
Moon Phase: 3rd Quarter   Moon Sign: Gemini
Color: White   Incense: Vanilla

16
SUNDAY
NIGHT OF HECATE (GREEK)
Waning Moon
Moon Phase: 3rd Quarter   Moon Sign: Gemini
Color: Green   Incense: Pine

17
MONDAY
Waning Moon   Moon Sign: Gemini
Moon Phase: 3rd Quarter   Moon enters Cancer 1:33 AM
Color: Yellow   Incense: Sandalwood

18
TUESDAY
DAY OF ARDVI SURA (PERSIAN)
Waning Moon
Moon Phase: 3rd Quarter   Moon Sign: Cancer
Color: White   Incense: Almond

19
WEDNESDAY
FEAST OF SANTA ISABEL (MEXICAN)
Waning Moon   Moon Sign: Cancer
Moon Phase: 3rd Quarter   Moon enters Leo 8:38 AM
Color: Peach   Incense: Fruity

20
THURSDAY
ST. EDMUND'S DAY
Waning Moon
Moon Phase: 3rd Quarter   Moon Sign: Leo
Color: White   Incense: Vanilla

21
FRIDAY
DAY OF CAILLEACH (CELTIC)
Waning Moon   Moon Sign: Leo
Moon Phase: 4th Qtr. 6:58 PM   Moon enters Virgo 7:33 PM
Color: Pink   Incense: Floral

Sagittarius

22 SATURDAY
YDALIR (NORSE)
Waning Moon
Moon Phase: 4th Quarter
Color: Blue

Moon Sign: Virgo
Sun enters Sagittarius 1:47 AM
Incense: Thyme

23 SUNDAY
SHINJOSAI (JAPANESE)
Waning Moon
Moon Phase: 4th Quarter
Color: Orange

Moon Sign: Virgo
Incense: Ginger

24 MONDAY
STIR-UP SUNDAY (BRITISH)
Waning Moon
Moon Phase: 4th Quarter
Color: White

Moon Sign: Virgo
Moon enters Libra 8:29 AM
Incense: Frankincense

25 TUESDAY
FEAST OF SANTA CATALINA DE ALEJANDRÍA (MEXICAN)
Waning Moon
Moon Phase: 4th Quarter
Color: Black

Moon Sign: Libra
Incense: Patchouli

26 WEDNESDAY
FESTIVAL OF LIGHTS (TIBETAN)
Waning Moon
Moon Phase: 4th Quarter
Color: Brown

Moon Sign: Libra
Moon enters Scorpio 8:43 PM
Incense: Cedar

27 THURSDAY
THANKSGIVING
Waning Moon
Moon Phase: 4th Quarter
Color: Violet

Moon Sign: Scorpio
Incense: Lavender

28 FRIDAY
DAY OF SOPHIA (GREEK)
Waning Moon
Moon Phase: 4th Quarter
Color: Blue

Moon Sign: Scorpio
Incense: Floral

November

29

Saturday
Sons of Saturn Festival (Roman)

Waning Moon
Moon Phase: New 9:14 pm
Color: White
Moon Sign: Scorpio
Moon enters Sagittarius 6:28 am
Incense: Almond

30

Sunday

Waxing Moon
Moon Phase: 1st Quarter
Color: Violet
Moon Sign: Sagittarius
Incense: Lilac

November Birthstones

Ancient: Topaz
Modern: Topaz

November Flowers

Chrysanthemums
Dahlias

Sagittarius

MONDAY
1 FESTIVAL OF POSEIDON (GREEK)
Waxing Moon
Moon Phase: 1st Quarter
Color: Gold

Moon Sign: Sagittarius
Moon enters Capricorn 1:38 PM
Incense: Myrrh

TUESDAY
2 FEAST OF SHIVA (HINDU)
Waxing Moon
Moon Phase: 1st Quarter
Color: Gray

Moon Sign: Capricorn
Incense: Sage

WEDNESDAY
3 ST. BARBARA'S DAY (BASQUE)
Waxing Moon
Moon Phase: 1st Quarter
Color: Peach

Moon Sign: Capricorn
Moon enters Aquarius 6:58 PM
Incense: Fruity

THURSDAY
4 Waxing Moon
Moon Phase: 1st Quarter
Color: Violet

Moon Sign: Aquarius
Incense: Lilac

FRIDAY
5 Waxing Moon
Moon Phase: 1st Quarter
Color: Green

Moon Sign: Aquarius
Moon enters Pisces 11:08 PM
Incense: Bayberry

SATURDAY
6 ST. NICHOLAS' DAY
Waxing Moon
Moon Phase: 1st Quarter
Color: Blue

Moon Sign: Pisces
Incense: Thyme

SUNDAY
7 BURNING THE DEVIL (GUATEMALAN)
Waxing Moon
Moon Phase: 2nd Qtr. 1:10 AM Moon Sign: Pisces
Color: Yellow   Incense: Musk

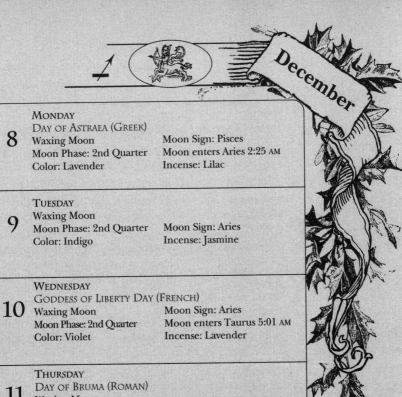

December

MONDAY
8
DAY OF ASTRAEA (GREEK)
Waxing Moon
Moon Phase: 2nd Quarter
Color: Lavender

Moon Sign: Pisces
Moon enters Aries 2:25 AM
Incense: Lilac

TUESDAY
9
Waxing Moon
Moon Phase: 2nd Quarter
Color: Indigo

Moon Sign: Aries
Incense: Jasmine

WEDNESDAY
10
GODDESS OF LIBERTY DAY (FRENCH)
Waxing Moon
Moon Phase: 2nd Quarter
Color: Violet

Moon Sign: Aries
Moon enters Taurus 5:01 AM
Incense: Lavender

THURSDAY
11
DAY OF BRUMA (ROMAN)
Waxing Moon
Moon Phase: 2nd Quarter
Color: Turquoise

Moon Sign: Taurus
Incense: Thyme

FRIDAY
12
SADA (ZOROASTRIAN)
Waxing Moon
Moon Phase: 2nd Quarter
Color: Rose

Moon Sign Taurus
Moon enters Gemini 7:36 AM
Incense: Floral

SATURDAY
13
ST. LUCY'S DAY (SWEDISH)
Waxing Moon
Moon Phase: Full 9:38 PM
Color: White

Moon Sign: Gemini
Incense: Almond

SUNDAY
14
FESTIVAL OF NOSTRADAMUS (FRENCH)
Waning Moon
Moon Phase: 3rd Quarter
Color: Gold

Moon Sign: Gemini
Moon enters Cancer 11:25 AM
Incense: Frankincense

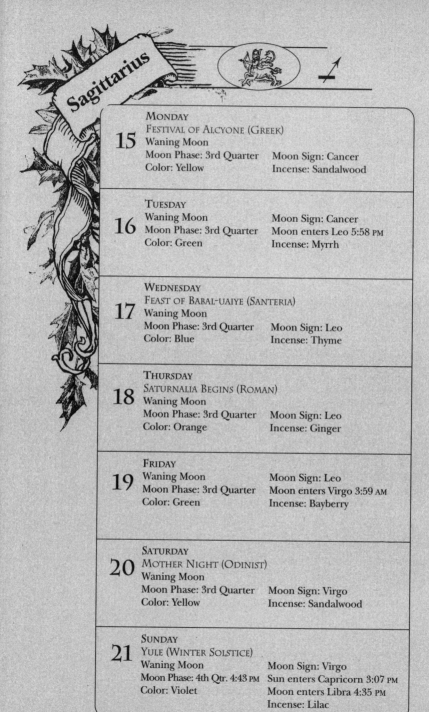

Sagittarius

15 MONDAY
FESTIVAL OF ALCYONE (GREEK)
Waning Moon
Moon Phase: 3rd Quarter
Color: Yellow
Moon Sign: Cancer
Incense: Sandalwood

16 TUESDAY
Waning Moon
Moon Phase: 3rd Quarter
Color: Green
Moon Sign: Cancer
Moon enters Leo 5:58 PM
Incense: Myrrh

17 WEDNESDAY
FEAST OF BABAL-UAIYE (SANTERIA)
Waning Moon
Moon Phase: 3rd Quarter
Color: Blue
Moon Sign: Leo
Incense: Thyme

18 THURSDAY
SATURNALIA BEGINS (ROMAN)
Waning Moon
Moon Phase: 3rd Quarter
Color: Orange
Moon Sign: Leo
Incense: Ginger

19 FRIDAY
Waning Moon
Moon Phase: 3rd Quarter
Color: Green
Moon Sign: Leo
Moon enters Virgo 3:59 AM
Incense: Bayberry

20 SATURDAY
MOTHER NIGHT (ODINIST)
Waning Moon
Moon Phase: 3rd Quarter
Color: Yellow
Moon Sign: Virgo
Incense: Sandalwood

21 SUNDAY
YULE (WINTER SOLSTICE)
Waning Moon
Moon Phase: 4th Qtr. 4:43 PM
Color: Violet
Moon Sign: Virgo
Sun enters Capricorn 3:07 PM
Moon enters Libra 4:35 PM
Incense: Lilac

184

December

MONDAY
PRYDERI'S BIRTHDAY (CELTIC)
22 Waning Moon
Moon Phase: 4th Quarter   Moon Sign: Libra
Color: Gold   Incense: Almond

TUESDAY
CHANUKKAH BEGINS (JEWISH)
23 Waning Moon
Moon Phase: 4th Quarter   Moon Sign: Libra
Color: Indigo   Incense: Jasmine

WEDNESDAY
SATURNALIA ENDS (ROMAN)
24 Waning Moon   Moon Sign: Libra
Moon Phase: 4th Quarter   Moon enters Scorpio 5:07 AM
Color: Violet   Incense: Lavender

THURSDAY
CHRISTMAS DAY
25 Waning Moon
Moon Phase: 4th Quarter   Moon Sign: Scorpio
Color: Rose   Incense: Floral

FRIDAY
KWANZAA BEGINS (AFRICAN-AMERICAN)
26 Waning Moon   Moon Sign: Scorpio
Moon Phase: 4th Quarter   Moon enters Sagittarius 3:08 PM
Color: Peach   Incense: Fruity

SATURDAY
FEAST OF ST. JOHN THE EVANGELIST
27 Waning Moon
Moon Phase: 4th Quarter   Moon Sign: Sagittarius
Color: White   Incense: Frankincense

SUNDAY
BAIRNS' DAY (SCOTTISH)
28 Waning Moon   Moon Sign: Sagittarius
Moon Phase: 4th Quarter   Moon enters Capricorn 9:49 PM
Color: Green   Incense: Bayberry

Capricorn

29	**MONDAY** BIRTHDAY OF RA (EGYPTIAN) Waning Moon Moon Phase: New 11:57 AM Moon Sign: Capricorn Color: Gray Incense: Sage
30	**TUESDAY** ISIS' BIRTHDAY (EGYPTIAN) Waxing Moon Moon Phase: 1st Quarter Moon Sign: Capricorn Color: Black Incense: Patchouli
31	**WEDNESDAY** NEW YEAR'S EVE Waxing Moon Moon Sign: Capricorn Moon Phase: 1st Quarter Moon enters Aquarius 1:59 AM Color: Brown Incense: Cedar

DECEMBER BIRTHSTONES
Ancient: Ruby
Modern: Bloodstone

DECEMBER FLOWERS
Narcissus
Holly

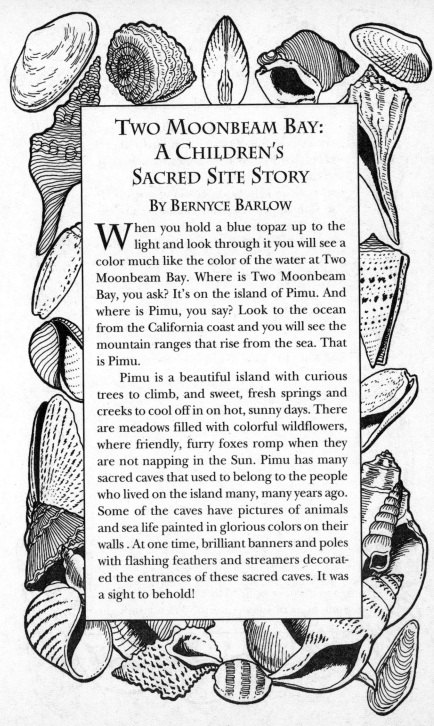

Two Moonbeam Bay: A Children's Sacred Site Story

By Bernyce Barlow

When you hold a blue topaz up to the light and look through it you will see a color much like the color of the water at Two Moonbeam Bay. Where is Two Moonbeam Bay, you ask? It's on the island of Pimu. And where is Pimu, you say? Look to the ocean from the California coast and you will see the mountain ranges that rise from the sea. That is Pimu.

Pimu is a beautiful island with curious trees to climb, and sweet, fresh springs and creeks to cool off in on hot, sunny days. There are meadows filled with colorful wildflowers, where friendly, furry foxes romp when they are not napping in the Sun. Pimu has many sacred caves that used to belong to the people who lived on the island many, many years ago. Some of the caves have pictures of animals and sea life painted in glorious colors on their walls . At one time, brilliant banners and poles with flashing feathers and streamers decorated the entrances of these sacred caves. It was a sight to behold!

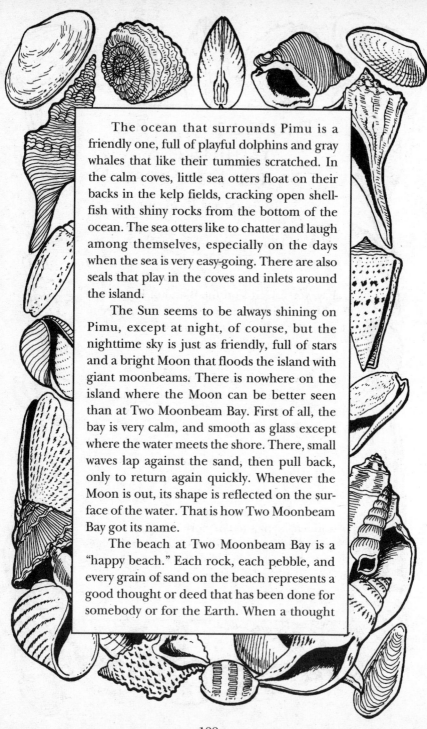

The ocean that surrounds Pimu is a friendly one, full of playful dolphins and gray whales that like their tummies scratched. In the calm coves, little sea otters float on their backs in the kelp fields, cracking open shellfish with shiny rocks from the bottom of the ocean. The sea otters like to chatter and laugh among themselves, especially on the days when the sea is very easy-going. There are also seals that play in the coves and inlets around the island.

The Sun seems to be always shining on Pimu, except at night, of course, but the nighttime sky is just as friendly, full of stars and a bright Moon that floods the island with giant moonbeams. There is nowhere on the island where the Moon can be better seen than at Two Moonbeam Bay. First of all, the bay is very calm, and smooth as glass except where the water meets the shore. There, small waves lap against the sand, then pull back, only to return again quickly. Whenever the Moon is out, its shape is reflected on the surface of the water. That is how Two Moonbeam Bay got its name.

The beach at Two Moonbeam Bay is a "happy beach." Each rock, each pebble, and every grain of sand on the beach represents a good thought or deed that has been done for somebody or for the Earth. When a thought

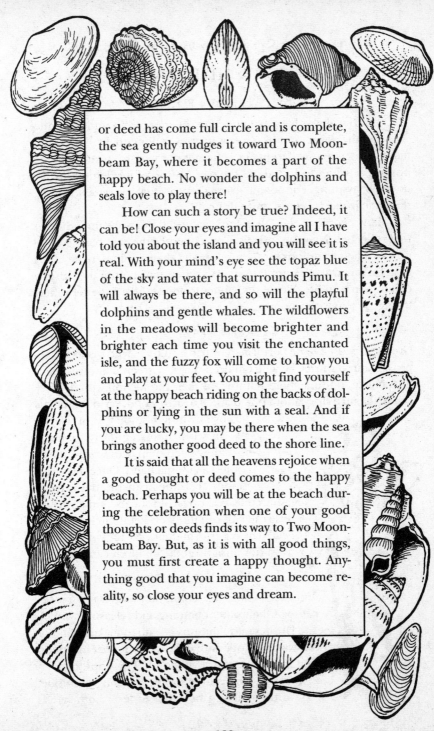

or deed has come full circle and is complete, the sea gently nudges it toward Two Moonbeam Bay, where it becomes a part of the happy beach. No wonder the dolphins and seals love to play there!

How can such a story be true? Indeed, it can be! Close your eyes and imagine all I have told you about the island and you will see it is real. With your mind's eye see the topaz blue of the sky and water that surrounds Pimu. It will always be there, and so will the playful dolphins and gentle whales. The wildflowers in the meadows will become brighter and brighter each time you visit the enchanted isle, and the fuzzy fox will come to know you and play at your feet. You might find yourself at the happy beach riding on the backs of dolphins or lying in the sun with a seal. And if you are lucky, you may be there when the sea brings another good deed to the shore line.

It is said that all the heavens rejoice when a good thought or deed comes to the happy beach. Perhaps you will be at the beach during the celebration when one of your good thoughts or deeds finds its way to Two Moonbeam Bay. But, as it is with all good things, you must first create a happy thought. Anything good that you imagine can become reality, so close your eyes and dream.

Pagan Summer Activities for Children

By Patricia Telesco

Children always have an abundance of energy, but somehow during the warm months it seems to grow exponentially. This leaves many conscientious parents in a quandary trying to invent enough positive activities to round out the day, instead of just letting the TV do the babysitting. For people striving for spiritual awareness, finding thematic projects is even more difficult.

Many people in the "New Age" sector did not grow up in homes that reflected "New Age" ideals. Consequently, they are having to invent or adapt traditions for themselves and their families. In an effort to help, this article examines some activities that you can try with any children in your life. Please remember to adjust them to better reflect the age group with whom you're working and playing.

Green Plays

Green plays used to be performed by tribal cultures who wished to appease natural spirits. Having children devise a green play gives them the chance to think about nature and their interaction with it. They can make up a story about one plant, a nearby wood, various animals or anything else they want. Check in with them regularly to see if they need help with words, ideas, or just a guiding hand. Once the script is done, costumes can be made from gathered leaves, twigs, old sheets, and anything else the kids can think of. Let them have a special day to perform their play for you, and see just how insightful the children can be!

Making Weather Ropes

In Arabia, knots were commonly used for magic because of their potent binding and releasing symbolism. During warm months it's fun to make a wind or rain weather rope with children that they can undo later in the season as needed. The rope chosen should be fairly sturdy so you can hang it outside. Have the children hold the rope in both hands while imagining the weather desired. If rain, have them add a drop of water to each knot made. If wind, have them tie a feather into the knot while they visualize the effects.

Traditionally, three knots were placed in these ropes, the first to bring a gentle wind or rain, and the second to bring a fuller gale and downpour. The third knot was never undone—that brought horrible storms to greedy people who abused nature's gifts! Once the knots are done, help the child mount the rope on a window sill, favorite tree, or any other accessible place.

EMBLEMATIC SHIELDS

Native Americans make medicine shields. In old Europe, knights carried shields that displayed the emblems of their families. These ideas can be used for an art project.

Depending on the ages of the children, they can make their shields with a paper, cardboard, or wood base. First, however, they have to decide what they want their shields to represent. Perhaps one child has nightmares and wants a protective shield. Perhaps a child wants to depict an animal with which he or she feels close affinity (which basically invites the spiritual creature as a guardian and teacher). No matter the decision, let the children take their time pondering this point, as this increases the energy that the finished shield will have.

Next, have them decide how to represent that desire artistically. You may have to help with some of the outline work here, but let them choose the colors, textures and other mediums that go on the shield afterward. Children have a natural talent for knowing what they need spiritually, even if they can't vocalize that awareness.

Once they're finished, use some art spray to protect the creation and then let the children put them wherever they wish. This is also a nice gift project for friends and family members.

KITE WISHES AND PINWHEEL PRAYERS

On a windy day all manner of wishes and prayers can fly on the edges of kites and pinwheels. Both items can be drawn on fairly easily, using symbols that depict your children's goals, needs, and hopes. Again, you may wish to help them in finding appropriate emblems.

In the case of the kite, when it takes to the air, the children should keep their wishes in mind so that energy flies. The pinwheel is basically a youthful substitute for a Buddhist's prayer wheel, where each turn of the toy represents a prayer being released to the universe.

GARDENING AND PLANT DIVINATION

I know of no child who doesn't have a natural affinity for playing with dirt. If you have a garden, take full advantage of this by allowing the child to help plant seeds, weed, till, and harvest. In itself, this is a wonderful learning experience right from the classroom of Earth. If you don't have a garden, consider letting the children have a small indoor window box that they can tend regularly. Their wishes can be planted with the seeds, repeated with each watering, then blossom with the plant itself!

Another fun pastime is plant and flower divination. This can be done one of two ways. The first way is having the children go to the garden, close their eyes, ask a silent question, then randomly choose one plant. Afterward, you help them look this plant up on a correspondence list to see the meaning, then (if necessary) show them the connection between those meanings and their query.

The second way is to help them create a natural oracle out of dried plants, flowers, and herbs that are glued to cards, stones or wooden pieces, then used like a tarot deck or rune set. For more ideas along these lines, see the *Victorian Flower Oracle* from Llewellyn.

SERVICE DAY

On service days, children put aside their normal play schedule and focus their attention on others. This is hard for young children especially, but it is a wonderful experience. Have them decide exactly how they're going to spend the day. For example, they could help an elderly neighbor with chores, go visit a sick friend and keep them company, or maybe give up meat for the day to thank the animals for our sustenance.

Service days can be repeated once a month to reinforce the idea that everyone and everything is connected. So, the more kindness we extend to others and our world, the better place it becomes.

Good Luck Day

Get together with your children and make a list of things associated with good luck, like horseshoes, old pins, four-leaf clovers, and found pennies. Once this list is assembled, conduct a treasure hunt in a safe area nearby to see who can find the most serendipity for themselves. Afterwards, help the children make their treasures into a special good luck charm to keep or carry with them regularly. The easiest way to do this is by placing everything into ready-made pouches or sachets.

Other Activities

This list is by no means complete. You can also consider projects like star gazing story time (where children learn about the myths behind visible constellations); taking weather omen walks to learn about nature's language and signals; seasonal bedroom decorating—in spring have them make a planter with flowering seeds, in summer bring in fresh flowers daily, come fall wax some leaves, and in winter gather some fallen twigs for a dream catcher; or fun with food—helping children make foods that have special meaning because of the magical associations of each ingredient, the shape of the finished product, the color of the food, or because of family traditions (see *Kitchen Witch's Cookbook* from Llewellyn).

As you try these and other activities for children, try not to worry too much about complexity. Truthfully, kids appreciate just having you around, so all the fun is like icing on the cake. Also, remember that if any of your inventive projects and games instill love, tolerance, self-respect and a one-world vision in our youth, then you have been very successful.

THE MAGIC OF PRAYER

BY ROSLYN REID

A person can seek the Gods through the active means of prayer; but formulating and efficient prayer can often be difficult. If your wish is diffused and unfocused, your prayer may not affect the desired outcome.

How then, does a person formulate an efficient prayer to achieve his or her desired ends? To start, we can divide the act of prayer into two categories: votive (or worship), and petition.

Votive prayer is usually a thank you, or it can be thought of as a maintenance program—honoring the God(dess) when things are going well, so they will continue that way. However, when we use prayer as a petition, we are requesting something specific from the God(dess). It may be something concrete, such as a place to live; or it might be abstract, such as relief from a burdensome emotion.

Frequently a petition prayer takes the if-then form—if the God(dess) gives me this, then I will do that. As you can see, in this particular form there is a votive prayer involved too. A petition prayer can also be just a straight and simple request without any offering made. In any case, what one needs when using prayer for petition is a narrow, concentrated focus on the desired outcome.

To achieve a narrow focus, lay a firm foundation before you even ground and center. First, try to consider all the consequences of your request, and its impact on everyone involved. Ask yourself very specifically what you think would be accomplished if your request were granted—what would it change? Obtain any appropriate input from others to get as many different perspectives as possible. This is the most important part, because in this manner you can identify your motives for desiring a particular result. It's always possible you are trying to deny an existing influence.

Next, strive to attain some measure of precision when you formulate your prayer. For example, if you ask for wealth, think of exactly what the term means to you. Do you want to have a wealth of children? If you are actually requesting money (and nothing else), use the more specific term. Write your prayer down and revise it until you feel it conforms to your exact wishes. Visualize your request as keenly as possible while praying. The narrower your focus, the more certain you are about what you want, the easier it is for the God(dess) to understand and help you achieve your wish. (Always remember, the God(dess) has veto power!)

In considering motivation, we can examine the second use of prayer, worship or votive. Do you wish to honor the God(dess), and why? He or She should be honored not just for granting wishes, but because in honoring him or her we honor ourselves and all life.

Not all votive prayer involves falling to your knees, face, or whatever, in formal ritual. Folding the laundry can be a votive prayer if we choose to dedicate this act to the Gods. In fact, honoring the Gods in this manner can inspire us to achieve our best.

You can offer all of your daily activities as votive prayers honoring the gods just by indicating a wish to do so at the beginning of the day. Or, you can choose to dedicate only specific acts to them. If you are having a particularly bad day, perhaps you would not consider any of your activities suitable to offer as a votive prayer! Perhaps in this case it would be better to employ the other type of prayer, petition, for help instead.

The choice is up to you—the Gods will always be there.

ETHICAL GARAGE SALING

BY ESTELLE DANIELS

There are several aphorisms which state that one should not haggle over price or barter for anything which is to be used as a tool for magic or the Craft. As an inveterate garage saler (for at least as long as I have been studying things occult and spiritual) I have a real problem with this "rule." I would like to share some thoughts which reflect my personal point of view about bartering.

First, the rule, when applying to unethical use of psychic talents or "occult" abilities, should stand. Using your "superior will" or "irresistible hypnotic eye" to coerce someone to selling to you at a better price, against their will or best interests, shouldn't happen.

To have a blanket stricture against bargaining over price, however, may be overstating the case. Remember, Gardner and company were British upper class, which has culturally disdained "those in trade" as being socially inferior. In America, our culture was consciously excised of those feelings, so our outlook is different.

In mainstream American culture, one can still bargain in one marketplace, in fact it is expected—that of the automobile market. The fact that so many people are intimidated about buying a car probably stems from inexperience at bargaining. Also, the perception of the unevenness of the abilities between buyer (amateur) and seller (professional salesperson) increases the anxiety. Add to that a whole array of psychological ploys which play on cultural stereotypes and intimidation (just who wears the pants in your family, anyhow?), and you have a set of phobias which have arisen from buyers' anxiety.

Surprisingly, as competition between retail stores for consumer dollars has increased, some stores now accept limited bargaining. "We will meet or beat any competitor's price" is a form of bargaining. Consumer reporters have even been known to advocate offering less on sale or clearance merchandise, or for last minute shopping (like just before the holidays). Some retailers are so interested in seeing it go out the door, they will willingly take less. And getting discounts on discontinued items or "floor models" is another form of bartering. So bargaining exists in the mainstream marketplace. Would you insist on paying full price for a magical item, even though it was on sale in a retail store? Of course not.

Intent is everything here. If you bargain as a way to feel psychologically superior ("I really got the best of that guy"), you are probably being unethical. However, if you enter into the spirit of the thing, you are not out of line.

If you really want the thing, but honestly feel the price is too high, then I wholeheartedly recommend you politely make an offer. The worst they can do is say no. If you garage sale, you are familiar with the phenomenon where a person will charge ridiculous prices for mediocre stuff, and not come down one cent in price. You still have the right to ask if they will take less, and your ultimate right is to not buy if the price is outrageous. You, too, can "just say no." My feeling is, if the gods want you to have it, you will find a way.

Personally, time and again, I have been to sales where a thing I wanted was overpriced and the seller would not take my offer. Then I would politely say, "well, I just can't make that price," and move on. And, if I really needed it, or really wanted it and was "playing by the rules," sooner or later I would find the same item, or a better one, at a better price. Ethics have their rewards. And I always silently say a heartfelt thank you to the Gods whenever I come across a particularly good buy.

I have lived by these ethical bargaining rules for many years and have never failed to see reward. When I would refuse to buy out of pure cheap meanness, I might end up with a dry spell. If I were just haggling to save a few pennies, I might have reverses. But when I went with feelings of respect and reverence for the process and the players, I would invariably come away with real bargains.

You also develop "instincts" for bargains. I got so I could literally "smell" a bargain, and when I acted on those hunches and dug a bit or gave a garage another look, I would invariably find the hidden treasure. That use of psychic talents is certainly ethical. Sometimes items become hidden in the clutter, and if the person wants to sell it, and you can "divine" that there is something neat you have missed, by all means, go for it.

Remember, haggling was a common practice of the folk of old. And one person's trash is another person's treasure.

I have gotten some of my best magical items from garage sales. These items I keep and use and treasure, and have never felt "bad vibes" or a "lessening of the power" because I might have bargained over price. With magic, intent is everything, and when I was polite and respectful, I invariably was rewarded for my actions. As long as both buyer and seller feel satisfied with the transaction, then no harm has been done.

KUAN YIN'S GARDEN

By Silver RavenWolf

Kuan Yin means She-Who-Harkens-to-the-Cries-of-the-World. Kuan Yin has been revered as a goddess of love for a thousand years throughout Korea, Japan, and China. She is a goddess of all, from lowly peasant to affluent royalty. The essence of Kuan Yin can be found in Avalokitesvara and Tara (two goddesses cherished by Tibetans), and the Chinese Princess Miao Shan.

The energy of Kuan Yin radiates compassion and universal harmony. She does not desire sacrifice of any kind. To emulate Her and the energies she represents, the most fitting act of honor grows from dedicating a small garden to Her.

Kuan Yin's garden does not have to be elaborate. If you live in an apartment, then design a window-box, or even a terrarium. If you have property, begin planning a small area in your yard dedicated to Her. Choose flowers that will grow well in the soil and lighting available. You don't have to purchase a statue of Kuan Yin to dedicate a garden to her. Simply cleanse, consecrate, and dedicate the area on the first day of spring, and as you plant your flowers, talk to Her. She will know of your attentions, and she will bless you accordingly. You can also leave offerings of honey and milk to the garden devas, as they will drink the essence to keep themselves strong. In return, they will send prosperous energy into your life.

As your small garden matures, you can meditate there or simply visit to fill yourself with the love of this gentle goddess. Petitions to Kuan Yin can be left under a stone, in a special vessel you place there, or beside a flower. Kuan Yin always has your best interests at heart. If you leave a petition to Her in your garden, and you receive something different than what you asked for, know that what you receive will be infinitely special, and chosen just for you.

A Tarot Recipe for Health and Well Being

By Marguerite Elsbeth

Creating wholeness is like baking a delicious cake. You need a recipe that contains just the right mixture of ingredients to accommodate your entire personality. The following recipe requires only the major arcana cards of a standard tarot deck and knowledge of your Sun sign and Ascendant (Asc). This combination of energies lets you know what it is that gives you the worst of a bad hair day. It also tells you how to reason things out clearly in order to resolve the issue. The problem and answer combined indicate the right path to take, so that you will not waste time moving in the wrong direction. All of these factors combine to bring you to recognize the good health and well-being that already exists within you!

THE RECIPE

Spread out the major arcana before you, and locate the tarot cards associated with your Sun sign and Ascendant, using the list of Sun sign tarot cards on the next page. Look to the Planetary tarot card list that follows to help you complete the recipe.

SUN PLUS ASCENDANT EQUALS PROBLEM

Find the problem by adding the numbers of the cards associated with your Sun sign and Ascendant (we'll use an Aries Sun with Leo Rising for our example). Four plus eight equals twelve, The Hanged Man. Neptune is your problem. (Continued after Sun Sign and Planetary Tarot Tables.)

SUN SIGN TAROT CARDS

Sign	Number	Tarot Card	Symbol
Aries	4	The Emperor	Authority
Taurus	5	The Hierophant	Sensuality
Gemini	6	The Lovers	Diversity
Cancer	7	The Chariot	Intuition
Leo	8	Strength	Creativity
Virgo	9	The Hermit	Analysis
Libra	11	Justice	Fairness
Scorpio	13	Death	Intensity
Sagittarius	14	Temperance	Truth
Capricorn	15	The Devil	Ambition
Aquarius	17	The Star	Humanitarian
Pisces	18	The Moon	Visionary

PLANETARY TAROT CARDS

Planet	Number	Tarot Card	Symbol
Sun	19	The Sun	Purpose
Moon	2	High Priestess	Memory
Mercury	1	The Magician	Cleverness
Venus	3	The Empress	Affection
Mars	4	The Tower	Passion
Jupiter	10	Wheel of Fortune	Prosperity
Saturn	21	The World	Control
Uranus	0	The Fool	Rebellion
Neptune	12	The Hanged Man	Dreams
Pluto	20	Judgement	Transformation

Sun Minus Ascendant Equals Answer

Assess the answer to the problem by subtracting the number of your Sun card from your ascendant card. Four minus eight equals four, The Emperor. Aries is your answer.

Problem Minus Answer Equals Path

Calculate the path to achieve wholeness by subtracting the problem card from the answer card. Twelve minus four equals eight, Strength. Leo is your path.

Problem Plus Answer Plus Path
Equals Wholeness

Formulate the wholeness associated with your destiny by adding together the cards representing your Sun, Ascendant, problem, answer and path. Four plus eight plus twelve plus four plus eight equals thirty-six. Three plus six equals nine, The Hermit. Virgo is your wholeness. (Any number greater than twenty-one is reduced by adding the digits together.)

Finally, learn all you can about the planets, signs and Tarot cards involved in your special recipe. Use your personal recipe for meditation, and "power" yourself up on a daily basis.

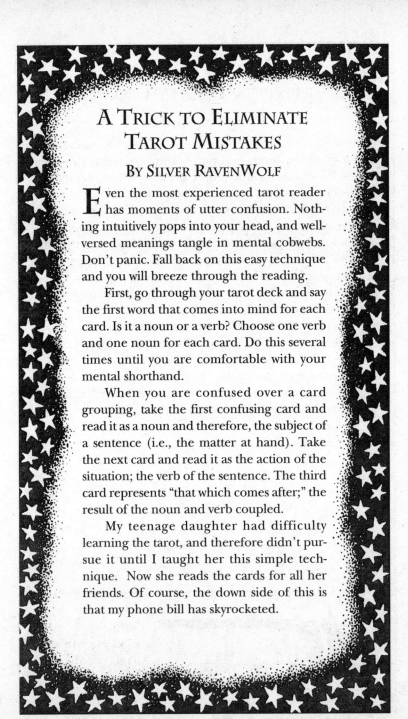

A Trick to Eliminate Tarot Mistakes

By Silver RavenWolf

Even the most experienced tarot reader has moments of utter confusion. Nothing intuitively pops into your head, and well-versed meanings tangle in mental cobwebs. Don't panic. Fall back on this easy technique and you will breeze through the reading.

First, go through your tarot deck and say the first word that comes into mind for each card. Is it a noun or a verb? Choose one verb and one noun for each card. Do this several times until you are comfortable with your mental shorthand.

When you are confused over a card grouping, take the first confusing card and read it as a noun and therefore, the subject of a sentence (i.e., the matter at hand). Take the next card and read it as the action of the situation; the verb of the sentence. The third card represents "that which comes after;" the result of the noun and verb coupled.

My teenage daughter had difficulty learning the tarot, and therefore didn't pursue it until I taught her this simple technique. Now she reads the cards for all her friends. Of course, the down side of this is that my phone bill has skyrocketed.

Tarot For The Artistically Challenged

By Edain McCoy

I have always envied people who can draw, translating onto
paper all the lovely and magical images birthed in their
minds. Never have I wished this more than when I hear about
some gifted soul who has been able to create his or her own
tarot card deck.

Creating a seventy-eight-card divination deck from one's
own subconscious is a daunting process even for the gifted, but
for those like me, the artistically challenged, it may seem downright impossible. Turning creative thinking in another direction, I came up with a method for making a tarot pack which
requires no more artistic talent than the ability to cut, paste,
and visualize.

For the foundation of your deck you will need some good
quality card stock, which you can find at a stationery store or
copy shop. Avoid using poster board for your cards since this
will make them too thick to handle with ease. You will also need
a pair of scissors, craft glue, and lots of old magazines.

Using a ruler to make uniform sizes and straight lines, cut
your cards into either 3" x 5" or 4" x 6" rectangles. When you
have the seventy-eight card-
forms all cut out, set
them aside while
you spend some
time—days, weeks,
or however long it
takes—visualizing
the symbols or oth-
er graphics you wish
to see on your
cards. Use any
decks you currently
have for inspira-
tion, and check

out books on dreams and archetypal symbolism for other images you may wish to incorporate. For instance, it is common in the Strength card to include the image of an animal of power, such as the lion. You might also want to embrace the images of the Sun, a bear, or a raging fire to conjure up the archetypal essence of strength. Pay close attention to your dreams during this period of exploration. Archetypal symbolism is the language your subconscious speaks, and you may find insights into the cards coming to you through  your dreams. Write down your impressions as they come so that you know just what it is you are seeking when you begin looking for pictures to represent these insights.

As you begin to search through magazines and catalogs for the images you want, it is best to browse with only one card in mind at a time so that your thoughts are not scattered. Cut out all the pictures or parts of pictures which reflect the essence of the card on which you are working. Place these in an envelope with the name of the card on the front so that, when you have gathered all the images for all your seventy-eight cards, you can go back through each one individually and make a final decision about the pictures you chose. At this point you may discard, alter, or add new images.

When you have succeeded in collecting all the symbols which sum up your personal impression of the card, glue them like a collage onto the cards. Trim around them to make the edges smooth, and then preserve them with craft shellac.

RUNNING WITH THE HORNED GOD

BY JIM GARRISON

The leaves dance on the autumn wind, a swirling, skirling waltz of orange, yellow, and brown. I can smell the coming rain. I stand in the twilight. Waiting. Listening to my heart—each moment I linger in this place I can hear the drumbeat of my ancestors in my blood more clearly. A sense of calm descends upon me, the calm before a storm.

He approaches.

The trees sway in the chill breeze that whispers to me of the coming winter, and the long sleep during which the trees dream the world back into being each year. I stretch my limbs and concentrate on my breathing—each exhale curling from my lips like wisps of smoke. My skin grows warmer despite the wind, and I almost lose myself to the rhythm of my breath.

He is nearly here.

The Sun sets behind iron-gray clouds, and darkness fills the air. I wait in the shadows, looking out over a lake teased by the cold wind. My breath comes to me with the pace of a dancer, and the fire within my bones kindles into a flame that must move. Swaying in the rapidly dimming twilight, I feel the call.

He is here.

No candles light this place. No circle marks the space. No incense fills the air, nor any chant—I stand surrounded

by silent trees and the whispering wind. My heart is my drum, my breath is the smoke I offer. With a shiver I feel the presence of the one I have sought. I see clearly in the gathering gloom, and the mist begins to fall, drops running off of my hair and beard. With a snort I stamp the ground and the urge to run overcomes my vigil as the familiar weight of antlers settles upon my shoulders.

We run in the twilight.

Lost to the animal pleasure of intense exertion we run through the trees, around the shores of a cold, black lake in the rain. We are as one; no thoughts do we share, only scents, sights, feelings, and sweat. Running in the dark, we both abandon the pretenses of the daylight world and embrace the truth, waiting for us all deep within our cells, our dreams, our souls. For an eternal moment, I know the awful bliss of truly being alive, and then I stumble.

We part.

Everything is quiet—there is only the patter of the rain on my back to distract me from the drum-beat within my chest. As if waking from a dream, perhaps another reality, I slowly become aware of my body, my surroundings, and the rain upon my face. Steam rises from my bare flesh. I get up from the moss and mud, and I feel the familiar weight of flesh and blood. The wind steals my heat from me and I stand, looking out over a black lake that shines with moonlight coming from a break in the clouds.

He still runs.

We've run full circle and I'm back where I started, only everything is different now. I've changed. I can hear His throaty laughter in the night, and something deep within me stirs with a deep longing to go running in the twilight once more.

THE LORD OF THE FOREST

BY KEN JOHNSON

As dwellers in a forest environment, most Pagan European peoples honored the Lord of the Wildwood or Master of the Forest. His names are many: in Celtic lore he is Cernunnos the Horned God, while in later English folklore he is known as Robin Hood.

Like the forest itself, the Wildwood Lord is sometimes benevolent and sometimes fearsome; at other times, he plays the trickster and works his mischief upon unwary wanderers in the woods.

In Eastern Europe, the forest spirit, or guardian, is called the Leshy. It is said that he looks "almost" human, though his flashing green eyes pop out of their sockets, his eyebrows are tufted, and he has a green beard. He doesn't cast a shadow.

His job is to guard the forest. He protects the deer, the birds, and all other forest creatures. Sometimes he is seen leading herds of wild animals, but he is especially fond of the bear, with whom he feasts and revels, and of the wolf, who is his totem.

The Leshy won't trespass on anyone else's land, but he jealously guards his own kingdom. He leads wanderers astray in the forest, removing or re-arranging signposts and markers. He especially hates loggers, and weeps over the death of every single tree in his domain. He seldom hurts anyone, for he is basically good-natured. He may appear to

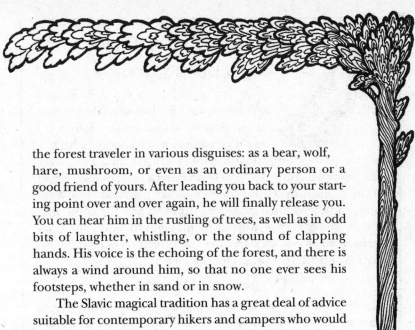

the forest traveler in various disguises: as a bear, wolf, hare, mushroom, or even as an ordinary person or a good friend of yours. After leading you back to your starting point over and over again, he will finally release you. You can hear him in the rustling of trees, as well as in odd bits of laughter, whistling, or the sound of clapping hands. His voice is the echoing of the forest, and there is always a wind around him, so that no one ever sees his footsteps, whether in sand or in snow.

The Slavic magical tradition has a great deal of advice suitable for contemporary hikers and campers who would like to make friends with the Forest Lord.

First of all, never whistle or shout in the woods; the Wildwood Lord hates noise.

If you want to avoid getting lost in the woods, sit down under a tree trunk, remove your clothes, and put them on again backward, remembering to put your left shoe on your right foot. Bend down and look between your legs. Now you can move on.

If you want to become really close friends with the Forest Lord, go into the woods on Midsummer's Eve (June 21) or St. John's Eve (June 23). Find a fallen aspen tree with its tip pointing to the east. Stand on the stump facing east, then bend over and peer back through your own legs, saying: "Forest Lord, come to me now, not as a gray wolf, not as black raven, not as a flaming fir tree, but as a man."

DOMINO DIVINATION

BY LILITH SILVERHAIR

Most of us have a set of dominoes around the house. Few people know, though, that dominoes were used as a divination tool in China as far back as the twelfth century BC. Back then, there were thirty-two tiles and the dots were both red and black. By the end of the eighteenth century, dominoes had gotten as far as England, and the colored dots were dropped and the blank tiles added. Today's sets consist of twenty-eight tiles, in pairs from blank/blank to six/six. Here is a simple method of domino divination and interpretations for the tiles.

DIVINATION METHOD

Lay the dominoes face down on the table in front of you. Concentrate on your question for a moment before selecting the three or four tiles that speak to you from the set. Interpret them according to the list below.

DOMINO INTERPRETATIONS

BLANK/BLANK: Trouble ahead, perhaps sorrow in love, a lost job, an accident, or loss of personal property.

ONE/BLANK: Your health will improve. Be careful not to waste money or other valuable resorces. A visitor arrives from over the water.

ONE/ONE: Parents and family offer happiness and support. A courageous decision needs to be made.

TWO/BLANK: Your upcoming trip goes well, and communications and sales skills serve you well also. Watch out for thieves, whether they are after your purse or your heart.

TWO/ONE: Upheavals in love and/or business life.

TWO/TWO: Be careful with your health. Dealings with others turn out well.

THREE/BLANK: Problems with spouse or family in the home. Jealousy threatens friendships.

THREE/ONE: Good news and/or a surprise comes your way. Gossip about an affair may land you in hot water.

THREE/TWO: A new project goes well. The trip you are planning is exactly what is needed. Don't take risks or tell white lies; both will get you into trouble.

THREE/THREE: Your love life is in an upheaval because of forces you can't control. Money comes your way through an inheritance, raise or bonus.

FOUR/BLANK: You change your outlook on life, possibly because of a close family member. That misunderstanding in your relationship is not going to go away easily.

FOUR/ONE: Debts come back to haunt you. A good marriage is in your future, but it may be childless.

FOUR/TWO: Unexpected events, both good and bad, cause major upheavals at home. Don't flirt back with that person no matter how much you want to.

FOUR/THREE: Sorrow because of children or an illness. Be careful with your vehicle.

FOUR/FOUR: Things go well for you if you are a craftsperson, but if you're "white collar" you're all thumbs. Young people and sports create happiness in your social life.

FIVE/BLANK: Be there for a friend in need, but don't forget your needs. Avoid risks.

FIVE/ONE: Your calendar is full, so you should be able to find someone to help you forget that charming rake. Money problems loom ahead.

FIVE/TWO: Your heart is breaking because of a marriage gone cold. New projects. Perhaps a child.

FIVE/THREE: Social and financial life are secure. Expect a visitor.

FIVE/FOUR: Money problems with your partner will end when you make your own money.

FIVE/FIVE: Things are looking up in all aspects of your life. Now is the time for that move.

SIX/BLANK: Accidents, gossip, jealousy and perhaps even the death of a person or animal.

SIX/ONE: Problems work themselves out. Middle age brings happiness.

SIX/TWO: Relationships go well, leading to possible marriage to a good partner. Bad business goes sour. A useful gift comes your way.

SIX/THREE: A good marriage is in your future. That trip will be successful. Good report about a vehicle. Middle-age illness.

SIX/FOUR: Though there may be legal problems in your future, all in all your life is a good one. Early, successful marriage brings children.

SIX/FIVE: The job is going well, but to have good relationships takes work. Children could bring trouble.

SIX/SIX: All parts of life are good. Business dealings in land and property are lucky.

212

RUNES

BY DONALD TYSON

Runes are the symbolic tools of a system of magic created around 500 BC by the shamans of warrior tribes living in the great forests of northern Europe. No one knows their origin. It is believed they resulted from a fusion between the native occult symbols of the shamans and the Etruscan and Latin alphabets.

Lured by the prospect of plunder, German mercenary clans crossed the Alps to fight in northern Italy. To the illiterate barbarians, written letters seemed magical. The shamans recognized a similarity between the letters used by the Etruscans and their own secret power symbols. Over generations, the shamans combined their own symbols with some of the Etruscan, and later Latin, letters, and developed a system of writing to convey their native language.

Runes serve the balanced functions of letters for writing and symbols for ritual magic. Other alphabets, such as Hebrew and Enochian, are used for magical purposes, but they remain written letters with secondary magical associations. Each rune is equally a letter and a living power symbol for a force in nature.

These natural forces were, in early ages, humanized as gods and spirits. Most of the names of the gods have been forgotten. Today, only a handful of runes can be linked with specific gods. Even so, there is good reason to believe that each of the forces represented by individual runes was looked upon as a mighty spirit by the shamans. This is supported by the ancient division of the twenty-four German runes into three families (aettir) of eight runes.

Thus each rune is the sigil or seal of a deity, and may be used ritually to summon forth and command that deity for human purposes. For example, the rune Teiwaz (↑) is the symbol of the warrior god Tew, after whom Tuesday gets its name. Teutonic warriors cut this rune into their own flesh over their hearts to invoke Tew into their bodies just prior to battle. In this way they sought to become possessed by Tew, who was renowned for his courage and war skill.

The use of runes was not restricted to a particular group in society. Any man or woman might employ the runes for purposes such as protection against poison, or to ease the pains of childbirth. However, ignorance carried a price. Each use of the runes involved a sacrifice to the rune gods, usually a sacrifice of blood. The gods were capricious and pitiless. If an insufficient payment was offered, they were thought to exact their own payment in kind. Rune spirits evoked to slay a foe might claim as their gift the life of someone beloved by the person who called them. It was generally considered prudent to leave runes to the shamans, who obtained the knowledge to use them through initiation.

After gashing himself upon the breast (and perhaps on the arms and legs) with rune symbols, the young shaman allowed himself to be tied to a wooden pillar or cross that represented the World Tree. He remained suspended for nine days and nights without eating or drinking. At the climax of the rite, Woden possessed the initiate and passed on to him the knowledge of runes. Perhaps this appearance of Woden was pantomimed by the master shaman wearing a mask, who whispered the secret wisdom into the ear of his disciple.

We do not know whether women were formally initiated into the mysteries of the runes. However, we do know that there were female rune masters, renowned for their powers of scrying, healing and cutting the runes for magical purposes. They enjoyed a position of authority in their tribes, but were regarded with a certain amount of dread by the people.

The purest set of runes that has survived to the present is the twenty-four symbol German futhark (a name that derives from the first six runes in the German rune alphabet: F, U, Th, A, R, K). Later rune alphabets which evolved in Scandinavia contain sixteen runes, and other alphabets which evolved in England contain twenty-eight (or thirty-three) runes. All these later rune sets were based upon the elder German futhark. For the purposes of ritual magic, this is the best rune alphabet to use, although Wiccans often prefer the English runes.

One ancient form of rune magic is divination. A branch was cut from a fruit-bearing tree, such as the apple, and divided into twenty-four short wands. The diviner carved a rune into each wand, then cast the wands onto a white cloth. Three wands were picked up in succession with the eyes directed heavenward, then interpreted.

All of the German runes can be made by simple vertical and diagonal strokes. They contain (in their purest, primal forms) no curved strokes and no horizontal strokes. This is a strong indication that they were designed to be incised into the thin green bark of a freshly-cut wooden sapling across the grain. Each sapling could thus carry a written message, and it seems likely one early use of runes was to convey messages between the leaders of nomadic tribes.

Shamans carried runes in their heads, and inscribed the runes wherever their magic was required. The thing upon which the rune was cut became infused with the spirit and power of that rune. When runes were written on carved yew wands and other objects for magical purposes, they were grouped into significant sets of repetitions and could not be read as words. Groups of three and nine runes occur frequently, but the meaning of these sets is not understood.

The inscription of runes on large standing stones arose when the use of runes for magic began to give way to the use of runes as a decorative, formal way of writing. Runes were carved on stones to commemorate important events, to mark the boundaries of land, and to preserve the names of great people. These rune stones had no magical function.

Modern rune pebbles or tiles are without historical precedent. They descend from the old rural custom of selecting animal hides by lot. Personal symbols were marked upon flat pebbles, then one was drawn randomly from the group. Some of these personal symbols were runes, but there is no indication that the medieval farmers who employed them as emblems understood their meanings or magical uses.

THE ELDER FUTHARK

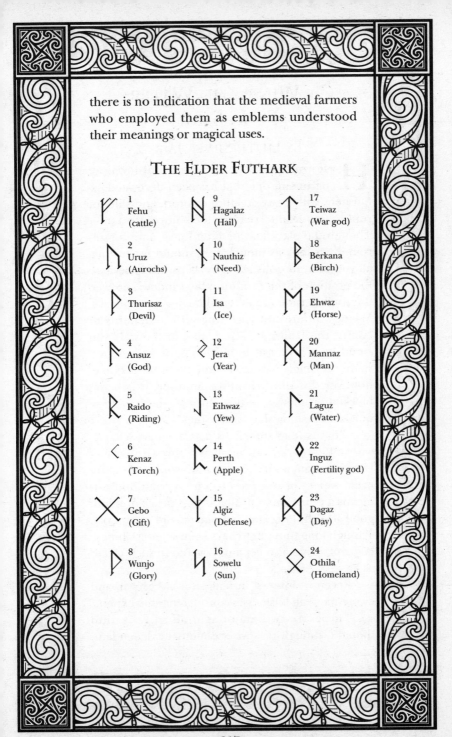

1 Fehu (cattle)	9 Hagalaz (Hail)	17 Teiwaz (War god)
2 Uruz (Aurochs)	10 Nauthiz (Need)	18 Berkana (Birch)
3 Thurisaz (Devil)	11 Isa (Ice)	19 Ehwaz (Horse)
4 Ansuz (God)	12 Jera (Year)	20 Mannaz (Man)
5 Raido (Riding)	13 Eihwaz (Yew)	21 Laguz (Water)
6 Kenaz (Torch)	14 Perth (Apple)	22 Inguz (Fertility god)
7 Gebo (Gift)	15 Algiz (Defense)	23 Dagaz (Day)
8 Wunjo (Glory)	16 Sowelu (Sun)	24 Othila (Homeland)

Of Wind and Water: Feng Shui

By Lilith Silverhair

Have you ever been in a beautiful home or apartment, one that has been decorated exquisitely, with every creature comfort, and still, for some inexplicable reason, feels uncomfortable? Though the place may be brand new, and the surroundings look as though they should be inviting, all you want to do is leave. Perhaps this is because the position of the furniture, the windows, or even the road outside are all encouraging you to leave. Maybe you are not receiving all the benefits of "Ch'i," the Universal Life Force, in the ways you could be. Ch'i exists in all things, and flows constantly through nature. In our theoretical home, however, for one reason or another, it is being blocked or allowed to flow through the home too quickly. The feng shui is all wrong.

What is feng shui? It is part art, part science, with a liberal dose of mysticism thrown in. Feng shui is an ancient Chinese philosophy. Relating every aspect of our lives to our surroundings, it means an environment that brings peace of mind, good health, long life, happiness, and prosperity. Though long thought to have been solely a Chinese concept, it has also been discovered in such places as Eastern Africa.

Recently, interest in feng shui has grown, and even American businesses consult feng shui experts.

There are two major schools of feng shui thought, though the two are mutually dependent.

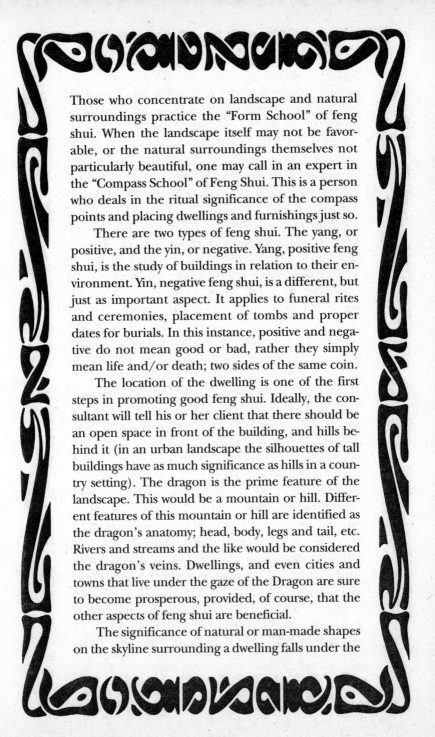

Those who concentrate on landscape and natural surroundings practice the "Form School" of feng shui. When the landscape itself may not be favorable, or the natural surroundings themselves not particularly beautiful, one may call in an expert in the "Compass School" of Feng Shui. This is a person who deals in the ritual significance of the compass points and placing dwellings and furnishings just so.

There are two types of feng shui. The yang, or positive, and the yin, or negative. Yang, positive feng shui, is the study of buildings in relation to their environment. Yin, negative feng shui, is a different, but just as important aspect. It applies to funeral rites and ceremonies, placement of tombs and proper dates for burials. In this instance, positive and negative do not mean good or bad, rather they simply mean life and/or death; two sides of the same coin.

The location of the dwelling is one of the first steps in promoting good feng shui. Ideally, the consultant will tell his or her client that there should be an open space in front of the building, and hills behind it (in an urban landscape the silhouettes of tall buildings have as much significance as hills in a country setting). The dragon is the prime feature of the landscape. This would be a mountain or hill. Different features of this mountain or hill are identified as the dragon's anatomy; head, body, legs and tail, etc. Rivers and streams and the like would be considered the dragon's veins. Dwellings, and even cities and towns that live under the gaze of the Dragon are sure to become prosperous, provided, of course, that the other aspects of feng shui are beneficial.

The significance of natural or man-made shapes on the skyline surrounding a dwelling falls under the influence of the five "elements," or forces. These five are: wood, fire, earth, metal, and water. Four of these are related to the four cardinal points, with earth in the center, relating to none and all.

Wood corresponds to all vegetation, and is related to spring, beginnings, sunrise, and the East. Its color is blue-green, and the associated shape is tall and narrow.

Fire corresponds to heat like that of the Sun, and is related to summer, midday, and the south. Its color is red, and the associated shape is triangular.

Earth is associated with stability and earthenware materials. As it is the center, it has no corresponding season or direction. Its color is ochre, and the associated shapes are flat.

Metal corresponds to swords or farming tools. It is related to autumn and the west. Its color is silvery white, and the associated shapes are circular.

Water corresponds to speech and communications. Its season is winter, its time is night, and its color is black. Irregular shapes represent water because the element has no form.

Each element, or force, is able to reinforce the next element, but also is able to destroy or neutralize an element. Thus wood burns, producing fire, which produces ash or Earth, from which is mined metal, which melts, like water, which nourishes wood. Wood takes away nourishment from Earth, which muddies and pollutes water, which extinguishes fire, which melts metal, which chops down wood.

How things are positioned inside a building is just as important as where the building itself is. For a positive atmosphere, Ch'i must flow effortlessly through the dwelling, without being caught in corners or dead ends, where it is stifled, thus creating a bad influence. Ch'i is a particularly Chinese philosophy, and thus cannot be easily translated. In very simple terms, it is a healthy flow of energy.

Ch'i can be deflected and helped along its course by the placing of mirrors in different strategic positions. This is done because it is not good for Ch'i to pass straight through a house (say, in a case where the front door and back door are at exact opposite ends of the house, with no obstruction in between), because it cannot permeate the rooms and leave its revitalizing forces.

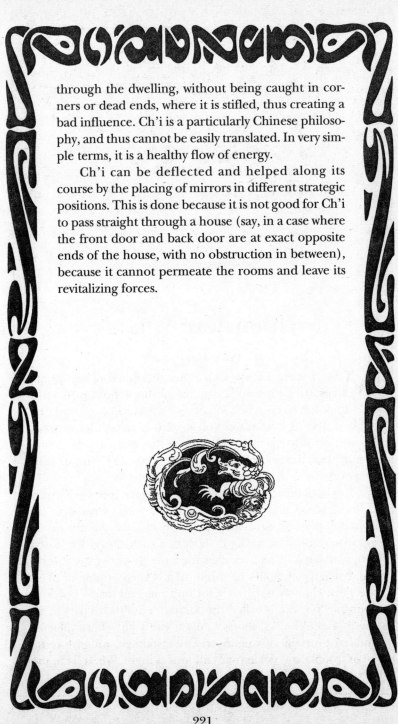

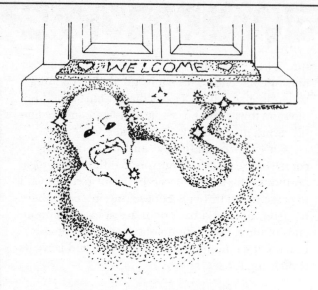

HOUSEHOLD SPIRITS

BY KEN JOHNSON

Most ancient European peoples recognized a special ancestral spirit who served as the household protector. This tradition has survived in parts of Eastern Europe until the present day. In Russia, the house spirit is called Grandfather House Lord. He usually appears in the shape of a departed family member, though sometimes he may take the form of your dog or cat.

It is both difficult and unwise to try to see your house spirit, though you may sometimes hear his voice. Ordinarily he speaks softly and caressingly, but he can also be abrupt or groan and sob. This means he feels neglected and is displeased with you. Usually, he lives near the stove or under the threshold, though sometimes he dwells in a branch of pine or fir in the yard. He may be a bachelor or a married man—in Slavic countries his wife is called the Kikimora and takes part in all the household tasks, though only if you yourself are diligent and hardworking. If you are lazy, the Kikimora will give you a lot of trouble and tickle your children at night. When seen, she is usually spinning; hopefully, however, you will never see her doing this, for it is a bad omen.

Your house spirits are useful Otherworld friends, and will help you in various ways, including promoting your prosperity, keeping things in order, and warning you, usually by howling and moaning, if trouble is approaching

Here are a few traditional ways to make friends with your house spirits.

✧ When moving into a new house, cut a slice of bread from your first dinner there and put it under the stove to attract your house spirit into the new place, saying: "Dear friend, come into the new house to eat our bread and listen to us."

✧ If you move from one house to another, you can take your house spirit with you. Have the oldest woman heat up the stove in the old house and scrape out the cinders. At noon, let her put them in a clean plate and cover it with a napkin, then open a window, turn toward the oven, and invite the house spirit to come to your new home. Let her take the plate to the new house. Have everyone waiting for her with bread and salt in their hands. Have them bow and again invite the house spirit into the new house. The old woman must then put the pan by the fireside, remove the cloth, shake it toward the four corners to frighten away any unwanted spirits, and empty the coals into the oven. Then let her break the plate and bury the pieces below the threshold.

✧ Sometimes, a house without a spirit may acquire one if you put on your best clothes, go outside, and say: "Grandfather House Lord, come and live with us and tend our affairs."

✧ For friendship's sake, hang your old shoes in the yard. House spirits really love this.

The Orishas
of Santeria

By Marguerite Elsbeth

Orishas are the African deities of Santeria, a rich and vibrant nature religion based on stones, seashells, water and herbs. The Yoruba slaves who brought the religion from Africa identified the orishas with the Catholic saints in order to preserve the tradition. Therefore, practicing santeros, or priests, recognize the saints as having the same supernatural powers as the orishas for healing and spell-casting.

As the practitioners of Santeria believe in one creative force, called Oloddumare, the orishas are worshipped as spirit guardians who offer divine guidance and protection to reverent followers, rather than as gods. Every individual in the Santeria religion has a personal orisha to help him or her along the path of life.

ELEGGUA (St. Anthony) is a trickster, tending to create confusion wherever he goes. Because he knows all things, he demands his due before all other deities. Eleggua brings us into balance and wholeness.

ORUNMILA (St. Francis of Assisi) is "one who lives both in heaven and earth." Divination is his gift to humankind. Because he knows our ultimate fate, he helps us to improve our destiny.

OBATALA (Our Lady of Mercy) is a male deity, embodying female aspects also. He is known for peace, purity, and the white robes in which he dresses. Obatala helps us to control our thoughts.

CHANGO (St. Barbara) is the patron of power. He wears a red coat covered with cowrie shells, and is fond of women, food, dancing, thunder, lightning—all things hot and fiery. He can help us to attain passion in our relationships.

OGGUN (St. Peter) is a warrior god, and the patron of all metals. Although he creates much chaos here on earth, he also helps us to gain employment and protects us against violent crime.

Ochosi (St. Norbert) is the divine hunter. He resides in the woods, sometimes "eating and living" with Oggun. Ochosi protects and assists hunters. He also has curative powers, and can help with relocation, as well as courtroom trials.

Aganyu (St. Christopher) is the volcano god, and the father of Chango through his union with Yemmu. One can only receive Aganyu's helpful control over harmful influences through Chango's intercession.

Babalu-Aye (St. Lazarus) is the patron of healing, and one of the most respected and well-loved orishas. He carries a bag filled with corn, and helps those in financial distress achieve prosperity.

Yemayá (Our Lady of Regla) is an ocean goddess, and a patroness of fertility. This much-revered orisha is very beautiful. She brings young girls to womanhood, and is associated with the Moon.

Oshún (Our Lady of Charity) is a river goddess, the Venus-Aphrodite of the Santeria religion. She is the patroness of love, marriage, money, joy, and abundance.

Oyá (Our Lady of Candelaria/St. Teresa) is the goddess of the winds and the cemeteries. Because she is a warrior, her behavior is very aggressive. She offers her followers protection against death.

References

González-Wippler, Migene. *Santeria: The Religion.* St. Paul: Llewellyn Publications, 1994.

ESSENTIAL OILS: AN ABBREVIATED FORMULARY

BY GWYDION O'HARA

To journey into the world of essential oils is to step out upon that undefined edge where magic, healing, and beauty seem to dissolve, one into the other. Because these functions are so interrelated, it would appear that any attempt at producing a formulary would be incomplete if it did not consider health and beauty as well as magic. Since the different applications of essential oils seem to develop out of the same arena, there are examples of each type of blend included below.

MENTAL AND PHYSICAL HEALTH

ANTI-STRESS: Bergamot, spikenard, jasmine, orange, apple, cedarwood, camphor.

BRONCHITIS: Lemon, sandalwood, lavender, camphor.

BRUISE OIL: Lavender, orange, rosemary, rose, camphor, eucalyptus.

COLDS: Lavender, orange, rosemary, rose, camphor, eucalyptus.

COUGH: Benzoin, galangal, frankincense, jasmine, eucalyptus, peppermint.

DEPRESSION: Jasmine, lavender, orange, oakmoss, pine.

SEXUAL STAMINA: Jasmine, musk, vanilla.

MAGICAL USES

ASTRAL TRAVEL: Frankincense, myrrh, cypress, jasmine.

ATTRACTION: Musk, cassia, sandalwood, myrrh.

BLESSING OIL: Myrrh, cedarwood, frankincense, lemon verbena.

CLEANSING: Lotus, frankincense, cedarwood, amber.

DIVINATION: Musk, ambergris, vetivert, violet, lilac.

FAST LUCK: Patchouli, carnation, mimosa.

GAMBLER'S OIL: Lily of the Valley, rose, sandalwood, mimosa, cinnamon.

LOVE: Gardenia, jasmine, muguet, sandalwood, musk.

MONEY DRAWING: Patchouli, pine, bay.

NEEDED CHANGES: Sandalwood, mimosa, hyacinth, cinnamon.

PROSPERITY: Patchouli, gardenia, cinnamon.

PROTECTION: Frankincense, sandalwood, amber.

PSYCHIC POWER: Cedarwood, myrrh, violet, musk, ambergris.

SUCCESS: Heliotrope, patchouli, lavender.

UNCROSSING: Rose, carnation, bay, clove.

CHAKRA OILS

CROWN: Myrrh, lotus, frankincense, camphor.

HEAD: Carnation, lavender, rosemary.

HEART: Cedarwood, mimosa, rosemary, clove.

THROAT: Violet, vanilla, ylang ylang, eucalyptus.

BELLY: Frankincense, honeysuckle, galangal, lemon verbena.

SPINE: Orange, oakmoss, sandalwood.

BASE: Civit, muguet, ambergris, cinnamon, musk.

BALANCING OIL: Lemon, orange, lavender, myrrh, clove.

How to Use
Planetary Hours

By Estelle Daniels

Planetary hours are helpful when you are in a hurry, or need to do a working today and want certain influences but the planets in the sky aren't cooperating.

To use planetary hours, determine what you want to do, and what you want to accomplish. Let's say you are doing a love spell. To use planetary hours to assist you, first you would look in the listing of planetary correspondences, and see love is listed under Venus. Therefore, you would do your love spell during a Venus hour, and possibly on a Friday also, since Friday is ruled by Venus. It's that simple. You can also use a standard astrology book which has word lists and planetary correspondences to find what planetary hour you should use.

If what you want corresponds to Uranus, Neptune or Pluto, the three planets not assigned planetary hours (because they were not known when the system was developed roughly 5000 years ago), there is a way to use them. Uranus is the higher octave of Mercury; Neptune is the higher octave of Venus; and Pluto is the higher octave of Mars: so for Uranus use Mercury; for Neptune use Venus; and for Pluto use Mars hours.

Planets Used for Planetary Hours

Saturn

Ruler of Capricorn and Aquarius. Saturn's metal is lead, its colors are brown, dark green, dark blue, and black, and it rules Saturday. It also rules barriers and limitations, time and clocks, the reaper, severity, contraction, business, karma, hermits, the Crone, the Father, control, mountains, pessimism, melancholy, things which require patience and endurance, long-term gains and goals, masons, decrease, spirituality, the teacher, rocks and stones, duty and responsibility, reputation, rewards which are worked for, work and career, darkness, death, debility, government and government leaders, bosses, silence, and endings. Its attributes include controlling, limiting, pessimistic, abortive, barren, enduring, frugal, paralyzing, selfish, serious, skeptical, tactful, punctual, and ascetic.

JUPITER

Ruler of Sagittarius and Pisces. (Note: Jupiter rules Pisces only in the case of planetary hours; Pisces' astrological ruler is Neptune.) Jupiter's metal is tin, its colors are purple and indigo, and it rules Thursday. It rules law, judges, physicians, religion, philosophy, expansion, philanthropy, gain and increase, ritual, gurus, freedom, fun and laughter, joy, confidence, optimism, generosity, sports, higher education, high magic, higher mysteries, favors, buying, lending, start of new undertakings, mercy, dharma, languages, foreign cultures, long-distance travel, large animals, and adventurers. Its attributes include pompous, jovial, benevolent, buoyant, confident, corpulent, generous, just, optimistic, reverent, naive, and abundant.

MARS

Ruler of Aries and Scorpio. (Note: Mars rules Scorpio only in the case of planetary hours; Scorpio's astrological ruler is Pluto.) Mars' metals are iron and steel, its colors are red, dark red, and magenta, and it rules Tuesday. It rules physical exertion, ego, self-assertion, energy, action, sex, males, war, conflict, anger, weapons, soldiers, courage, danger and excitement, pain, burning, poisons, wounds, violence, police, accidents, fire, passion, and quarrels. Its attributes are amorous, aphrodisiac, burning, combative, cruel, dangerous, exciting, explosive, fearless, forceful, rough, sharp, bloody, violent, and wounding.

SUN

Ruler of Leo. The Sun's metal is gold, its colors are golds, yellows and oranges, and it rules Sunday. It rules leaders, people in authority, vitality, life, men, the God, self expression, executives, heart, confidence, the will, ambition, individuality, hobbies and amusements, acting and the stage, children in general, speculation, the stock market, employment, promotion, rulers in general, the center of things, authority, and the body as a whole. Attributes are forceful, life-giving, rhythmic, strong, structural, diurnal, active, open, generous, and fiery.

VENUS

Ruler of Taurus and Libra. Venus' metal is copper, its colors are bright blue and pastels, and it rules Friday. Venus rules love and romance, art, music, social matters, marriage, beauty, jewelry and ornament, refinement, sensuality, females, peace, Maiden, compromise, negotiation, indolence, pleasure, creature comforts, money and possessions, values, charms and amulets, perfumes, philters, cosmetics, and sweets. Its attributes are lazy, indulgent, amorous, artistic, cheerful, dissolute, erotic, fertile, graceful, immoral, musical, relaxing, soothing, and soft.

MERCURY

Ruler of Gemini and Virgo. Mercury's metal is mercury (quicksilver), its colors are blue, gray and patterns, and it rules Wednesday. Rules communication, writing, words, The Magus, education, neighbors, relatives, merchants, business people, messengers, mind, mentality, magic, books, short-distance travel, thieves, manual dexterity, consciousness, speech, coordinating, dualities, buying and selling, radio and television, lying, reason, low magic, lower mysteries, books and reading, cars and all vehicles in general, small animals, and knowledge. Its attributes are wit, worrisome, dual, impulsive, quick, irrational, intelligent, nervous, rational, reasoning, restless, and moving.

MOON

Ruler of Cancer. Cancer's metal is silver, its colors are pearl, green and iridescent hues, and it rules Monday. It rules the public in general, food and drink, water and liquids, domestic affairs, home, family, country, short journeys, Mother, temporary plans, women, emotion, unconscious, mediumship, the past, Goddess, memory, soul, altar, magical tradition, real estate, fertility in general, and weather. Attributes are changeable, dissolving, fertilizing, fruitful, periodic, sensitive, visionary, wandering, imaginative, impressionable, instinctive, nocturnal, and passive.

THE MODERN PLANETS

Here are the modern planets for further reference, although they are not used in planetary hours.

URANUS

Ruler of Aquarius. Uranus' metals are uranium and rainbow-hued metals. It rules electricity, metaphysics, occultism, revolution, upheaval, divine inspiration, television, genius, mental insanity, the unusual, the future, astrology, freedom, democracy, chaos, explosives, the aura, catastrophes, impulses, animal magnetism, reformers, suicide, and telepathy. Its attributes are original, erratic, unusual, eccentric, irreverent, abortive, chaotic, independent, non-conformist, and anarchistic.

NEPTUNE

Ruler of Pisces. Neptune's metals are neptunium and the noble gases. It rules fog, illusion, deception, emotional insanity, visions and voices, magic, psychism, spirits, merging with God/dess, spiritualism, martyrdom, empathy, earthquakes, oils, poisons, perfumes, secrets, addiction, alcohol and drugs, oceans, idealism, saints, conmen, large institutions, dreams, and imagination. Its attributes are subtle, abstract, psychic, magical, musical, impressionable, willing to see only the good, imprisoned, confined, unfortunate, hospitalized, handicapped, spiritual, idealistic, charismatic, and sensitive.

PLUTO

Ruler of Scorpio. Pluto's metals are plutonium and radioactive elements. It rules volcanism and plate tectonics, resurrection, death and rebirth, obsession, archetypes, research, upheavals and radical transformative changes, rape, metamorphosis, mobs and riots, the Mafia, chaos, alchemy, ESP, black magic, force and willpower, phoenix, depths and heights, sex, and merging with a partner. Its attributes are violent, regenerative, reincarnating, chaotic, forceful, excessively violent, reforming, rebuilding, redeeming, initiatory, stripping down to basics, explosive, subtle, deep, unknowable, and intimidating.

INTAGLIOS

BY BERNYCE BARLOW

More often than not, when we think of Native American rock art we think of pictures or symbols that have been etched into a community of boulders, a cliff face, or a cave wall. There is another category of rock art, however, called intaglios. These are giant ground pictures, reaching lengths of 300 feet, which are scattered along the desert floor of the west.

The word intaglios refers to a type of etching used in jewelry making, block prints, glass cutting, and architecture that was perfected by the Italians, but whose techniques can be traced to early Egypt and China. A cameo is an example of a type of intaglio. The word was adopted for the ground pictures because their technical method of creation was similar to intaglio art.

There are two kinds of intaglios; rock alignments and gravel effigies. Rock alignments were created by stomping, grinding, or pounding small stones into the desert pallet in the form of a picture. The ground would be prepared by removing any rocks or boulders that would interfere with the illustration's outline; creating a blank, clean canvas, so to speak. Then small rocks were gathered for the immense task of sculpting the alignment into whatever form had been agreed upon.

The second type of intaglio is called a ground effigy. These were made by creating an outline with rocks the size of a child's fist or smaller, then raking the topsoil away from the illustration, leaving a three-dimensional picture on the ground. Both alignments and effigies can be representational or abstract. Representational intaglios, such as those at Blyth, California, are easier to understand. They are pictures of

Blyth Intaglios site, Southern California

animals and people—things we recognize. Abstract intaglios represent the ancient power symbols of the Desert Culture. At best, we can guess they probably have to do with rain, fertility, hunting, and prosperity. There are over 100 significant intaglios scattered throughout the Colorado river drainage basin, beginning in Baja and continuing into California, Nevada, and a small portion of Arizona.

The ground pictures were created during different centuries, hundreds of years apart sometimes, by diverse migrating peoples. Because of this, distinct legends from different tribes shroud the mystique of the intaglios. The intaglios were not created by one people, and their artistic style was adopted by many. One of the tales surrounding an intaglio has to do with the Hopi. They say one giant ground picture, a Fire Clan deity figure with its arms stretched out to its side (barring return) represents the quarrelsome split that happened in this area between the Fire Clan and the Water Clan during their migrations.

The Mohave and Quechan tribes also have legends telling us about the identity of some of the giant ground pictures.

Mostambo (or a name derived from Mostambo) was the name of the creator in some native tongues. Halakulya (sic) was his helper. Halakulya could take the form of a mountain lion and sometimes did, while helping to create the earth and the human race. To be able to take the form of an animal was a gift only shamans possessed, so Halakulya was revered as a power symbol on many levels. Present Desert Culture tribes recognize some of the representational intaglios near Blyth as Mostambo and Halakula.

Then there are the abstract intaglios, like those found in Wildrose Canyon (Inyo County, California), a rock sanctuary we know little about. Stone carins and packed gravel circles complement the Wildrose grouping, giving them an air of mystique. The compacted circles at Wildrose play an intricate part in the layout of the intaglios site. They are typically three to seven feet in diameter, and were made by leaving a gravel base, packing it tightly, and pounding finer gravel into the formation. Circles are found more frequently near rock alignments, as are carins.

The carins are made of larger rocks piled on top of each other, averaging two feet wide and five feet tall. The meaning behind their construction has been lost. Wildrose Canyon has eighteen carins, interplaying with circles and abstract alignments.

There have been very few artifacts found near the intaglios, although nearby villages, hunt trails, and petroglyphs (especially along the banks of the Colorado river between Needles and Blyth), have contributed substantially to our understanding of the cultures who

made them. It is obvious that the intaglios were ceremonial sites, which explains why so little was left behind.
The priests and shamans of the desert carried and kept
the medicine bundles of the community. They would
not be left on site. Indeed, this would be considered by
some as foolish, because a spirit charm could be used
against its owner with the right magic. There is little to
find at an intaglios site, unless it is an offering or a fetish
of some kind buried to protect it. Heaven help the person who finds this kind of a charm and pockets it!

Unraveling the mystery of the intaglios is intriguing.
I believe part of the key will be found in the comparison
study of rock paintings, petroglyphs, and oral history
with those further north. The Desert Culture was one of
migration. They followed game, agricultural opportunity, and water. The similarities of the intaglios' symbols to those painted or pecked into rocks that are
found in the Great Basin and the Southwest are uncan-
ny. How can they not be connected?

There is yet another field of study concerning the
intaglios, and that has to do with the astronomical alignment or placement of certain sites. The Desert Culture
people were wizards of the sky, and are known for their
star charts and solstice and lunar observations. It would
not be at all surprising to find that at least a few of these
sites have to do with celestial observations. Many spiritual ceremonies began and ended when the Sun, Moon,
or stars were in a specific position. If there was no natural landmark to keep track of celestial time, one was
made. In the Southwest, kiva sipapu (sipapuni), pueblo
doors, windows, and notches were cut into temple walls
in order to frame certain celestial positions. This practice is also seen throughout the Great Basin.

The intaglios are a wonderful mystery whose complete story we may never know. Earthquake and erosion

have taken their toll, although some of the ground pictures have semi-permanently settled into the desert pavement. The human race, on the other hand, has been very respectful to these pieces of art.

If you visit an intaglios site, bring lots of water, a topography map, and a spare tire. Four-wheel drive is preferable, except at Blyth, which is a very accessible public display. Fine intaglios examples can also be found in California's Chocolate Mountains, Death Valley, Yuha Wash, and there is one on the side of a mountain in the Valley of Fire, outside of Las Vegas, Nevada, that was spotted by plane some years ago. Ranger check-in is advised. Rangers can also answer any questions you may have about the intaglios site you are visiting. It is also a good idea to be aware of perimeter weather conditions when hanging out in the desert. Although it may not be raining where you are, a flash flood can occur if it is raining in the mountains above you. Flash floods can last only a few minutes, but their path can be treacherous. Last word? Happy hunting. I am convinced there are many more intaglios sites we do not yet know about whose discovery will help define the mystery and intrigue of the giant ground pictures of the desert.

REFERENCES

Barlow, Bernyce. *Sacred Sites of the West*. St. Paul: Llewellyn Publications, 1996.

Sofaer, Anna. "A Unique Solar Marking Construct." In *Science* 206, no. 4416, Oct. 19, 1979.

Swan, James. *Sacred Places*. Santa Fe: Bear & Co., 1990.

Watson, Lyall. *Beyond Supernature*. New York: Bantum Books, 1988.

A Sensuous Journey into the Garden of Dreams

By Sirona Knight

Her partner's voice echoes somewhere in the imending darkness. "Remember! As you drift to sleep, give yourself the suggestion to let your dream body follow me, and I'll take you somewhere you have never imagined, even in your wildest dreams." She allows her mind to flow alongside her dream lover, down a winding path laced with the soothing scent of lavender. They move gracefully through the shadows of mighty oak and ash trees. Looking up, she catches a glimpse of the Full Moon floating overhead. Together they stop, momentarily gazing at the silver candle-like orb, their attention captured by the silent spell of moonlight.

Joining hands, the two lovers continue their journey along the narrow earthen path, both intuitively moving through the enveloping mist that hangs like a thin, moist blanket in every direction. She feels his strong hand in hers and his touch is warm on her skin in the cool night air.

Soon they approach a granite archway, looming out of the mist. The stones are partially covered by the white, bell-shaped blossoms of moonflowers, whose vines climb up both sides of the archway. As the lovers move closer to the dream gate, she sees two white quartz dragons standing guard like watchtowers on either side of the archway. Their eyes glow ruby-red in the brilliant light of the Moon. In the middle of the dream archway is a filigreed iron gate with three stone markers hanging from the thick bars. She watches as her mate touches one of the stones hidden by the weaving moonflower vines, and the giant iron doors begin to swing open. She shades her eyes as a flood of sunlight suddenly pours out from behind the archway. Moving through the open gate and into

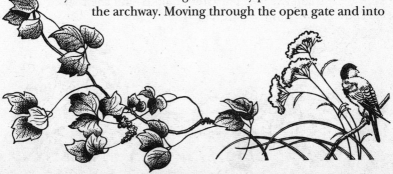

dream, she notices the inside of the stone arch is covered by violet morning glory blossoms, and all around her, in surreal splendor, stands a garden filled with the rainbow of life. Roses of every size and color adorn the parameter, their delicate scent, mixed with the sweet smell of honeysuckle, present an olfactory banquet, which in turn stirs her other senses to a heightened delight.

Her lover picks a sprig of honeysuckle and crushes the pale flowers between his fingers. Standing in front of her, he first rubs the oil of the crushed flower on her forehead, stimulating her psychic senses. He then moves his arms around her shoulders and gently strokes her hair with his scented fingers. Embracing, their lips meet. They stare intently into each other's eyes before he beckons her to follow him on the garden path. They glide more deeply into dream and move down the rock-edged path.

As they saunter into the depths of the garden, past peach trees laden with fruit, hollyhocks, and cosmos, she spies a giant ash tree with thick branches stretched out like massive arms reaching for the sun-soaked sky. Growing up between the moss-covered arms of the ash is a tall sugar pine, symbolically joined with the ash. The long cones of the sugar pine dot the ground like flowers beneath the ash.

The two of them move closer to the trees. A tiger-striped cat startles her as it looks knowingly down at the two lovers from its perch in the ash. She stares into the cat's citrine eyes, and for a moment her perception catapults into another dimension. All around her the flowers and plants begin whispering in the tongue of the ancients. The birds and insects join in the cosmic song, chanting in cadence with the soft breeze as the tones blend together and strike a harmonious chord within the vast web of oneness. Merging with this feeling of boundlessness, she becomes the garden and the garden becomes her. There are no separations or boundaries. For an instant she sees life without limits, and she is awed by the infinite possibilities.

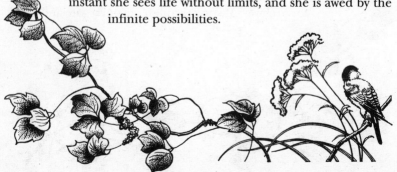

Once again her lover takes her hand and leads her farther down the dream path until they reach a small natural circle. Milky-white stones of varying sizes and shapes mark the rim of the circle. She spies a dark green malachite sundial standing at the north point of the circle and watches as the shadow of the Sun drapes across the timekeeper's face, pointing halfway between the top and bottom. To the south, opposite the sundial, lies a small verdant meadow covered with white and rose-colored alyssum. In the middle of the small dream meadow is a tartan blanket, woven from different colored threads of light. Spread around the blanket is an assortment of fruits from the garden. The two lovers glide over to the waiting feast.

Lounging on the soft blanket, they lie side by side, feeding each other ripe purple grapes. They take turns biting into a crisp red apple and then indulge in the sweet succulence of a juicy peach. Each piece of fruit whets their appetites for more, until soon they set the fruit down and begin to consume each other in escalating passion. The nectar of their lovemaking drives them to new heights of awareness as their bodies entwine like the oak and sugar pine trees they saw earlier. Like Goddess and God, they spark the renewable flame, consummating the timeless link of polar energies inherent in us all—life pulsating to a climax, only to be renewed again and again.

Lying back, bathed simultaneously in the Sun's rays and moonlight, she realizes for dream to become reality it must permeate every facet of life, until no division exists between the waking and the dream. Absorbing the light, the lovers' unconscious and conscious thoughts become one, as the energy polarities of the cosmos weave together into the synthesis we call life. She understands now that as we open the dream gate and become more adept at patterning the energy and light that makes up our world, we begin to dream our reality and, in turn, live our dreams. Remember, when you plant and nurture the seeds, your garden of dreams will grow beyond your wildest dreams!

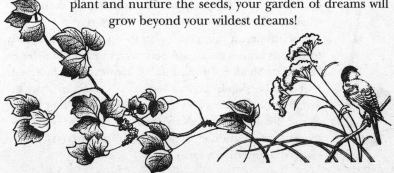

SCOTT CUNNINGHAM

BY deTRACI REGULA

Scott Cunningham was born on June 27th, 1956 to Chet and Rosie Cunningham. Chet was a successful freelance writer, the son of farmers who for generations had eked out a living on the land.

Although Scott never claimed to be a hereditary witch, believing that many such claims were simply wishful thinking, several of his own ancestresses fit the popular conception of a witch. One of these was Abby Pointer, his red-haired, green-eyed great-great grandmother. Abby's "superstitions" were noted by the other relatives, and recorded in some detail in the family history. She and her husband Ben adhered to the old practice of planting by the Moon, and followed the Moon phases to determine the best times for moving or butchering livestock. In *The Magical Household,* Scott included Abby's insistence that it was unlucky to move a broom from one house to another. She believed that it brought the bad luck of the previous household to the new residence. Abby also advised bringing one's purse to the new house first of all, to ensure prosperity.

The surname Cunningham is said by some to be derived from cunning man, the male equivalent for the term wise woman. Just as some authorities derive "Wicca" from the old root word for wise, cunning carries the Middle English meaning of knowing or knowledge.

The suffix "ham" would most likely mean "a village." One who bore the name Cunningham would be someone from the village or place of knowledge, a definition which could describe a temple or sacred site.

Scott was an initiated high priest in several magical traditions and wrote or assisted in the writing of several "Books of Shadows" in use today. However, he believed that membership in a coven was not necessary in order to worship the Goddess and the God. His bestselling book, *Wicca: A Guide for the Solitary Practitioner,* provides an eloquent guide to individual practice for hundreds of thousands of modern Wiccans.

His passing in 1993 from a combination of ailments, including the return of the lymphatic cancer he had conquered ten years before, was mourned by thousands of Wiccans in the United States and abroad. He was, however, an ardent believer in reincarnation, as he states in *Wicca: A Guide for the Solitary Practitioner:*

> Reincarnation is one of Wicca's most valuable lessons. The knowledge that this life is not our only one, that when our physical body dies we do not cease to exist but are reborn in another body, answers many questions...So fear not death, seeker; it is the door to birth, and as you rise and fall upon this plane of existence, know that death is but the beginning of another life.

His own words in the closing of his book *Earth, Air, Fire, and Water,* written while he was ill, best sum up his philosophy of magic:

> If you would be a magician, honor the Earth. Honor life. Love. Know that magic is the birthright of every human being, and wisely use it....This book of magic is ending. Yours, however, is continuing. May it be a book of joy.

May it be so for all who follow the path of the God and Goddess, and may we always remember Scott Cunningham, the guide whom they lent to us for a short while.

FURTHER READING

Cunningham, Scott. *Hawiian Religion and Magic.* St. Paul: Llewellyn Publications, 1994.

Cunningham, Scott. *Living Wicca.* St. Paul: Llewellyn Publications, 1993.

Cunningham, Scott. *Wicca: A Guide for the Solitary Practitioner.* St. Paul: Llewellyn Publications, 1988.

Harrington, David and deTraci Regula. *Whispers of the Moon: A Biography of Scott Cunningham.* St. Paul: Llewellyn Publications, 1996.

HAVE A MAGICAL BON VOYAGE

BY EDAIN MCCOY

Whenever we venture far from home, we naturally worry about safety until our return. Magical folklore has passed down to us a variety of methods to invoke protection as we travel in an increasingly dangerous world.

- Mugwort is a travelers' herb of old, one which confers protection upon the one who carries it. Make a simple travel talisman by placing some of the herb in a white cloth, which can be carried in a purse, glove box, or suitcase throughout your journeys.

- Irish Moss is another herb which protects travelers. Place pouches of it in suitcases and pockets to take advantage of its energies.

- To ensure a safe return home, pick up three small stones from your property and tell them that you wish them to accompany you on your travels and that, at journey's end, you shall return them to their resting place. The stones will look after you as long as you keep your promise to them. This magical protection probably has roots in Irish legends about homing stones. These are stones which go home by themselves if moved.

- Carry a bloodstone in your left pocket to protect yourself from thieves.

- To keep your suitcases from being opened and items stolen from it, put a pouch of comfrey into each one.

- If you will be traveling to an area you might contract a disease, carry posey petals in your pockets.

- To protect yourself as you sleep in a strange place, turn your pajamas inside out.

- To prevent evil spirits from following you as you set out on your journey, spin three times counterclockwise just as soon as you step outside of your house.

- To protect your car, and all those traveling within it, make a small medicine bag out of cloth or leather and fill it with protective herbs, stones, symbols, and some mugwort. Charge it with your need and place under the driver's seat or in the glovebox.

- Hang a protective symbol, such as a pentagram, from your rearview mirror to cloak your car with protective energy.

- Before you set out on a long car trip, wash your car with security by adding protective herbs to the rinse water. These include rosemary, dill, thyme, pepper, basil, cinnamon, and bay.

- A small pouch of salt on the floor of your car will ground any harm which comes at your car, either intentional or accidental. When you get home, flush the salt down a drain to get rid of any negativity it has absorbed.

- For long hikes or walking tours, place a little flax in your shoes to ensure a safe journey. Bury the herb when you return to your hotel or campsite.

- Carry along some bladderwrack or rue to protect you on sea voyages, just as many generations of sailors have done.

- If you will be flying, take along some gorse or hawthorn to protect the plane from lightning strikes.

- To help prevent plane crashes, carry some mugwort, an herb related to "flying" (read astral projection) travels, as well as physical journeys.

Fast Magics for Witches Without Tools

By Silver RavenWolf

We can't always cart our magical tools with us wherever we go. Many of us work at jobs where we either can't bring out your magical hardware, or where we are in a production environment, and taking a lot of time to work magic isn't feasible. Here are some ideas to keep in mind if you find yourself in a situation where you don't dare use any magical tools.

- ✪ Memorize the Banishing Ritual of the Pentagram and do it in your mind. (This ritual is at the end of the article.)

- ✪ Carry several packets of salt that you have empowered at your altar. You need only use a pinch to consecrate an area or item.

- ✪ Use a lighter to call on the element of fire.

- ✪ Use repeated sounds to set yourself in alpha, then use those sounds to trigger positive affirmations, or even spell casting. For example, if you work as a cashier at a grocery store, most likely you use the scanner cash registers. Each time an item is scanned the register emits a sound. These repetitive sounds help you to reach the alpha state faster.

✪ Any time you clean your work area, banish and consecrate the cleaning fluid, then wipe in a widdershins pattern to banish all negative energy from the area.

✪ If you are responsible for large amounts of money, such as the position of bank teller or cashier, banish your till by dropping a few bits of salt in the tray, then ward the tray for safety. Empower every coin roll you open, sending blessings and love into each coin.

✪ Is a customer or boss giving you a bad time? Put a bit of sugar where you can get at it quickly. Lace it on papers, money, charge receipts, whatever the grumpy person will touch. Sugar helps to sweeten the situation.

✪ Remember that whatever you formulate in the astral affects this plane of existence in some manner. Keep a running dialogue of positive thought-forms, rather than negative ones.

THE BANISHING RITUAL OF THE PENTAGRAM

There are four parts to the rite: the Qabalistic Cross of the Hebrew Sages; the Pentagrams and Sacred Names; the Invocations of the Archangels of the Directions; and the Qabalistic Cross, repeated.

It is an article of faith among the Witches of England that at the time the King did expel the Jews from England, the Witches of the countryside did shelter many of them, wherein certain sacred names and chants were taught by the Jews' sages to us for our use, and rudiments of their system of magic, which they call Qabalah. Herein is one such part.

1. The Qabalistic Cross of the Four Elements

Draw the fingers of your right hand from the heavens to your forehead. Say:

Ah-tah

Touch your chest or stomach below the heart.

Mal-koot

Touch your right shoulder.

Ve-geh-boorah

Touch your left shoulder.

Ve-ged-oolah

Clasp your hands at your heart.

Lay-olam
Amen.

2. The Pentagrams and Sacred Names

Facing East, trace the Banishing Pentagram of Earth with hand or athame and say:

Yod-Hay-Vow-Hay (YHVH or Tetragrammaton)

Facing South, trace the Banishing Pentagram of Earth.

Ah-do-noy

Facing West, trace the Banishing Pentagram of the Earth.

Eh-ay-Eh

Facing North, trace the Banishing Pentagram of Earth.

Ah-gee-lah

3. The Invocations of the Archangels and Directions

Facing East, extend the arms to the sides to form a cross with the whole body and say:

Before Me, Raphael
Behind Me, Gabriel (seen as feminine)
On My Right is Michael
On My Left is Auriel

Before Me (or around me) flames the Pentagram
And above me Shines the Six Rayed Star
Honor (Touch head)
Divinity (Touch heart)
Service (Touch thigh)
Shekinah descend upon me now!

4. QABALISTIC CROSS

Repeat the Qabalistic Cross. This completes the banishment.

I wonder if the Banishing Ritual of the Pentagram works on dirt...

THE SPRINGS AT POPCORN ROCKS

BY BERNYCE BARLOW

The drive around Pyramid Lake to Popcorn Rocks, Nevada, is stark. Everything stands out. Around the lake are several springs, each individual in its character and purpose. Pyramid Lake is sacred, as are its springs. Ask anyone who has been there.

Popcorn Rocks, a popular stop, undoubtedly got its name due to the unusual likeness of its rocks to popcorn. The curious formations consist of crystalline calcium and silica deposits and are created by underwater springs in the saline and alkaline lake. There are no trees around the shoreline, except one, which is also sacred. When the Moon is Full, the boulders look almost ghost-like, silently standing sentry, drifting in and out of the shadows. Their mystique fits the surroundings. Across the lake are the rock formations Basket Woman and the Pyramid Needles. Pyramid Needles is an area where springs well up from beneath needle-shaped rocks, is there too, as are more sacred springs.

There is a long beach for the Popcorn Rocks to adorn. The land crunches under foot. Thousands of small shells cover the ground—a reminder of change. They finally give way to firmer sand and silt rooted in stickers.

The springs are tucked away among the boulder community. At one time they were completely under water. Now that they are exposed, the first thing one notices is their blue-black sand lining. It is jet, the color of protection. Approaching the spring, one can smell the ether of the Earth. Small, granular bubbles bulge from the spring bed, rise, then disappear to rise again inches away, allowing the Earth to slowly percolate. The spring follows the lay of the land; flat, spread out. Finally it disappears, absorbed by the shells and sand, and once in a while by the lake itself.

Shaman Springs near Popcorn Rocks

Surrounding the springs are giant webs made by the orb weaver spider. The orange spiders with the long spindle-like legs are the males. The spiders live communally, stretching and joining their webs across giant boulders and partaking together of the sparse food supply. This familiarity only applies for hunting and dining, otherwise the spider colonies are independent. Their webs catch the sunlight, and look like enchanted gates protecting the sacred springs. Rainbow hues glisten off the life taking/giving fabric, enticing the unaware.

It is the character of the springs, and the legend and myth that gird themselves to them, that brings life to these waters, or perhaps I should say brings life to us. The springs at Popcorn Rocks have long been known for their healing properties and purification abilities. They are a shaman's springs, if you will, as many are around Pyramid Lake. It is no secret that life is given and can be taken at this place, just as in the orb web.

When a healer comes to the springs, it is with an attitude of respect and humility. Curiosity has no place here, yet child-like wonder does. A good shaman/healer understands balance, can find it and come back to it. A blind innocent cannot. Sacred springs are there not to be conquered, but to submit to accordingly. That is why attitude is so very important.

The springs are an outside connection to the inner Earth, emerging deep from within, interconnecting with the surface. They are a path for the healer to follow during the inner journey, as well as a route back from it. The jet sand is sometimes painted on the healer's body so he/she may become invisible or protected during a dark underworld pilgrimage. The sand is also a purifying sand. It is used by shamans to absorb the leftover residues of sickness or disease that may have clung to their auras while healing others.

The shaman is to find the imbalance in a person's life, the reason for the illness, and if possible, correct it. In order for this to happen, the healer must be spiritually clear. The springs serve as a focus for spiritual ecstasy by providing a potent ritual spot that is already a powerful healing center.

The springs at Popcorn Rocks are, as mentioned, one of many that bless Pyramid Lake. Each spring site is treated as an intrinsic personality with its own knowledge, power, and song. Tribes such as the Washoe and Paiute, as well as earlier aboriginal communities, relied on the specific character of these springs to bring things like balanced health, increased hunting, and rain.

If you have the chance to visit this site, do so. The orb weaver will no doubt be there to greet you at the gates. Follow the path carefully until you come to the inner Earth, and watch your step.

Coyote Stories

Retold By Marguerite Elsbeth

Coyote is the Trickster of Native American culture. His antics are often outrageous, thoughtless and just plain strange—Coyote is definitely not to be trusted! He is always a teacher, however, and a very magical one at that, with much wisdom and humor to share.

Coyote Puts His Nose In It

The Kalispel Indians say that at one time someone stole the Moon. They asked Coyote if he would be the Moon. Coyote liked this idea, thinking that he would be able to see everything on Earth.

For a while, the people thought he was doing a good job. But soon Coyote could not contain himself when he saw people doing things they weren't supposed to do. He would shout loudly when he saw someone stealing meat or cheating at the moccasin game. So the people who did secret things got together and took Coyote out of the sky. Someone else became the Moon, but Coyote has kept his nose in everybody else's business ever since.

Coyote Almost Uses It and Loses It

The Crow Indians tell a story about Old Man Coyote and Mouse. The young women danced as the young men watched. One pretty woman asked the men to expose themselves, as she wanted to marry the man with the smallest penis. Old Man Coyote couldn't resist tricking her, so he asked Mouse to trade penises with him. Of course, the young woman unwittingly picked Old Man Coyote to marry, thinking his penis was small.

But soon Mouse came by, dragging along Old Man Coyote's penis, covered with dust. It was huge, much bigger than Mouse. The people laughed at Mouse and poked at the penis until he cried out, "This isn't mine!"

It was soon determined that Old Man Coyote was wearing Mouse's penis. The young woman heard about Old Man Coyote's big penis and ran away.

CIRCLE CASTING OF THE WINDS

BY SILVER RAVENWOLF

I f you haven't guessed by now, one of my favorite pastimes is to collect, invent, and practice unusual circle castings. Although the casting of the winds is not unusual (our ancestors probably did it all the time), the excitement of calling the four winds gets me every time.

The technique is very simple. Stand at the north (or east if you are so inclined) and call the winds of the north. Envision the winds coming toward you, bringing stability and prosperity. In your mind, visualize the north wind circling clockwise around you. Turn it into a leafy hedge that pulsates with energy around you. Now call the east wind in the same manner. This wind stands for intellect. In your mind, see the east circle around you, then join the north (still circling), making the visualization of the leafy hedge stronger. Next call the south wind, with its powers of creativity and passion. As before, visualize the south wind circling you, then joining the other two winds, making the hedge stronger. Call the west wind, that of love, devotion, and honor. Visualize the west wind circling clockwise around you, then joining the other four winds. Your circle should be very dense by now. Finally, visualize the breath of spirit coming down from above, circling about you, then joining the other winds. This wind carries the energy of the divine. Clap your hands or stamp your foot to seal the circle.

Once the circle is cast you can call the quarters if you so desire, however some would say this is a bit redundant.

Do your magical working inside the circle, or just sit and enjoy the energies flowing around you. When you are finished, be sure to bid hail and farewell to the winds, one at a time, counterclockwise. Stamp your foot or clap your hands to open the circle.

Angels, archetypes, and ancestral spirits enjoy the energy of the winds. You can also turn this circle casting into a quickie (when you need to conjure up something super fast and don't have your tools tucked up your nose). All kidding aside, try your hand at this unique and ancient circle casting. I think you'll love it.

DRUMMING

BY KEN JOHNSON

When you think of a drumming circle, what image springs to mind? A bunch of hairy guys, perchance, pounding away in search of a wildness they may never have had?

In fact, drumming is one of the oldest human activities still going, and one of the most magical. A log and a stick formed the first drum set, and still work just fine. Native American drums are painted and decorated in an entirely different way than African tribal drums; the differences can give you a hands-on feeling (literally) for the cultures that produced them. The sounds are unique too. A Scottish bodhran drum sounds altogether different than a Caribbean drum.

Not only is the drum the earliest of all musical instruments, it is still used for magical purposes in cultures where only two instruments, the flute and the drum, make up the native orchestral assembly. Shamans beat on drums to induce a state of trance, which will help them travel to the Otherworld, as well as to summon the spirits into their sphere.

Because drums make magic, they should be treated as ritual implements. Of course, if you have an expensive tribal drum produced by a Native culture, you won't want to change it, but if you have a plain and simple drum, you can make it your own. Try making your drum both more magical and more personal by painting a picture of the magical universe on its head; and tie some bones, feathers, stones, or other magical objects to it in order to represent whatever spirit speaks to your heart and soul.

Drumming circles are a great way to stir up positive energy with other people, but try not to be competitive about it. Just because you happen to be a music school drop-out capable of imitating twelve different complex tribal time signatures, that doesn't mean you should impose your talents on everyone else! Bringing people together in a circle of energy is far more important than showing off.

And if you can't keep time to save your own life, don't worry about it. Just shut your windows and listen to the beat of the "different drummer" that is you.

CREATING A POWER-SINK STONE

BY D. J. CONWAY

Building an emergency reservoir of power is a form of magic not used much any more. A power-sink stone is a rock which has been carefully saturated with magical power over a period of time. When a magician is low on energy, or the Moon is in the wrong sign for a particular magical endeavor, the magician can draw upon the stone's stored energy to boost his or her powers. This makes it possible to do a ritual for prosperity under a waning Moon, for example, and have a much better success rate than without the power-sink stone.

If you plan to keep your power-sink stone on your indoor altar, choose a rock that is not too heavy or large. You need a stone you can lift and hold. My own power-sink stone is about ten and a half inches long, six inches wide, and an inch thick. I prefer flat stones so that I can set objects on them, but you don't have to search for a flat stone if you prefer a different shape. If the stone is small enough to handle, wash it thoroughly in a mixture of water and salt. Rinse and let dry.

The best time to begin energizing your stone is during the week before the Full Moon. The night of the Full Moon is excellent for adding large amounts of energy to the stone. One very important thing: don't pour energy into your stone if you are feeling negative or pessimistic! You want positive energy in your stone. Whatever type of energy you put into your stone is exactly what you will get back. It is nice if you can go outside for this ritual, but this isn't always possible or safe to do so. If inside, light a white candle and sit near a window so moonlight can fall upon you. If the skies are cloudy, don't worry. Hold the stone in your hands, or sit beside it and place your hands on the stone. Close your eyes and picture the Full Moon with its streams of energy falling upon the Earth. Chant softly:

Powerful Moon, Goddess of Light,
Empower this stone, I ask You tonight.
Fill it with magic and energy bright.
Make it a storehouse of power and might.

Chant this three, six, or nine times, and while you are chanting, rub your hands lightly over the stone. When you are finished, put the stone in a safe place where others won't handle it.

This empowering ritual should be done for seven days, ending on the night of the Full Moon. You should be able to detect a definite increase in the aura and power of the stone the first week. It is advisable to empower the stone for at least three Full Moons before drawing upon its energy for the first time.

After the stone has been fully empowered, the magical energy within the power-sink stone can be used whenever you want to charge candles, jewelry, or any such object with power. Use whatever ritual you usually do, but place the candle or jewelry directly on the stone, at least for a period of time when the main part of the ritual is finished.

If you are depleted of much of your energy, and have a need to do a ritual anyway, you can place your hands on the stone just before you begin. Close your eyes and concentrate on the Moon-power within the stone. Chant:

I ask you to share your energy which came from the Moon.
At the next Full Moon I will return what I have borrowed.

Feel the energy rising out of the stone, entering your hands and going up through your arms into your body. Breathe deeply, and feel the energy continue to rise until it reaches the top of your head. Then release your connection with the stone and begin your ritual.

You could use a crystal cluster as your power-sink stone. If you decide to do this, be very certain that the crystal can be programmed in this manner. Some crystals seem to be pre-programmed for certain tasks, and you will only scramble the results if you try to make them go against their inborn nature. A few of the regular variety of stones will, on rare occasions, also have pre-programming, so always hold your hands on a stone and see what your instinctive feelings tell you.

THE ISLAND
OF PIMU

BY BERNYCE BARLOW

Statue dedicated to the first islander of Catalina (Pimu)

The island of Santa Catalina, one of eight in the Channel Island chain, lies less than twenty-five miles off the mainland of Southern California. Today, it serves as a vacation resort. However, there was once a time when the paradise of Santa Catalina was not a destination, but a home to no less than five aboriginal tribes. The Pimugnan, who were heavily influenced by the Chumash culture and the Chingichnich cult, were the last of the Native cultures to live on Catalina in peace. They called their island Pimu, or "mountains that rise from the sea."

Because the residents of Pimu were so isolated, their religious/political practices did not shift as the practices of those on the mainland did. Constantly exposed to the integration of new or changed practices, the mainland people saw many discrepancies in Chingichnich laws and rituals depending on the resident priests' dispositions, and their political counterparts' preferences. Through geographical separation, the Pimugnans remained a very intact, uncorrupted reflection of the Chumash/Shoshonean culture at its finest for centuries.

It was believed by the coastal tribes that the Pimugnans were wizards who possessed great powers over certain forces of nature. The tribal mainlanders became somewhat weary of the Pimugnan's power, even though trade between the two was brisk. The Chingichnich cult could be exacting, and to anger their gods was the act of a fool. By word of mouth, lore about the supernatural control the Pimugnans had over certain elements was passed on throughout the medicine circles of the West and Southwest. Stone talismans made from the obsidian that came from Pimu were revered as potent. It was believed that obtaining such a commodity would bring great power and control to the individual who possessed it. Charms from the desecrated soapstone hill near what is now called Empire Landing were also considered sacred, and were used in rituals to call rain by the shamans of the island.

Adding to the mystique of Catalina are its sacred caves, decorated with paintings inspired in part during visions brought on by the hallucinogenic drink Taolache. Within the Chingichnich cult, there were many ceremonies requiring altered states of consciousness. Some of the records of

*Classic architecture of
Catalina Island*

these experiences are neatly tucked away into both island and sea caves. When the priests and shamans were not in the sacred caves seeking answers or carving sacred talismans, they could be found in the holy, tent-like structure called the Y'auve. It is not hard to close your eyes and see this open air tabernacle, high on a hill with its banners of brightly colored feathers, suspended from painted poles planted around its sea pelt and fiber entrances. Only the priests and chiefs of the Chingichnich were allowed in this structure.

The mystique and sacred history of Pimu is undeniable, its physical appearance endearing, and its spirit of place ancient. The sites at Little Harbor and Two Harbors are good places to begin your adventure if you plan to camp Catalina. They are two of the larger settlement sites of the Pimugnans. Avalon Bay provides a more recent look at Catalina, and affords the voyeur a full perspective of the Catalina of today.

Regardless of how you see the island, you will come away with a feeling of captivation. Pimu, the island whose residents were thought to be powerful wizards who could calm the Pacific and call lightning and swordfish; the island whose medicine power was sought throughout the ancient West; is an island that continues to entice the imagination with understanding of a long ago mystic culture and its people.

HORSE LORE

BY EDAIN McCOY

Horses have figured heavily in mythology, folklore, and superstition. Sacred to many goddesses, they symbolize the night, the Moon, the dream world, and archetypally represent those beings which can travel back and forth between the seen and unseen worlds.

- To dream of seeing someone ride a black horse means illness or death, especially if they are seen riding over water.

- To see a man in dark clothing mounted on a white horse which is traveling west is another sign of impending death.

- To dream that you are riding a horse means that the Otherworld has opened itself to you and that you are free to travel there, as long as you stay safely on the horse's back.

- To dream that you cannot dismount a galloping horse indicates the presence of a sexually abusive spirit called a succubus or incubus. This is the origin of the term "hag ridden," meaning to be burdened under a Witch's curse.

- Horse goddesses are the original night "mares." The Irish goddess Mare is said to be the bringer of dreams, both pleasant and ugly.

- In rural, western Ireland there persists a legend which says that if you sit at a perfectly oriented crossroads just before dawn, light fires at the four corners, then ride three times around the intersection on a besom, you will see a dark woman upon a white horse—the Night Mare—fleeing west from the waxing morning light.

- Horseshoes have long been regarded as symbols of good luck, and are often hung over thresholds or above barn doors to bring good fortune to those who pass through them. The origin of this custom is said to have come from Irish Leprechauns, who hold horses in high esteem.

- The sole occupation of the Russian faery known as the Vazila is to care for horses.

🐴 The malevolent Manx goblin known as the Glashtin is half horse and half cow. If the head part is that of a cow, he is stupid; if the head part is that of a horse, then he is smart and cunning.

🐴 The Welsh god Gwyn Ap Nuad rides his otherworldly horses through the night sky, following the baying of his hounds. This "Wild Hunt" is a metaphor for the gathering of souls to take back with him to the Otherworld.

🐴 To dream of riding a horse traveling east, or up a mountainside, means that you are taking spiritual gifts and manifesting them in your physical world.

🐴 Horses are symbols of sexual prowess. To increase your sexual stamina, take three hairs from a horse's tail and three hairs from your own head and tie them together with a red string. Carry this in your right pocket or place under your bed.

🐴 To increase your sex appeal to others, weave some horse hair into a ring. Wear it on the middle finger of your right hand.

🐴 Horses are also fertility symbols. To help you conceive, make love in a horse's stall, or clip some hair from its mane and weave it into bracelets for yourself and your mate.

🐴 Irish horses were used as goddess symbols to bestow sovereignty on kings, who once had to endure rituals which "married" them to horses.

🐴 The ancient hill-cut drawing of a horse at Uffington, England, is thought to have been a shrine to a revered horse goddess.

🐴 The Welsh horse goddess Rhiannon was forced to ferry people back and forth on her back from the Otherworld to the earth realm when she was falsely accused of killing her son.

VISION QUEST

BY MARGUERITE ELSBETH

The vision quest is a spiritual rite of passage practiced by many Native American tribes. It is a very powerful ritual. It takes courage and patience to venture forth alone into nature without food, water, or supplies, and remain in one particular place for days with nothing to do but pray, wait, and hopefully receive a vision. Because the wild, primal forces of the natural world are much stronger than the human mind, they can change your concept of reality, and perhaps even frighten you if you don't know what to expect. The quest is successful if, during this time, a vision comes to you that will help you to unravel a part of the Great Mystery, find yourself, and determine your future.

The vision may be visual, like Hawk swooping low overhead, or it may come in the form of sound, such as Coyote laughing in the distance. Perhaps Brother Wind will rise to chill you with rushing fingers, or Sister Rain will fall over you, gently washing away your doubts and fears. Some Indians believe that if an animal or elemental spirit comes to you in this way, it could be your totem. Sometimes the quest might result in your being given some form of medicine power, a gift that you could use to help others. If a vision does come, you may seek out a medicine or wise person to help you to interpret its meaning, if this is necessary. If no vision comes at all, you may go on another quest at a later time.

THE MINI-QUEST

The "mini quest," a twelve-hour, daytime version of the traditional vision quest (which can last up to four days), is an excellent way to familiarize yourself with the spiritual process of scrying for a vision. It is a safe, effective alternative for city folk, working people, and those who simply need to overcome their fear of the unknown.

Prepare by eating lightly, fasting, or, if possible, participating in a sweat lodge ceremony.

Arrange to have a trusted companion drive and/or hike with you into the outback. Find a place that feels sacred to you, such as the middle of an open meadow or a hill top.

Prepare a circle. Bless the area with sage or cedar smoke. Use tobacco ties or stones to mark the four directions —east, west, north, and south—around the circle. Keep nothing with you, except perhaps a blanket and a little water. Instruct your companion to come back for you in twelve hours.

Use your alone time to pray, chant, or just be. Stay in the circle, and be sure to remain awake and alert. An animal might come or a spirit might appear. Perhaps you will receive a vision.

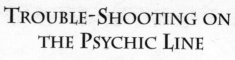

TROUBLE-SHOOTING ON THE PSYCHIC LINE

By Marguerite Elsbeth

It's 2:00 AM and you're headed into an emotional tailspin. Who ya gonna call? Well, Ghostbusters notwithstanding, sometimes it's me—psychic trouble-shooter on an 800 telephone line.

Usually, a major emotional crisis indicates a crossroads in life and, while chaotic change breaks new ground for good things to come in, the process is painful and decidedly unsettling. Times like this demand extreme measures, so I've acquired a broad repertoire of magical techniques to expedite emotional rescue. The following balancing tricks of the psychic trade are immediately effective and come from a mixed bag of Earth-based traditions.

Psychic Trouble-Shooter Number One

First, calm down! Anxiety cannot exist where there is conscious breath, so take three deep breaths; on the third exhale, say the name you ascribe to the Creator (Great Spirit, God/dess, etc.) seven times. Then take seven breaths and name the Creator; then do it again.

Psychic Trouble-Shooter Number Two

Next is grounding, because you can't find solutions if you're out of psychic whack. Find a cardboard box big enough to put both feet into and small enough to fit under the bed. Take the box and a digging utensil, and go out to the back yard or local park. Fill the box with fresh Earth dug from six inches down. Place the box under your bed and step into it every morning. Replace the dirt every thirty days.

Psychic Trouble-Shooter Number Three

Take the egg test to determine what ails you. Get two fresh eggs in their shells. Ask permission to use them for psychic diagnosis. Holding one egg in each hand, rub them all over your body, front, back, sides, head to toe. Take the eggs into the bathroom and crack them, one at a time, against the inside wall of the toilet, watching the albumin and yolk slide into the water.

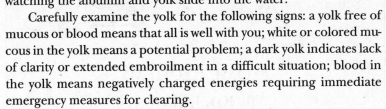

Carefully examine the yolk for the following signs: a yolk free of mucous or blood means that all is well with you; white or colored mucous in the yolk means a potential problem; a dark yolk indicates lack of clarity or extended embroilment in a difficult situation; blood in the yolk means negatively charged energies requiring immediate emergency measures for clearing.

Psychic Trouble-Shooter Number Four

Draw a clearing bath (recommended for all manner of psychic upsets). Purchase liquid bluing (non-toxic/bio-degradable) and a bottle of rum or whiskey. Add one-half cup each to hot-as-you-can-stand-it bath water. Completely immerse yourself seven times. Rinse off in an ice-cold shower

Psychic Trouble-Shooter Number Five

Jump in a lake (for extreme cases of psychic duress). Take a trusted friend, towels, extra clothes and a bathing suit to a secluded lake (river, ocean) area. Sit quietly and commune with the water spirits. Throw some silver money into the water as a spirit offering. Disrobe and jump into the water, immersing completely seven times.

HOME ALCHEMY

By Ken Johnson

H ere are two alchemical recipes you can use to help develop psychic senses such as clairvoyance (psychic sight), clairaudience (psychic hearing), and clairsentience (psychic feeling, and perception):

RECIPE ONE

¼ liter distilled water

2 teaspoons chamomile flowers

1 teaspoon *herba euphrasia* (eyebright) leaves

Heat up distilled water. When it boils, add chamomile flowers and eyebright. If you can't find eyebright leaves, use the eyebright liquid, available in health food stores. After a few more seconds of boiling, remove the mixture from the fire and cover it with a lid. Let stand for ten minutes, then strain the liquid into a new container.

Take some willow or hazel switches which you have gathered outdoors, stripped of their leaves, and tied into a small bundle of about seven to nine pieces. Light one end of the bundle and let it burn for a bit.

Dip the burning willows into the liquid until the fire goes out. Strain the liquid into yet another container, making sure that all the ashes and pieces of charcoal are filtered out. Store the mixture in a sterile container in the refrigerator.

To use this preparation for developing clairvoyance, pour some of it into a bowl. Meditate on heat and warmth, feeling your body becoming filled with an inner fire. Breathe your inner fire into the bowl, knowing with certainty that the liquid is now filled with the power of fire. Moisten a cloth with the charged liquid and place it over your eyes (it is better not to apply the liquid directly to the eyes with a dropper). Continue to breathe in the power of fire and heat and, using your imagination, direct that heat into your eyes. This will enhance your ability to "see" in the spiritual realms.

RECIPE TWO

To develop clairaudience and clairsentience, you can use an even simpler formula:

⅛ liter water

2 teaspoons chamomile flowers

Add chamomile flowers water and boil. Strain the liquid into a new, sterile container and store it in the refrigerator. To use this formula, proceed as before, with the following variations.

To develop clairaudience, fill yourself and the liquid with the power of air by breathing in lightness and clarity until you can virtually feel yourself floating. Then moisten two cotton balls with the potion and place them in your ears, continuing to draw that airy lightness into your body and allowing it to settle in your ears. This will help you to hear the spirits speaking all around you.

To develop clairsentience, fill yourself and the liquid with the power of water, breathing in coolness and moisture until you can actually feel your body becoming cooler. Moisten a washcloth and place it on your solar plexus, breathing the power of water into that part of your body. This will aid you in all kinds of psychic perception that involves feeling or touch, including psychometry.

MODERN MAGIC CARPETS

BY ESTELLE DANIELS

When I was a kid I read all the Arabian Nights stories about the magic carpets. The hero would ride through the air to all sorts of wonderful places, with only a single magical word needed to command the carpet. I would dream of having a neat thing like that, but as I grew up I realized that it was not to be. The magic carpet was a thing of fantasy, and existed only in fairy stories.

But then I became a Witch, and discovered that some of those magical things in fairy stories can and do exist in the real world. Today, it might seem impossible to have a magic carpet of your very own, but I will let you in on a little secret: I do have a magic carpet, and furthermore, you can too!

In my living room, which doubles as my temple room, I have an oriental carpet. It's domestic and contemporary; nothing really fancy. The pattern is an old Persian pattern called the "Tree of Life." This is a common pattern for oriental carpets. In fact, it is the classic pattern for oriental rugs. The colors may vary, but the design has several regular features. It is symmetrical, no matter which axis you measure from. It has a central design, which branches out to the edges of the rug. This is the tree. It is bordered with designs, and usually has some design in the exact center of each side. The carpet may be most any size, from nine by twelve feet to twelve by sixteen feet (or larger); rectangular, octagonal, round, square, or a long runner for a hallway. Traditionally, the best carpets were made of silk, but nowadays they are made also of cotton, wool, and acrylics.

After years of doing magic in the living room on the carpet, I came to discover that my carpet has come to hold quite a bit of magical energy by itself. I can lie on the rug, centered on the tree, and feel a circle ready to be activated. Sitting in the center of the carpet, I can meditate and travel to wherever I want, both within and without this world. Divination on the carpet is better; stronger, more clear, and centered. I get better results while studying or reading on occult and magical subjects there than in other rooms of the house. Some days, I can feel the carpet both in the solid mundane world and simultaneously in the magical world.

The carpet seems to work better for my magic when it is freshly vacuumed. As I clean it, admittedly with a thoroughly modern tool, it seems to realign the energies to where they should be, straighten out any stray influences, and reset the circle for use.

My magic carpet just happens to be oriented north-south in the long axis. It's wool, and the colors are light blue, cream, gold, black and pink. When I do circles in the living room, I put the quarter candles on the designs in the border at the center of each side in the rug, where the "quarters" of the rug are. The carpet is big enough to easily hold eight people in a circle, but rarely do we limit our circles to just the area of the carpet. Still, when magic is done there, either solo, in class, or in groups, the carpet is in the center of the circle.

This is a really interesting phenomenon: I have several oriental rugs in the house, and two others have some residual energy potential while the others do not. The ones that have traditional Persian patterns are the ones with energy potential.

It would seem that those ancient Persian rug makers, along the silk trade routes, developed more than just pretty patterns those millennia ago. These traditional Persian patterns carry magical potential, and can act as batteries for magical energy, when used for ritual purposes. I think of them as magical energy battery sigils. I have found that it seems to matter little what colors or fabrics are used; even acrylic rugs exhibit battery potential. This might seem impossible, but I have friends who swear by their Lucite® wands, also. The pattern itself holds the magical potential, and though it might operate better if executed by hand in traditional silk and colors, it still has quite a bit of potential.

So next time you are out driving and see one of those roadside rug vendors or a garage sale, think about purchasing yourself a magic carpet. It takes a bit of time and energy investment, but with work and intent, you too can have your very own magic carpet, to ride the ether on your magical journeys. Blessed Be.

Take a Magic Carpet Ride

By Marguerite Elsbeth

The Oriental carpets of Persia, Afghanistan, Turkey, the Caucasus, and Morocco are truly magical productions. Beyond the rich, bold, natural colors drawn from dye plants—madder for pink, rose, apricot, scarlet, and purple, indigo for blue, weld for yellow, oak gall and acorn cup for black—every piece is hand-woven with esoteric symbols, mysterious designs and deeply spiritual meanings.

The patterns are created in an arabesque style of weaving common to Islamic or Arabian art, and contain details which repeat, intertwine, and turn back on themselves to confuse evil spirits. Silver plate, earring, yellow-head, mouse tail, four fish, boxes, arrows, scorpion, and footprints are some of the nicknames given to the designs.

Patterns which date back to an ancient, pre-Islamic shamanic concept of the world are divided into three levels, or worlds: upper, middle (our world) and lower. A medallion dominating the middle of a rug shows the metaphysical center of the universe which, according to Arab culture, can be anywhere. From this orientation point, a person can make a connection with the upper world, the source of light and order, or with the lower world, dwelling place of the ancestral spirits. Sometimes the pattern in the center signifies the sun at its zenith, and appears as a tree or pillar surmounted by a disk or ball. This tree is the sacred Tree of Life.

The four corners of a carpet represent space as well as the four directions—east, west, north, and south. Corners marked by endless knot patterns indicate the "four suns" or the rising and setting Suns at the vernal and autumnal equinoxes.

Islamic weavers commonly add strange colors or inconsistent patterns to their rugs, a reminder that only Allah is perfect, while tribal peoples weave amulets made of hawk bones and feathers, tiny mirrors, silver coins, or herb-filled pouches and buttons into rugs for protection.

Perhaps most exotic is the long-held belief that carpets can be made to fly. Why not cast this authentic Turkish spell on your musty, old Persian rug and go on a magic carpet ride?

Facing east, on wild and open ground
Sit you cross-legged, gazing at the sky.
To small bowl made of silver, add
A pinch of fennel
A bud of thyme
A hand of rue
With fire set and breathe the cleansing smoke.
Now shield your face with paint of saffron,
And your body with the scent of ambergris,
And cry you:
Ali-kazan, by night we fly!

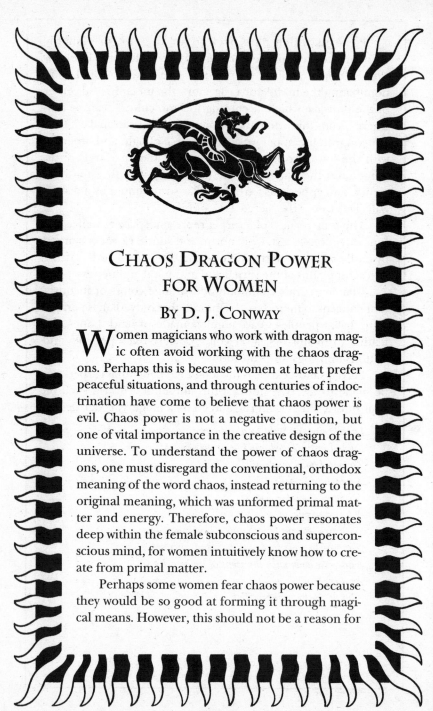

CHAOS DRAGON POWER FOR WOMEN

BY D. J. CONWAY

Women magicians who work with dragon magic often avoid working with the chaos dragons. Perhaps this is because women at heart prefer peaceful situations, and through centuries of indoctrination have come to believe that chaos power is evil. Chaos power is not a negative condition, but one of vital importance in the creative design of the universe. To understand the power of chaos dragons, one must disregard the conventional, orthodox meaning of the word chaos, instead returning to the original meaning, which was unformed primal matter and energy. Therefore, chaos power resonates deep within the female subconscious and superconscious mind, for women intuitively know how to create from primal matter.

Perhaps some women fear chaos power because they would be so good at forming it through magical means. However, this should not be a reason for avoiding one of the most powerful forms of dragon energy. All magicians must take care with whatever power they are tapping into. Magicians are responsible for every creation they bring into existence.

One way to begin your acquaintance with the chaos dragons is to call upon Tiamat. The great black dragon Tiamat is primarily thought of as a feminine entity. She is called upon when the magician needs to work magic for retribution of wrongs, protection from physical and non-physical beings, to bring justice to a specific case, or to stop violence.

Learning to understand Tiamat's energies and work magic with her help is very important to any magician. However, many women magicians shy away from making contact with her, because contact with the intense emotions of this particular dragon can be difficult, and because the emotions evoked often conflict with subconscious programming. Although one cannot say that all dragons can be classified as being male or female, it is very true that a great many of them respond more readily to male or female energies within the magician. These energies within the magician do not correspond in any way to the physical sex of the magician, but rather to the energy projected by a specific frame of mind. Most women working dragon magic appear to be able to do this with great clarity, once they have grasped the idea. For women to realize their full potential in dragon magic, they must learn how, and be willing, to unleash certain emotional reservoirs of energy from within. Some of these emotional energies may be ones they have seldom, if ever, allowed out. These

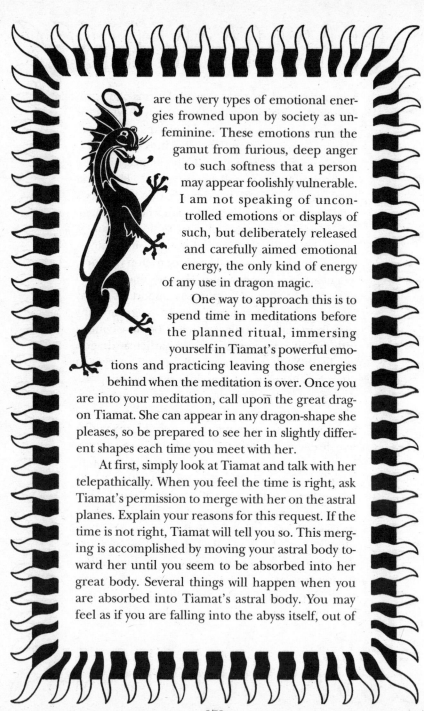

are the very types of emotional energies frowned upon by society as unfeminine. These emotions run the gamut from furious, deep anger to such softness that a person may appear foolishly vulnerable. I am not speaking of uncontrolled emotions or displays of such, but deliberately released and carefully aimed emotional energy, the only kind of energy of any use in dragon magic.

One way to approach this is to spend time in meditations before the planned ritual, immersing yourself in Tiamat's powerful emotions and practicing leaving those energies behind when the meditation is over. Once you are into your meditation, call upon the great dragon Tiamat. She can appear in any dragon-shape she pleases, so be prepared to see her in slightly different shapes each time you meet with her.

At first, simply look at Tiamat and talk with her telepathically. When you feel the time is right, ask Tiamat's permission to merge with her on the astral planes. Explain your reasons for this request. If the time is not right, Tiamat will tell you so. This merging is accomplished by moving your astral body toward her until you seem to be absorbed into her great body. Several things will happen when you are absorbed into Tiamat's astral body. You may feel as if you are falling into the abyss itself, out of control and helpless. You will find yourself in the center of an emotion-cyclone, a whirling mass of intense emotions. These will not all be of anger, but also may be of overwhelming love, depression, intolerance of human stupidity and cruelty, great compassion, etc. As soon as you are over your first shock at the strength and intensity of these emotions, observe your personal feelings about each very carefully. You will find that Tiamat is showing you what is within yourself. Call each emotion to you and look at it carefully in terms of your own experiences. If you are truthful, you will be able to connect each of Tiamat's revealed emotions with past or present experiences in your own life. Most often there is some part of these experiences unresolved. Do not deny these emotions, but accept them as part of yourself. Emotions are energy, a valuable personal resource which you can control or release as needed. Recognizing, accepting, and exploring these personal emotional patterns may well take several meditations.

When you have finished your communication with Tiamat for this time, feel your astral body move back until you once more see that you and Tiamat are two separate entities. Although you may still be shaking from the experience, thank the great dragon for teaching you. End your meditation.

Before returning to normal activities, making three cutting strokes with your hand in front of your solar plexus area helps to sever any remaining astral threads to that part of Tiamat's energy pattern. This is necessary to avoid being inundated constantly with every type of emotional energy. It is better to try to explore only one personal emotion pattern at a time, for many of them may well leave you emotionally sensitive and drained for up to a week, sometimes more, depending upon what effect that particular emotion had in your life.

The reason for doing all this is to familiarize you with Tiamat's energy patterns, which match certain similar patterns within yourself. When working magic and needing to tap into a specific energy, you can recall the feelings you experienced with the emotional energy. You can then deliberately open or close the conduit to that energy as needed in ritual. All magicians need to know how and when to loose or bind emotional energy called forth from the dragons and themselves. All magic is accomplished through the deliberate application of energy. Magical energy is primarily created through emotions. Thus, emotional energy forms astral matter, or a desired result, which must first be born in the astral realms. Formed astral matter must eventually distort space, or come into physical existence in our realm. By learning from the feel of energy patterns of emotions. The magician can create that emotion on demand, shape its energy into a specific form out of astral matter, and know that the desired result will appear in the physical.

MEN AND ISIS WORSHIP

BY deTraci Regula

The attraction of men for the worship of Isis has existed since early times. While there has always been an abundance of priestesses of Isis, the official temple staff was predominately male, both in Egypt and in the many temples of Isis in the Greco-Roman world. These priests did not lead an unremittedly ascetic life. Like most other Egyptian priests, they rotated their service at the temple with periods spent with their families in the ordinary life of the local community. Many priesthoods were hereditary, and religious offices were passed on to the sons and daughters of the priests and priestesses.

Looking at the mythology of goddesses, it's not surprising why Isis holds a special attraction. In Greek, Babylonian, and Middle Eastern myth, many goddesses are hostile to or contemptuous of males. Diana's hounds tear apart Actaeon for spying on her at her bath; Venus' lover Adonis castrates himself for love of her; Ishtar, though initially willing to go the Underworld to save her love, ultimately will not sacrifice herself to save him and returns to the physical world alone, leaving her lover to his fate.

Isis, on the other hand, is deeply and romantically in love with Osiris. To Her, he is Usar-un-Nefer, the "beautiful being," with whom she shares love, pleasure, and the throne of Egypt. When Osiris is torn into bits by their treacherous brother Set, Isis travels the length of Egypt looking for the pieces. All but his phallus is found. This is regarded as a catastrophe by Isis, who desires that her partner be her erotic equal. She promptly makes him a new one out of pure gold. Using her healing magic, she attaches this new, imperishable phallus to him and lays herself on top of him, successfully becoming pregnant with their son Horus.

Apuleius, a second-century novelist believed to have been an initiate of Isis, describes his vision of Isis in terms that vividly evoke her erotic, majestic beauty and power. She appears to him rising from the waves on a moonlit night, Her dark, curling hair streaming over her shoulders, and fragrant with the perfumes of Egypt.

Cleopatra, a woman whose reality and legend have moved many men, was a priestess of Isis, and saw herself as the goddess incarnate on Earth. It was as the avatar of Isis-Hathor (or Aphrodite) that she approached both Julius Caesar and Marc Antony, offering to them in turn both pleasure and power in return for their aid in holding the throne of Egypt.

Soldiers and sailors were certainly not immune to the attraction of Isis, and many of these men left dedications and inscriptions at her temples, thanking her for healing, for victory, or for a safe passage through perilous waters. The transmittal of the faith of Isis throughout the Roman Empire was largely due to her followers in the Roman Legion, who built temples and shrines to Her wherever the legions travelled.

Several male authors composed hymns to Isis. Four hymns of Isidorus of the Fayum still exist on the stones of a ruined temple to Isis at the site now called Madinet Madi, in the Fayum region of Egypt. In the prayer, known as Hymn III, Isidorus writes what men who believe in Her can expect:

> ...the best of men: sceptre-bearing kings and those who are rulers, if they depend on You, rule until old age, leaving shining and splendid wealth in abundance to their sons, and their sons' sons, and men who come after...

There are many ways modern priests of Isis relate to Her. Some, like the fictional character Dr. Rupert Malcolm in Dion Fortune's initiatory novel, *Moon Magic,* see themselves as an Osiris, her equal and opposite power, lending their masculine power to Her in exchange for her gift of bountiful life. Many others see themselves functioning as Her servant, tending Her altars and temples and seeing that Her rites are performed, as tens of thousands of priests of Isis have done

in the past. Still others see themselves as Her child, Her brother, or as Her husband.

It's not necessary for a man to confine his relationship to Isis to only one aspect. The Pharaohs, who were not only divine rulers of Egypt but were also the supreme high priests, in whose name the temple priests performed the sacred rites, saw no conflict with any of these relationships to Isis. They are depicted on Her lap, as Her son Horus, nursing at her breasts, or with Her standing behind the throne, perhaps with Her hand on their shoulder, guiding them and supporting them as a loving wife and magical mate, calling forth their power to answer Her own. For many modern men, Isis offers no less today.

FURTHER READING:

Fortune, Dion. *Moon Magic.* London: Aquarian Press, 1990.

Fortune, Dion. *The Sea Priestess.* New York: Weiser, 1979.

Regula, deTraci. *The Mysteries of Isis.* St. Paul: Llewellyn, 1995.

Vanderlip, Vera Frederika. *The Four Greek Hymns of Isidorus and the Cult of Isis.* Georgia: Scholars Press, 1974.

Witt, R. E. *Isis in the Graeco-Roman World.* New York: Cornell University Press, 1971.

NATIVE AMERICAN PROPHECY

BY MARGUERITE ELSBETH

Indian people have never lost their connection to Mother Earth. They believe that all creatures and things are her children, living on her giant turtle-back. However, these days there is much concern among the various tribes about the future of Mother Earth and her children. Native American prophecies say that the two-legs and four-legs, the winged and creepy-crawlies, the rivers, stones, sky and plants are in trouble, because technology has taken over Nature and we are sleeping when we should be awake. The Indian people ask only for the chance to pass on their way of life and their love for the Great Spirit to their children and grandchildren. Therefore, they have much to say about the coming Earth changes.

The Hopi believe that Nature will speak to them through mighty winds, earthquakes, floods, seasonal changes, fluctuating weather patterns, and endangered wildlife, as well as spiritual and political unrest.

The Six Nations Iroquois Confederacy says that the Earth changes will be upon us when the trees start dying from the tops down. They predict that there will be no corn, that nothing will grow, and that the water will be unfit to drink. Then a great wind will come to cleanse the Earth and return it to its original state. Some Lakota believe that an increase in volcanic eruptions, such as Mount St. Helens, as well as hurricanes and earthquakes affecting the west, south and east coasts of the United States, are a sign.

Mayan tradition marks December 21, 2012, as the end of one vast cycle of time and the beginning of another. It is said that the great spiritual teacher Feathered Serpent may return during the transitional era, sometime between 1993 and 2012. The Hopi have a similar prophecy concerning Pahana, the "lost brother."

The Seminoles think that two things will happen to announce the coming Earth changes: their children will no longer speak the old language, and their people will forget how to make the sacred fire from flint and metal. Like the Hopi and Lakota, they also believe that an increase in earthquakes and volcanos will show that certain prophecies may come to pass.

Despite the changing times we live in, Indians are hopeful that Mother Earth will bloom again and be healed of her woes, and that all people will unite in peace and harmony for many moons thereafter. Meanwhile, here's what you can do to help Mother Earth in her time of need:

- Nourish your connection with the Earth by learning to know and appreciate the heritage and ecology of your area.

- Use medicinal plants that are native to your region.

- Make conscious choices to preserve endangered species.

- Buy local produce and products.

- Support organic farmers and ranchers.

- Join an environmental organization.

- Use a natural alternative to household chemicals.

- Read labels and learn what to avoid.

- Grow an organic garden.

- Recycle!

SHEDDING SKIN

BY JIM GARRISON

We can shed our old habits, our fears, and our pain like a snake sheds its skin. The process doesn't make everything go away so much as it gives us a new start, a renewed perspective. We have to let go of the past in order to touch the future, and that is the work of the present.

When it is time to let go of the past—formally and through ritual magic—the following rite may be of some use to you. It is offered in the spirit of compassion. May you never need it.

Cleanse yourself. In a dark place go to the north. Scribe a circle moving clockwise. Walk around the circle three times, drawing the boundary with luminous gray fog. You are creating your own place within a place, a sacred space within which to work magic. Each step takes you farther away from the world, and deeper into the darkness which waits for us beyond. Feel something infinitely older than you stir beneath the surface.

Reflect upon why you are in this place, why you have drawn this circle and what must be done in order for you to release the past, as well as for it to release you.

When you are ready, close your eyes (or don a blindfold). This is the beginning of all things, for it is from darkness that all things come forth. Turn to the east and visualize a swirling blue disk, or ball of blue mingled with yellow sunlight, clouds, and other forms of weather according to the season and climate of your surroundings. When you can feel the presence of the element of Air, give the symbol permission to open the way to its realm and recite the following words, or something similar:

I stand within the triple-coil of the serpent, in this place between the worlds and beyond. I face the east, and recall all my words, everything I have said in this past year. I own these things and they are of my making. Eating these echoes of my passions and opinions, I taste the truth of my will, however obscured by ego or emotion it may have become. I pray for clarity, and by this act of self-sacrament I seek to speak honestly, openly, and fairly, with compassion and understanding from this moment onward. So mote it be.

Turn to face the south. Feel the warmth and visualize a flaming, red triangle before you, as large as you can manage. Give the symbol permission to open the way into the realm of fire, and recite the following words, or something similar:

To the south I turn, and by the flames of my actions, the light I have brought into the world, I warm my soul and open my eyes to the truth of my acts, the integrity of my courage, the fierceness of my mad anger and the pettiness of my insecurities. I own these acts, these expressions of my innermost self. I kindle the flames of self with the breath of clear intent, and in recalling and reliving these things I seek to know my true direction, the real expression of what I am here to do. I seek to dance the dance of my soul in harmony and beauty. So mote it be.

Turn now to the west and visualize a droplet of water. Let it grow in size until it becomes the size of a pond, a lake, an ocean. When you can feel the depths within this element, give the symbol permission to open the way into the realm of water and recite the following words, or something similar:

To the west I turn, the song of my ancestors in my blood, the truth of my work in my sweat and tears. I feel the sorrows and happiness, the waves and tides of my emotions wash over me, through me in this deep place of recollection and rebirth. I lower myself, willingly and completely, into the cauldron, and here I transform these feelings into memories, which shape me and guide me to bring about those feelings I most dearly hunger for, to share those things I most eagerly seek, and by these acts I shall finally find what I need through building what I might give and share. So mote it be.

Turn to the north and visualize a square of green and black and other colors of the soil. Bring this symbol into your circle as with the others, and when you can feel the presence of this element, give the symbol permission to open the way into the realm of earth. Recite the following words, or something similar:

To the north I turn, shaken to my roots, washed clean of pride, and in humility I look out upon the fruits of my labors. What have I wrought with my hands, my heart, my will? In silence I see the true harvest of my soul, the treasures I've crafted for my people, the gifts I've left for those coming after me, the things I have made and fashioned—the manifestations of my desire and the accomplishments of my efforts. Grateful for my life, for my talents and the challenges which form my life, I thank the ancestors and the gods, and from this fertile foundation I will grow and nurture a life to be lived: my life. So mote it be.

Feel the elemental power within your circle and meditate or relax and let the energy soak into you. Let it wash through your mind, body, and soul. Then quiet yourself, listen to your heartbeat or your breath, and after a time recite the following words, or something similar:

I reach down into the roots of my soul, the deep realm of the ancestors and the dead. I am a shadow of the past being cast into the future. I am the one who follows and shall in time be followed by those who come after. I am one of you, you are within me, the memories whispering in my blood, the secrets written upon the coils within my cells. I honor you and stand before you as a child in the darkness. I rely upon you for my foundation, my refuge from the storm. Your wisdom guides my steps and challenges my choices as I collect my own experiences to in time become one of you who stand watching. With thanks and a perspective born of shared insight, I walk onward with your blessing. So mote it be.

Reach upward and feel the space which surrounds you. Listen to its unique rhythms and sounds. Recite the following words, or something similar:

I extend my hands upward into the future, that which is ever-becoming, the crest of an eternal wave rolling forever onward and away from us. I touch the wild magic of creation and destruction, the forces of nature which shape us all, and define our lives. Grasping the lightning and breathing the wind of change, I shed the old skin of my past, I let go of those things which I've outgrown and make a new life from the old. I am reborn, renewed, and I let the lightning loose into my circle that it bring the light deeper into me, that I might make the great leap across the abyss and enter into a new life of light, love, and freedom. I stand here a free (wo)man. So mote it be!

Remove the blindfold if you chose to use one. Open your eyes and begin your renewed life by reciting the following words, or something similar:

Ever mindful that as we come into the world, we are not alone. I relinquish this circle and restore the energies of this sacred place. I thank the powers of the four directions and the ancestors. I thank the serpent for its protection and the chance to renew myself through its special gift.

Retrace your steps in scribing the circle and restore the space as it was before you began, all the while reflecting upon the changes deep within you that are even now beginning to manifest. Over the course of time these changes will emerge, and you will grow and your life will transform.

How to Figure Planetary Hours

By Estelle Daniels

To use this method to figure planetary hours you will need planetary hours tables such as the example found on page 285. Complete sets of planetary hours tables can be found in the magazine *Dell Horoscope*.

Using Planetary Hours Tables

To figure planetary hours, you first need to know what your latitude is (how far north or south your town or city is from the equator). Good places to check are your local library, city hall (they probably have records, or the local city engineer or city planner would also have it), or a good atlas. Once you have the latitude (and longitude, they come as a pair), write these numbers down and save them where you can refer to them again. They make a nice addition to a book of shadows. Round to the nearest whole degree.

Next, find the times for sunrise and sunset at your latitude and for the day on which you would like to use planetary hours. To do this, consult the sample planetary hours table on page 287. Sunrise is the first time listed under your latitude in the day hours section, and sunset is the first time listed under your latitude in the night hours section. You will also need to get a local newspaper, where the sunrise and sunset are shown for each day. The information may also be on TV in the weathercast. If they do not show sunrise and sunset times, you could call the station and ask the weather person for the sunrise and sunset times for the day.

Once you have both sets of sunrise and sunset times for a particular day of the year, note whether it is daylight saving time or not. In the U.S. the national standard starts daylight saving time at 2:00 AM on the first Sunday in April, and it ends at 2:00 AM on the last Sunday in October. The U.S. is on daylight saving time longer than it is on standard time. The following is an example showing how to compute planetary hours. (Continued on page 286, after table at right.)

PLANETARY HOURS FOR MAY 1–7, NORTH LATITUDE

Day Hours: Sunrise to sunset, top group. Night Hours: Sunset to sunrise, bottom group.
Saturn ♄; Jupiter ♃; Mars ♂; Sun ☉; Venus ♀; Mercury ☿; Moon ☽

Lat 27°	29°	31°	33°	35°	37°	39°	41°	Su	M	Tu	W	Th	F	Sa	Lat 43°	45°	47°	49°	51°	53°	55°
5:22	5:19	5:16	5:13	5:10	5:06	5:03	4:59	☉	☽	♂	☿	♃	♀	♄	4:54	4:50	4:45	4:40	4:34	4:28	4:21
6:28	6:25	6:23	6:20	6:18	6:15	6:12	6:09	♀	♄	☉	☽	♂	☿	♃	6:05	6:01	5:57	5:53	5:48	5:43	5:37
7:34	7:32	7:30	7:28	7:26	7:23	7:21	7:19	☿	♃	♀	♄	☉	☽	♂	7:15	7:13	7:09	7:06	7:02	6:58	6:53
8:40	8:38	8:37	8:35	8:34	8:32	8:30	8:28	☽	♂	☿	♃	♀	♄	☉	8:26	8:24	8:21	8:19	8:16	8:13	8:09
9:46	9:45	9:44	9:43	9:42	9:40	9:39	9:38	♄	☉	☽	♂	☿	♃	♀	9:36	9:35	9:33	9:32	9:30	9:28	9:25
10:52	10:51	10:51	10:50	10:50	10:49	10:48	10:48	♃	♀	♄	☉	☽	♂	☿	10:47	10:47	10:45	10:45	10:44	10:43	10:41
11:58	11:58	11:58	11:58	11:58	11:58	11:58	11:58	♂	☿	♃	♀	♄	☉	☽	11:57	11:58	11:58	11:58	11:58	11:58	11:58
1:03	1:04	1:04	1:05	1:05	1:06	1:07	1:07	☉	☽	♂	☿	♃	♀	♄	1:08	1:08	1:10	1:10	1:11	1:12	1:14
2:09	2:10	2:11	2:12	2:13	2:15	2:16	2:17	♀	♄	☉	☽	♂	☿	♃	2:19	2:20	2:22	2:23	2:25	2:27	2:30
3:15	3:17	3:18	3:20	3:21	3:23	3:25	3:27	☿	♃	♀	♄	☉	☽	♂	3:29	3:31	3:34	3:36	3:42	3:42	3:46
4:21	4:23	4:25	4:27	4:29	4:32	4:34	4:37	☽	♂	☿	♃	♀	♄	☉	4:40	4:43	4:46	4:49	4:53	4:57	5:02
5:27	5:30	5:32	5:35	5:37	5:40	5:43	5:46	♄	☉	☽	♂	☿	♃	♀	5:50	5:54	5:58	6:02	6:07	6:12	6:18
6:33	6:36	6:39	6:42	6:45	6:49	6:52	6:56	♃	♀	♄	☉	☽	♂	☿	7:01	7:05	7:10	7:15	7:21	7:27	7:34
7:27	7:30	7:32	7:35	7:37	7:40	7:43	7:46	♂	☿	♃	♀	♄	☉	☽	7:50	7:54	7:58	8:02	8:07	8:12	8:18
8:21	8:23	8:25	8:27	8:29	8:32	8:34	8:36	☉	☽	♂	☿	♃	♀	♄	8:40	8:42	8:46	8:49	8:53	8:57	9:02
9:15	9:17	9:18	9:20	9:21	9:23	9:25	9:27	♀	♄	☉	☽	♂	☿	♃	9:29	9:31	9:34	9:36	9:39	9:42	9:45
10:09	10:10	10:11	10:12	10:13	10:14	10:15	10:17	☿	♃	♀	♄	☉	☽	♂	10:18	10:20	10:22	10:23	10:25	10:27	10:29
11:03	11:04	11:04	11:05	11:05	11:06	11:06	11:07	☽	♂	☿	♃	♀	♄	☉	11:08	11:08	11:10	11:10	11:11	11:12	11:13
11:57	11:57	11:57	11:57	11:57	11:57	11:57	11:57	♄	☉	☽	♂	☿	♃	♀	11:57	11:57	11:58	11:57	11:57	11:57	11:57
12:51	12:51	12:50	12:50	12:49	12:48	12:48	12:47	♃	♀	♄	☉	☽	♂	☿	12:46	12:46	12:45	12:44	12:42	12:41	12:40
1:45	1:44	1:43	1:42	1:41	1:40	1:39	1:37	♂	☿	♃	♀	♄	☉	☽	1:36	1:34	1:33	1:31	1:26	1:26	1:24
2:39	2:38	2:36	2:35	2:33	2:31	2:30	2:28	☉	☽	♂	☿	♃	♀	♄	2:25	2:23	2:22	2:18	2:14	2:11	2:08
3:33	3:31	3:29	3:27	3:25	3:22	3:20	3:18	♀	♄	☉	☽	♂	☿	♃	3:14	3:12	3:09	3:05	3:00	2:56	2:52
4:27	4:25	4:22	4:20	4:17	4:14	4:11	4:08	☿	♃	♀	♄	☉	☽	♂	4:04	4:00	3:57	3:52	3:46	3:41	3:35

EXAMPLE

The day is Monday, May 5th, and the paper lists sunrise at 5:48 AM and sunset at 7:44 PM. You are in Chicago. Note that calculating planetary hours will vary as you move from place to place—100 miles or more makes a difference, and you have to re-figure if you are in a different place from where you originally figured it. The latitude and longitude of Chicago are 41° N 51' and 87° W 39'. The latitude rounds down to 41°N in the tables. In the tables, for 41°N between May 1–7, sunrise is at 4:59 and sunset at 18:56 (or 4:59 AM and 6:56 PM).

Subtract 4:42 (the sunrise time from the sample table on page 278) from 5:48 (actual sunrise, from the paper), and also subtract 7:02 (the sunset time from the sample table on page 278) from 7:44. The differences are :46 (46 minutes) and :42 (42 minutes).

Add :46 (or :42) to the times in the table to convert to clock time (during daylight saving time) or subtract :46 (or :42) from clock time to get the times in the tables. Do not be surprised if the conversion varies from the sunrise and sunset times; it could be up to three minutes. Pick which seems closest to you. With this method, you are rounding here and there, so it is best to give a five-minute slop either side of the change of the hours. Once you have your conversion number, you can then figure the clock time for any planetary hour using the tables. If you figure from the table in this book that the Jupiter hour is at 10:48 AM, and you add :46 to that to get a clock time of 11:34 AM, you should wait at least until 11:39 AM to assure you are really into the Jupiter hour.

This conversion number works for all days and hours during daylight saving time (:46 in Chicago). You have to get a different number for standard time conversions. Just do the same calculactions for a sunrise and sunset on a day which is not daylight saving time. You then have two conversion numbers, which will work forever for your location. It is a bit of a pain to work out, but once you have the conversion numbers written down, you never have to do the figuring again, unless you move 100 miles or more.

A NOTE ON CALCULATING BY HAND

Another method for figuring planetary hours is to save newspapers for a year and get exact sunrise/sunset times for each day of the year (they vary little from year to year—even in leap years) and figure out the planetary hours by hand. Find out how many minutes there are of day and night (they will be differing amounts except at the equinoxes), and divide each amount by twelve to get the number of minutes in each planetary hour.

Starting with sunrise, add the number of day-hour minutes to get each successive hour until sunset, then start with sunset and add the number of night-hour minutes to get each successive hour until the next sunrise. This method has no conversion from the tables, and will be in clock time automatically. You will even have the daylight saving time conversion built right in, but be careful on the actual days of the conversion, because the papers list the clock times, which will be daylight saving time for one day, and standard time for the next. The following sunrise will be an hour "off" if you do the figuring right. Also, though the sunrise and sunset times for the date in successive years will be the same, the day of the week that date falls on will change yearly. In 1997 May 5 is a Monday, in 1998 May 5 is a Tuesday. So the times of the planetary hours will remain the same, but the planetary designations of each hour will be different, 1997 May 5 starting with the Moon, and 1998 May 5 starting with Mars.

EDITOR'S NOTE: To learn more about computing planetary hours by hand, see the almanac section of this book.

SITE DUALITY: CHILD NEST ROCK

BY BERNYCE BARLOW

In the state of Nevada, within the confines of the Great Basin, there is a rock formation that juts out from the earth like a massive stone cradle. For mile upon desolate mile, the desert floor is barren, except for this rock. I was first introduced to this site by a ranger for Douglas county, Nevada, Ted E. Dailey. From the very beginning, I felt the site at one time was a women's place. Part of that feeling came from instinct, and part from intellect, as there was a single group of fertility symbols pecked into the base of the formation. There were no other peckings or paintings on the rock; just the lone fertility records shouting at me. At the top of the formation was a natural bowl one could climb into and lie down. Later research uncovered an ancient name for this site: Child Nest Rock. It was appropriate.

My initial impressions from the site indicated disrespect. Bits of plastic, paper, and glass littered the base of the rock and stuck in sandy crevices. Spent cartridges lay on the ground next to aluminum cans, torn ragged by the hit. The rock, too, was grazed, zinged here and there by stray bullets. I felt indignation and compared it to the treatment of women and children on many levels. The image stayed with me for a week.

Ranger Dailey, on the other hand, had a completely different experience at the site. His perception was oriented toward his own "spirit of place" impressions. The trash did not bother him; it was simply a reminder of people's impertinence. It did not take away from the power of the formation. Dailey found himself drawn to an area east of the rock, awash with stone cores of chert and obsidian. There were flakings from well-honed tools used by the ancient Desert Culture scattered about the encampment. We also discovered a number of stone circles, yards from the Nest, that were perhaps the foundations for sweat lodges or menses huts.

My next few visits to Child Nest were spent documenting and expanding the perimeters of the site. During this time, burial grounds, slabs, foundations, more circles, tool sites, and en-

Child Nest Rock: The ancient crone

campment areas were uncovered. Some of the graves at the burial center were very small, and suggested a place of rest for those little ones who did not make it out of the Nest. I contacted the Stewart Indian Museum and Cultural Center, whom I had been working with at another site. Their cooperation and enthusiasm is always a joy. They assisted with further documentation of the area with their usual good-natured style.

Understanding the history of the Desert Culture, how its people prospered in this region over thousands of years, leads me to expect the site has been sanctified many times, for many reasons. The duality of the site speaks for itself as layer upon layer of history is peeled back. The spirit of place at Child Nest Rock shows us the raw nature of both birth and death. Where the knowledge of the site becomes collective is in the nest, that curious natural cradle at the height of the rock, large enough for a person to lie down, dream, give birth, or die in. While lying in the nest, deeper dimensions unfold, leaving one hidden and safe, nurtured and empowered, within the rock womb. After a while, one can hear their heartbeat, a night bird, Gaia, then the Spirit within; collective and universal. Duality is put to rest, albeit as it so often is at sacred sites!

Putting Magic in Your Wardrobe

By Edain McCoy

Many grimoires, both old and new, teach students the art of making and using magical clothing, usually in the form of robes reserved for spellwork and rituals. Magical dressing does not have to be reserved for the ritual circle, however, nor does it have to involve the creation of new garments. With few exceptions, clothing is something we all have with us at all times, so it makes a great magical tool to see us through a crisis when nothing else is available. With a little visualization and creative imagination, your own wardrobe can be used to help fulfill almost any immediate magical need.

- Don't have any magical protection when you find yourself passing through that bad part of town? Then charge your white tennis shoes as talismans of protection to lead you safely away from any danger.

- Want to attract attention? Charge a red outfit with the projective energies of fire, and visualize it as a silent siren pulling eyes in your direction.

- Have a battle to fight today? Empower red clothing, the color of fire, energy, and combat, with extra strength on which you can draw if your own power reserves run low.

- Do you want to be viewed as intelligent? Let yellow clothing, empowered by your will, project to others the extent of your brain power.

- Need to relax, or to project a relaxed image to others? Become a walking "green room" and charge a green outfit with calming, competent energy.

- Want to be seen as mysterious? Wear black, empowered with a visualization that links your outfit to the absorbing energies native to its hue, to the Moon, and to magical mysteries.

- Do you feel that flu bug coming on, but today you just have to go to work? Empower blue or purple clothing to take advantage of the natural affinity of those colors with healing powers. Pause during your busy day and draw upon these power reserves when you feel drained.

- If you suddenly find yourself put on the defensive, empower that broach, pin, or tie tack you are wearing as a tool of power to assist in your defense.

- Going through bouts of grief or depression and want some extra uplifting energy to draw upon during the day? Choose orange or yellow clothing and charge it with cheerful energy.

- Do you feel as if someone is deliberately sending negative energy your way? Ward it off with spiked heels, white or gold clothing, or metallic fabrics, which can be empowered to deflect unwanted energies.

- Want to go unnoticed today? Wear black so that its protective powers can absorb your personal energies so they will not attract attention.

THE WORLD TREE

BY MARGUERITE ELSBETH

The World Tree grows in the center of the universe. It is an ancient mythological symbol for all of creation and our relationship to it, and stands as an otherworldly roadmap, which may be used to observe and measure our existence. It is a guide which we may use to navigate through the crossroads of life. To all people, the World Tree symbolizes life and death, growth and development, and is the center of the cosmos.

Some traditions, such as Theosophy and Hinduism, claim that the tree grows upside down, its roots touching the sky, and its foliage reaching deep into primal earth. But most affirm that its branches grow upward while it sends its roots down into the very core of Earth, to brush the cold darkness of hell, like the cosmic tree Yggdrasil in Norse mythology. Shamans of many cultures travel the axis of the World Tree to the three worlds: The upper world of spirit; the middle world in which we live; and the lower world of soul.

Although the concept of the tree is generic, various cultures may recognize a particular tree as being the sacred World Tree. The European Celts worshiped the oak, as did the California Indians. Scandinavian people agreed with the Iroquois Nation that the ash tree was the "tree of life." The tribes of Siberia venerate the larch, while Plains Indians revere the cottonwood, and place an eagle, a symbol for Father Sky or the Great Spirit, on top of the tree during the sun dance ceremony. Maple is the World Tree to some Northeastern tribes; others believe it is an evergreen tree that grows on the back of a turtle, a symbol for Mother Earth. Despite the difference in genus, however, the essential meaning of the World Tree remains unchanged. This is because the real World Tree grows inside each and every one of us.

Healing Caves of Nevada

By Bernyce Barlow

Tucked away in Nevada's Comstock Historical District in Lyon County are three mystical caves, set high off the basin floor on top of a thrust of basalt. Protected only by their anonymity and private property, these caves form one of the most spectacular petroglyph sites in the west. Starting about one-third up the height of the basalt, peckings of big horn sheep, suns, circles, horned toads, snakes, hunting symbols, lizards, birds, and clan markings begin to appear, becoming more prevalent the higher up you climb. There are also a number of figures of medicine men with bird-like feet and hands, intricately pecked into the rocks.

In addition to the peckings, there is an enchanted gallery of painted artwork, done in orange ochre, near the entrance of the caves. Ochre is a regional mineral that was used as a paint thousands of years ago by the people of the Desert Culture. The rock paintings depict sheep, mountains, and important clan and migrational symbols. Located in one cave there is an ochre lizard painted on the inner wall directly over the entrance. The figure is extremely clear. Another cave entrance painting is less defined, weathered by centuries of elements. It may be a bird. Further into the caves, the color of the walls is jet from hundreds of fires. This jet may be covering other paintings that once existed, but have since been blackened. The inner caves are not large; a five-foot person could perhaps stand in portions of two of them. They are in height, at least, more befitting to the coyotes, porcupines, and pack rats whose nests sit in the shallower corners.

Above the caves is a high mesa, with game trails leading down a steep slope. The tableland is ablaze with desert color, and medicine plants are abundant there. Sun-colored lichen cling to steppe boulders, and wildflowers bloom profusely, even in summer, which is an oddity for the Great Basin region.

On the back side of the outcrop are Chinese characters, probably left by Chinese coolies, or priests, from the 1700s. Also from this time period are some elaborate markings belonging to miners, including

names, dates, and in one instance, a meticulously pecked American flag.

With so many petroglyphs and paintings to decipher, one could become overwhelmed with all the information recorded at the site. Sacred centers are just that, however, sacred, and what you need to know will be shown to you if you are focused. In the beginning our fascination with this site revolved around questions involving the identification of who had been there and why. Some answers were soon revealed. A pecking of Spider Woman on a rock below the entrance to the caves was discovered, then another on the mesa. Spider Woman is undeniably Hopi. From this point on, part of the puzzle of the caves was taking a form, a picture, if you will, of holy history. But it was also apparent that many people had visited this site; Paiute, Washoe, and others, leaving their records etched in stone, each with their own stories to tell and colorful traditions. The Washoe left figures of shamans performing ceremonies, and pictures of the big horn sheep symbolizing healing power. Some peckings were ancient, others newer, but by studying the area it was apparent a steady stream of people had been there and left their marks.

Spectacular recordings depict clan markings and power symbols for healing.

Petroglyphs, old style scratchings, paintings, and peckings have an interesting life span. Because of the nature of their application upon stone, they change in color and mineral composition by leaching certain elements over hundreds of thousands of years. It is this

change that allows researchers to evaluate the approximate time of the origin of the recordings, similar to how rings on a tree can reveal its age. The rock art at the cave site dates back 500 to 10,000 years, and research is ongoing.

Some of the earliest recordings at the site are scratches in the shapes of circles and lines on the outlying boulders. As time went on, the rock art at the site became more intricate and involved. Tribal symbols developed and stories were drawn telling of events. Later, star charts and celestial signs became a part of the Desert Culture's recordings as the people mapped the heavens. These too can be found at the site.

Unraveling the mystery of this site is like putting together a puzzle whose pieces are strewn across the basin floor. It is both a challenge and a joy. Of course, there are many levels of study here. The petroglyphs only give us a hint as to the healing character of the spirit of the place.

Then, there is the electrical energy of the formation. The last time I visited the caves I was joined by two representatives from the Stewart Indian Museum. None of us were able to sleep after spending a few hours at the site, a phenomena I had previously encountered there. The center is a knockout wellspring of energy patterns that super-charge the mind, body, and soul. A place where visions are made!

There is a handful of people who are working on a way to protect these caves and their untold treasures. It's early in the game, but things look promising. In the meantime, I will work on documenting, deciphering, and translating the site with a "little help from my friends," in order to reconstruct as much of the picture as can be gathered. It is something I am looking forward to!

THE WILD MAN

BY KEN JOHNSON

Lately, we've all heard a lot about "the Wild Man within," though most of us may not be too certain who he is and what he's all about. Men tend to be curious, but shy, as if they're not quite certain they really have a Wild Man in there (must be some other guy's Wild Man, not mine). Feminists regard him with suspicion, as if they're not convinced this hairy howler will be inclined to play the Goddess' sweet little baby boy (that mocking smile and those crazy eyes have a rebellious look to them, don't they?).

BUT WHO IS THE WILD MAN, REALLY?

In Babylonian mythology, he puts an appearance as Enkidu, who lives outdoors like an animal, and is covered with hair; he becomes the best friend of the hero Gilgamesh, a faithful and reliable companion. In ancient Greece, he appears as Pan, the goat god who roams the woods in a state of sexual arousal and perpetual intoxication. The earliest known incarnation of the Tarot Fool was a Wild Man. In medieval England, the best-known Wild Man is Robin Hood, who, like Pan, lives in the woods and who scoffs at society's rules.

Though the Wild Man loves the woods, you can't find him just by taking a camping trip with a well-mannered bunch of New Age guys who feel daring when they beat a few taps on a drum. A Wild Man is at his best in nature, where he doesn't have to follow all those rules and regulations, but he exists in urban men as well. In a way, Wild

Man is an attitude—and not necessarily a proper one. Here's how you can tell.

When Civilized Man feels nagged by his family, he retreats to the garage with his tail between his legs to drown his sorrows in power tools. Wild Man just laughs, turns up the stereo, and dances to his own tune like some kind of a nut.

Civilized Man lives by the clocks; Wild Man regards clocks as excellent targets for his slingshot.

Civilized Man represses his anger, his sexuality, and his inherent craziness with a schedule and a tie; Wild Man revels in sex, dreams of kicking the boss's behind, and acts silly when he's alone outdoors.

Though the Wild Man's behavior may frequently seem bizarre and not at all polite, women shouldn't be afraid of him (and neither should men), for it's not the Wild Man who drives men to violence or despair; it's the absence of the Wild Man that causes all that pain, frustration, and general imbalance. Without his antlers, his badge of arousal, and his ticket to ecstasy, a man just isn't a man.

THE WITCH'S PYRAMID

BY JIM GARRSION

The Witch's Pyramid is a traditional teaching for successful magical practice. Each side of the Pyramid is a gift from one of the four quarters. By bringing these four elements into balance, our efforts at making changes in our lives will be more successful. This teaching has been passed down for a long time, and consists of bits and pieces drawn from Gnosticism, Qabalah, and other esoteric systems. The four sides of the Pyramid form a foundation from which we can climb toward the fifth—the Spirit/Akasha, and the realm of the gods.

TO KNOW

Quiet your mind and find yourself. Who are you? What do you bring to the world? Why are you here? What path do you follow? Who do you want to be? Every answer brings a hundred more questions into being. Cultivate doubt, if you have the courage, and question everything. Especially, question yourself. Wisdom begins when you realize that you know less than you thought, that we really know very little. But we can learn. To walk the Path of the Wise is to love learning, to defend truth and to teach by actions, not mere words. The most profound statements are sometimes made without words. This is the gift of Air, and reflects the Qabalistic world of Atziluth.

TO DARE

Do you have the courage to look deep within yourself? Can you accept the responsibility you have only begun to feel? Will you falter or will you pass through the veil? Can you surrender the lies and ego-poison of the old life you once knew? Can you abandon the outworn and take up the Great Work? Are you brave enough of heart and soul to face the screaming emptiness which lurks deep within each of us, and to pass that threshold unto the life that awaits you beyond? Better to thrust yourself upon the tip of the blade before you than to pass this portal falsely, or with wrong intent. This is the gift of Fire, and reflects the Qabalistic world of Briah.

TO WILL

This is the cornerstone of true magical practice—right action and the responsibility for one's words and deeds. The most ancient secret of the most powerful magic known to mortal kind is hidden within this one word: Will. There are no excuses when every action, or inaction, is decided by the choices and responses of our own selves. Discipline is not punishment, nor is structure restriction, save to those self-imprisoned. All things change, Nothing lasts forever, such is the nature of life. This is the gift of Water, and reflects the Qabalistic world of Yetzirah.

TO REMAIN SILENT

We must endure to succeed. All things pass, but it is within our power to determine how we shall pass through our time. We are truly known by those things we bring about. Change is the only constant. What came before us will come after us. There will be a harvest for every seed spilled or planted, after its own fashion, in its own way. The wheel turns and the tides wash away the residues of the past, that a new future can take root within the fertile soil of all who have come before. This is the gift of Earth, and reflects the Qabalistic world of Assiah.

Magical Study Aids

By Silver RavenWolf

At some point in our lives we all have to buckle down and study. Whether it be for a high school exam or a part of your master's degree, you can't get away from those tense hours of mental application.

According to the learning behavior people, you study best in short bursts. Your retention capability is better when you study ten minutes, then break. Another trick for memory retention is to pick a special object and set it on the desk while you study. When it is time for recall (such as a test) carry the object with you and place it on the test table. Of course, you would need to choose something like an unusual eraser, a pen, or pencil, as most teachers will not permit you to have junk lying all over your desk when taking the test. My teenage daughter, Echo, has come up with several magical tips for studying:

- Empower and dress a white candle to bring you clarity of thought. Burn it while studying.

- Choose a favorite incense and burn it while studying. Carry a stick of the incense with you when taking a test. Right before the test, roll the incense in your fingers. The smell of the incense on your hands will help you to recall those needed answers.

- Use runes to help you study. Doodle them on your notebook while memorizing long passages. Later, the sight of the rune will help you to recall the information as well as bring its magical application to bear.

- Do deep breathing exercises before you begin to study, and at every break. Ground and center at the end of each exercise.

- Magic your books to bring knowledge and understanding to you. See them in your mind as an opportunity to abundance.

- Use positive self-talk and hypnotherapy techniques, such as goal programming, to improve your overall class standing and keep your self-esteem intact.

- Learn to become what you are studying. If you are reading about the Saxons, visualize life at that time. If you are studying biology, see yourself as the organism. If you are studying math, move into the equation with your mind. Studying is fun and easy using this technique.

- Learn to reward yourself for studying. Take a break and drink a soda, or go for a walk and enjoy the evening air. Pick up a favorite magazine and read an article or two. If you learn to reward yourself for your hard work, studying will be much easier.

Talocan, the Aztec Underworld of Dreams

By Marguerite Elsbeth

The Nahuat Indians of central Mexico, descendants of the Aztecs, say that although everything on Earth exists in the underworld as well, we cannot see it with ordinary sight. It is too dark. This is why Talocan, the Aztec underworld, is thought to be a great flower of darkness. The Aztec people believe that we can journey to Talocan, the "Most Holy Earth," in dreams.

The Aztec witch, or *naoalli*—a shape shifter, a healer, and a wise person—is the one who dreams in Talocan. However, before the Witch undertakes a journey, many offerings are made to the spirits. Cigars and cigarettes are a must, as the Nahuat believe that the smoke of the tobacco plant is sacred. Flowers, candles, fresh tortillas, *aguardiente,* or cane alcohol, and many heartfelt prayers are also important if the Witch is to properly beseech the spirits of Talocan for aid. These offerings are left at the entrances of caves, streams, pools, sinkholes or wells, which, to the peoples of Mesoamerica, are mythical points of origin, as well as doorways in and out of Talocan.

Once inside, the *naoalli* may journey north to the Cave of the Winds and the Land of the Dead, or east to the Water Place, the Great Sea. He or she may travel south to the Land of Heat, or west to the House of Women in the Place of the Sun. Sometimes the business of healing the sick and saving souls takes the Witch to the center of the flower, the true heart of Talocan.

There are many different deities and spirits living in Talocan.

- Water Woman, the Lady of the Eastern Waters.

- Wind Woman, the Lady of the Winds of the North.

- The "water ones," spirits of Talocan living in every pool and stream of Central Mexico.

- The "water keepers," who release waters of streams, waterfalls and springs.

- The "hill heart ones," who reside in caves and mountain shrines, embodying the hills.

- The "lightning ones," who can live anywhere, but generally reside in the Cave of the Winds.

- The Aztec deities, saints and virgins, who live in the sky.

The Nahuats do not openly discuss their beliefs about the underworld with outsiders, but if they are asked about it in their own language, their eyes may light up and they may answer, *"Ticmati ipan in talocan"* (Ah, you know the underworld).

BIBLIOGRAPHY

Knab, Timothy J. *A War of Witches: A Journey into the Underworld of the Contemporary Aztecs.* San Francisco: Harper Collins Publishers, 1995.

HONORING THE RESTING PLACES OF LOVED ONES

BY EDAIN MCCOY

Adorning the final resting places of loved ones is a custom that has been practiced since ancient times, and in many cultures it is still done at designated points in the year, when the spirits of the dead are deemed to be roaming in the world of the living.

Most traditional grave offerings have roots in a Pagan past, and are symbolic of the eternal cycle of life, death and rebirth. Many speak of ancient reincarnation beliefs. The wreath, sometimes adorned with flowers, is one such item. A perfect circle with no beginning and no end, it represents the wheel of life; the ever-turning cycle of birth, death, and regeneration on which we all spin.

Lanterns, candles, or other light sources are sometimes offered. These symbolize illumination of truth, and a wish to light the pathway of the spirits as they travel between worlds.

Bowls and urns, which likely held food or wine, have been found in ancient burial sites. Providing sustenance for the deceased is still practiced in Paganism today, when feasts or libations are offered to spirits on certain holidays or during specific rituals. Modern food offerings usually include apples or eggs. The apple is the symbol of eternal life in the Celtic traditions, and the egg is an ancient token of new life or of life renewed.

Items of protection are also offered to the dead by way of grave offerings. This may be something as simple as a protective stone or pentacle, or a flower or oil. Over time, folklore has taken these items, once meant to offer protection to the soul as it journeyed to new adventures, and turned them into items of protection for the living, to guard them from the marauding spirit of the one who is buried. Modern Pagans might occasionally offer mirrors, which can be used magically as portals between worlds. Mirrors express their desire that the soul escape the grave, or any other earthly bonds which tie it to the physical world, so that it may move onward.

Fresh flowers are the most frequently seen grave offerings today, and are used in many religions and cultures. Archaeologists have found many neolithic gravesites containing fossilized flowers, which they believe to symbolize the spring and rebirth.

Masks make excellent grave offerings, and death masks, either cast from the face of the deceased or crafted as a representation of a wish for the departed, are still used in many cultures, including Africa, South America, and Polynesia. These are best made from substances like wood, or food which will decompose and become part of the Earth again. Avoid plastics, which will be around longer than the grave itself.

The anointing of graves with perfumes or precious oils is a very, very old practice whose precise meaning is unclear today. It may have been done to offer homage to the deceased spirit, to protect or purify the gravesite, or in preparation for a death ritual. Olive oil was commonly used for this task in the ancient Middle East, and perfumes made of native oils were, and in some cases still are, used in Africa and the Caribbean. Modern Pagans can choose from a wide variety of essential oils with a long history of use in death rituals and spirit contact, such as olive, jasmine, patchouli, rosemary, or tuberose.

Whatever way you chose to honor the resting place of your loved ones, paying tribute to their graves links us with magical people of generations past, who saw their burial grounds as halfway points between the worlds of the living and the dead. By remembering them we forge our bonds with our Pagan past, and light our own pathways to the Otherworld.

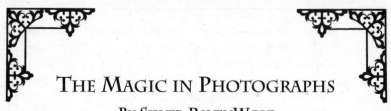

THE MAGIC IN PHOTOGRAPHS

BY SILVER RAVENWOLF

One of the most enjoyable evenings I've spent with my circle sisters centered around a special exercise involving ancestral photographs. Before circle night, each of us gathered old photographs of our families. There was one requirement: for a photo to be submitted to the circle, the individual pictured had to be deceased.

After our normal circle work, we brought out the photos. Only one photo was passed around the circle at a time. The owner of the photo could not tell any details about the individual pictured. Each of us wrote down our impressions of the photos on a piece of paper, using our intuition and psychic senses. When the last person put her pencil down, we went around the circle and shared our intuitions. The owner of the photo would tell us if we were right or wrong. After all thoughts had been shared, the owner of the photo told us the life story of the pictured individual.

This little exercise fulfilled several interesting functions. First, we got to know each other better, and enjoyed the spicy snippets of gossip and a few monstrous skeletons. Secondly, we learned to think together as a group mind. Finally, several of us learned to psychometrize old pictures through repeated practice. The trick is to meld your intuition with the impression you receive from the eyes of the individual in the photograph. An added benefit was learning what life was like for individuals separated from us by generations.

Several of the younger women in our group went to great lengths to obtain their photographs. They visited parents and grandparents, asking questions on the history of those pictured. Many had never showed an interest in their personal history before. As a result they not only felt closer with their Craft sisters, they also became enamored with their own family history.

Try sharing old photographs with your friends as a part of a Samhain ritual, then follow up by honoring the dead through verse or magical act.

ANCESTOR CIRCLE

BY JIM GARRISON

I begin in the north. The wind blows cold from the darkness before me. I reach into the veil between our realms and begin to scribe the circle. Icy flickers of something other than shadows move across my hands and arms. By the time I have made the entire circuit around the circle I am enveloped in the energy, a nimbus of aurora-like shimmers and gleams. It is good.

At the center, atop a small wooden box covered with an old blanket, I light the candle I have been using for the past three years for these sorts of things. It sputters, but soon takes light and glows with a soft blue flame in the darkness. I can feel their prescence, sur-rounding my circle, staring at me with eyes I cannot see. I consecrate the space with rainwater, salt, sage, and the candle flame. It is good.

I take my place, facing away from the candle flame, out toward the north, toward the way to the Underworld. It is cold here, but I am not alone, not in this sacred place. I call forth the ancestors, the grandfathers of my grandfathers, those who are still a part of me, they who are still remembered in my blood. They hear me. They too sit in the north, facing toward the other side, facing toward me. It is good.

Our various totems and allies flit about the edges of my vision, some teasing, others sitting in serious poses as though they, too, were in council, Crow picks at some roadkill. I hear the drum of my heart. It beats faster and louder as my vision clears, and I can see the grandfathers more clearly. Each one is unique, spe-cial. They look upon me with kind eyes. What words can suffice at a moment like this? We share visions, images born of sage-smoke and our wills. We share an unspo-ken communication which is of the heart, not the mind. We share silence, and for a time I taste serenity. It is good.

Crow laughs loudly, I shiver and come back to my-self, full of the reason I am alive—something inex-pressable except by the doing. I smile, and arise from the cold floor to close the circle. It is time to get on with life, to go back to the world. It is good.

THE TROLL-TEAR

A CHILDREN'S STORY FOR SAMHAIN

BY D. J. CONWAY

The night was very dark, with a Full Moon hanging in the cloud-filled sky above. The air was crisp with the feel of late Autumn and the doorway between the worlds was wide open. Carved pumpkins sat on the porches of the houses in the little town, and the laughter of children dressed in costumes could be heard from the streets.

It was a sad time for Beth as she climbed the little hill behind her house. In her arms was her cat and friend Smoky, carefully wrapped in his favorite blanket. A little grave was already dug on the hill, waiting, for Smoky had died that day.

"Do you want me to go with you?" Beth's father had asked. "I dug his grave beside MacDougal's at the top of the hill." Beth clearly remembered when their dog MacDougal had died after being hit by a car.

"No, I want to go by myself," she answered.

Beth stopped at the top of the hill and knelt beside the little grave. She carefully laid Smoky's blanket-wrapped form in the earth and covered it with dirt, laying several large rocks on the top . Then she cried and cried.

"Oh, Smoky, I miss you so much!" Beth looked up at the Moon, tears streaming down her cheeks. "Why did you die?"

"It was his time to rejoin the Mother," said a deep, gentle voice in the darkness.

"Who said that?" Beth looked around but saw no one.

"Dying is part of the cycle of life, you know." One of the boulders on the hill stirred into life.

"Who are you?" The moonlight shone down on the little woman, and Beth could see she was not human.

"I'm a troll-wife," said the creature as she came to sit across from Beth. "This is a sad night for both of us, girl. I, too, came to this hill to bury a friend." The troll-wife wiped a crystal tear from her cheek. "The squirrel was very old. Still it makes me sad."

Beth stared at the troll-wife. The little woman was the color of rock in the moonlight, her hair like long strands of dried moss, her bright eyes like shining crystals. She wore a dress woven of oak leaves and tree bark.

"The squirrel and I lived together for a long time," the troll-wife said. "We often talked to your cat when he was hunting here on the hill. Smoky and I were friends. I shall miss him, too." The little woman patted Smoky's grave gently. "Sleep well, little friend. When you are rested, we shall talk together again."

"But he's dead," Beth said, her voice choked with tears.

"Child, this is Samhain. Don't you know the ancient secrets of this sacred time of year?" The troll-wife motioned for Beth to come and sit beside her. "It is true that our friends have gone into a world where we can no longer physically touch them, but the Mother has given us other ways of communicating with them. We can do this any time, but the time of Samhain is the easiest."

"I don't understand how this can be done," Beth said, "or why Samhain makes it easier."

"At this time of year," the troll-wife answered, "the walls between this world and the world of souls and spirits are very thin.

If we are quiet and listen, we can hear our loved ones and they can hear us. We talk, not with spoken words, but with the heart and mind."

"Isn't that just imagination?" Beth looked down at Smoky's grave, tears once more coming into her eyes. "Like my thinking I can feel MacDougal get up on my bed at night like he used to?"

"Sometimes it is, but mostly it is not imagination, only our friends come to see us in their spirit bodies." The troll-wife reached up her hand and patted something Beth couldn't see on her shoulder. "Like my friend the raven. He is here now."

Beth looked hard and saw a thin form of hazy moonlight on the troll-wife's shoulder. "I've seen something like that at the foot of my bed where MacDougal used to sleep," she whispered. "I thought I was dreaming." She jumped as something nudged her arm. When she looked down, nothing was there.

The troll-wife smiled. "Close your eyes and think of Mac-Dougal," she said. "He has been waiting a long time for you to see him."

Beth closed her eyes and, at once, the form of her little dog came into her mind. His tail wagged with happiness. She felt a wave of love come from him, and she sent her love back. Then she felt the dog lie down against her leg.

"Can I do this with Smoky?" Beth asked.

"Not yet," the troll-wife answered. "He needs to sleep a while and rest. Then he will come to you. This gives Smoky time to adjust to his new world and you time to grieve for him. It is not wrong to grieve, but we must not grieve forever."

"I never thought of it that way," Beth said. "It's kind of like they moved away, and we can only talk to them on the phone."

"It is this way with all creatures, not just animals." The troll-wife stood up and held out a hand to Beth. "Will you join me, human girl? Although I buried my friend squirrel this night, I still must dance and sing to all my friends and ancestors who have gone on their journey into the other world. For this is a time to honor the ancestors."

Beth joined the troll-wife in the ancient slow troll dances around the top of the little hill in the moonlight. She watched quietly while the troll-wife called out troll-words to the four di-

rections, words Beth couldn't understand. Deep in her heart the girl
felt the power of the strange
words and knew they were
given in honor and love by
the little troll-wife.

When the troll-wife
was finished with her ritual, she hugged Beth.
"Go in peace, human
child," she said. "And
remember what I have
told you about the ancient
secret of Samhain."

"I will," Beth answered. "Will I ever see you again?"

"Whenever the Moon is Full, I will be here," the little troll-
wife said. "And especially at Samhain."

"I wish I had something to give you." Beth hugged the little woman. "You have taught me so much." She felt the tears
come to her eyes again.

"Let us exchange tears for our lost friends." The troll-wife
reached up a rough finger and caught a tear as it fell from
Beth's eye. The tear glistened on her finger. The troll-wife gently touched her finger to her cloak, and Beth's tear shone there
like a diamond in the moonlight.

Beth reached up carefully and caught one of the troll-wife's
tears as it slid down her rough cheek. It turned into a real crystal in her hand.

"Remember the secret of Samhain, and remember me,"
the troll-wife said softly as she disappeared into the darkness.
Beth walked back down the hill, the crystal clutched in her
hand. Her father was waiting for her on the porch.

"Are you all right?" her father asked as he gave Beth a hug.

"I will be," she answered. She opened her hand under the
porch light and saw a perfect, tear-shaped crystal lying there.

"Did you find something?" her father asked.

"A troll-tear," Beth answered, and her father smiled. For he
also knew the little troll-wife and the secret of Samhain.

ASIAN VAMPIRES

BY deTRACI REGULA

When we think of vampires, usually our imaginations conjure up a dark night, ominous bats fluttering through the air, and the silhouette of a Gothic castle suitable for Count Dracula and his pale companions. An Eastern European origin is often suggested for the Lord of the Night, but to find what may be the true origin of the vast vampire lore, we have to travel farther east.

The land of Asia has given birth to many legends of spirits who live off of the vitality of the living. While Western lore favors a wolf or a bat as the animal incarnation of a vampiric spirit, in China the overwhelmingly popular choice is the fox. Fox-spirits are considered common, especially in the province of Shantung, near the sacred mountain called Tai-Shan. To placate them, "fox-spirit-towers" were scattered across the countryside, where the fox spirits were believed to dwell. Only a few of these towers still exist. Some are to honor playful, benevolent fox spirits, but others are erected in the hopes that by honoring them, the dreaded, malevolent *hu-li ching* will leave the area in peace. These spirits sometimes attach themselves to Taoist monasteries, preying on novices, possibly because they realize that while the Taoists will do battle with them when necessary, they prefer to let them survive. Taoist exorcists believe in the sanctity of all existence, including "evil" entities. This sometimes results in situations which lead to the death of the fox-spirit's victim, since both victim and fox-spirit are considered to have equal rights to continued existence.

In Japan, shrines and full temples have been erected to these spirits, who drain the vitality from their victims, but who do so in such a pleasant and erotic fashion that their victims almost never dream of anything but complying with their wishes. Unlike their counterparts in China, Japanese fox-shrines and temples are carefully kept up, and the offerings to these spirits continue unabated by modern times. The fox is considered to be the messenger of the Inari, or rice-god, and is present at all of the more than thirty thousand Inari shrines in

present-day Japan. The largest and best-known is the Fushimi Inari shrine near Kyoto, a massive and busy precinct crammed with vendors of fox-related items for offerings or reverence at home. This temple culminates in a hillside tunnel, formed of thousands of sacred tori gates leading to the summit, which is allegedly haunted by fox-spirits.

Another variety of spirit which finds its echo in European myth is the *Ti Mo*, a black blob which emanates from the lid of a coffin. These blobs follow humans, but supposedly do not cause them harm.

The *Nueh Chi Kuei* attack the spinal column and are believed to be the evil spirits behind the debilitating attacks of malaria. Like the consumption-like wasting victims of Western vampires, those afflicted with the *Nueh Chi Kuei* are believed to be able to pass on their condition to those around them.

Forest tree-spirits can also be vampiric, pressing themselves on passersby who then feel a sense of oppression and suffocation. These entities intend to drain their victims of blood, breath, and semen.

Perhaps one reason why many vampiric spirits in the East appear to prefer ingesting sexual fluids, rather than blood, lies in the alchemical sexual mysticism of Taoist and some branches of Tantric Buddhist belief. The proper preservation and mingling of sexual fluids is considered essential to the practice of immortality or, at least, for the dramatic elongation of life. By extension, loss of these precious fluids is believed to contribute to general debility and early death. When an individual is following the prohibitions against

loss of sexual fluids and still seems to be in decline, a supernatural being is suspected of using that individual to obtain nutrients for its own survival.

A typical Chinese vampire is covered with white hair, with eyes glowing like coals and sharp teeth. Vampires are believed to be created when the primitive *p'o* spirit, one of the components of the human soul, is unnaturally strong, and survives after the death of the body, clinging to the bones, especially the skull.

Standard Chinese vampires seem to be relatively easy to dispose of. Burning of the corpse is efficacious, but so is simply removing the lid of the coffin to a place some distance from the box while the vampire is prowling about. The Chinese believe that simple fresh air will ruin this refuge for the vampire, and cause the corpse to decay on its return. To thwart a vampire in the act of returning to its coffin, no holy water is needed—just cast rice, red peas, and bits of iron around the coffin. These are supposed to stop or distract the vampire long enough for it to be captured.

One Chinese vampire didn't stop at collecting blood; this *kiang-shi* (corpse-spectre) decided he preferred his meal "to go" and collected the head of his victim. When the uncorrupted corpse of the vampire was discovered, he still held the head, drained of blood, in his arms. The vampire was dismembered and burned. The wife of the victim, who had originally been held for the beheading of her husband, was released from prison and that corner of the province of Kiangsi returned to normal, at least for a time.

As in the west, religious symbols hold power over the vampire, and the statue of one Buddhist deity called Wei To, the Protector, figures in a vampire tale where the would-be victim, Li Chiu, is awakened from a deep sleep with a warning from Wei To. When a vampire suddenly emerges from a coffin temporarily stored in the temple courtyard, Li pushes a statue of Wei To at the vampire. The startled bloodsucker bites the hard arm of the statue instead and retreats back to its coffin, where it is then destroyed by the priests of the temple.

These stories of Eastern vampires, with their familiar elements of incorruptible corpses, draining of blood and other vital fluids, and

the power of religious symbols, may have come west with the Huns and other invasions. More likely, however, is that inhabitants of the western regions of China were pushed west by these marauding hordes. Migrations of Asian settlers are known to have reached into both Romania and Hungary, two regions where vampire tales are prevalent. Can it be that the original Count Dracula, whose name can be translated as "The Dragon," is a misplaced Chinese spirit?

Recycling Your Jack o' Lantern

By Edain McCoy

B oth magical and non-magical folks know it is best to carve your Samhain-Halloween jack o'lantern at the last possible moment, so the meat will stay fresh long enough to be made into a delicious variety of autumn pies, cakes, and breads. But what do you do with all those pumpkin seeds? Recycle them into catalysts of magic!

The pumpkin is a fruit governed by the element of earth, and because of this association, it shares the magical influences of the earth element: fertility, prosperity, home life, peace, and health.

- Make a fertility talisman by tying up nine pumpkin seeds with a small handful of earth inside a green cloth. The number nine draws on the fertile powers of the moon while the earth is the element of fertility. Charge it with your need, and carry it until you conceive.

- For a talisman of home protection, bury some of the seeds at each corner of your property, or place them in a centrally located planter inside your home. As you bury them, chant a charm invoking the protection of mother earth on your home.

- To evoke prosperity on your purse, take a small glass jar and place some coins inside along with a handful of the dried seeds. Shake the two together while visualizing the earthy element of the seeds increasing your wealth. Keep the jar nearby throughout the year as a reminder of your goal. Shake it occasionally to stir up its magic.

- Carry some of the seeds inside a coin purse or wallet to help attract more money to your coffers. Or keep a single

seed inside your bankbook or checkbook to the same end.

- Make a prosperity talisman by tying up four seeds inside a gold cloth along with a single dollar bill. Place the bundle in your place of employment or under your bed.

- To stop a battle between two people in your household, place two seeds under each person's mattress while visualizing their quarrels being grounded. When the fighting is over, burn or bury the seeds to eliminate the negative energy they have absorbed from the combatants.

- Use the seeds as a catalyst for healing by soaking them overnight in a pan of water until they are soft enough to be threaded with a needle onto heavy thread. This chain of seeds can be charged with healing energy and worn as a necklace or bracelet, or hung up in a bedroom as a healing charm.

- Using visualization and personal contact, invest a small handful of seeds with the energy of an illness. When you feel this has been absorbed by the seeds, burn or bury them to help rid yourself of the disease.

If you have no immediate magical need for pumpkin seeds, they can be preserved by washing them in cool water to remove all the pumpkin meat, then spreading them out on paper towels to dry. When they are dry, but not dried out, spread them out on a cookie sheet and place them in a warm oven, at about 200°F, for 5–10 minutes. Or you can place them between two sheets of wax paper and microwave them on defrost for about 5–7 minutes. Transfer the seeds to a clean, air-tight glass jar for later use.

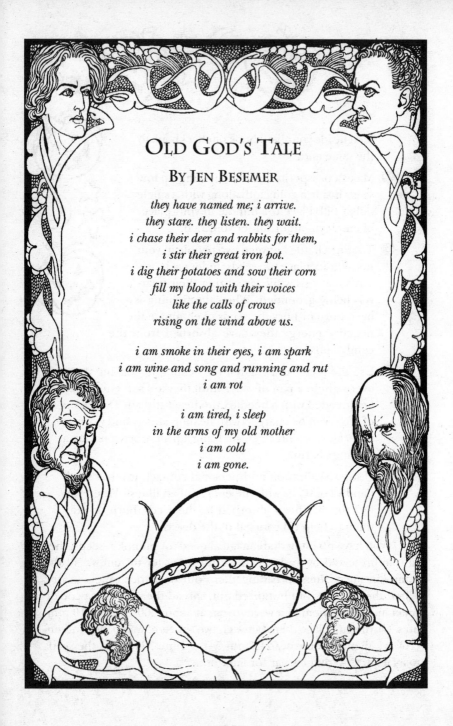

OLD GOD'S TALE

BY JEN BESEMER

they have named me; i arrive.
they stare. they listen. they wait.
i chase their deer and rabbits for them,
i stir their great iron pot.
i dig their potatoes and sow their corn
fill my blood with their voices
like the calls of crows
rising on the wind above us.

i am smoke in their eyes, i am spark
i am wine and song and running and rut
i am rot

i am tired, i sleep
in the arms of my old mother
i am cold
i am gone.

Dark Goddess

By Jen Besemer

Dark Goddess
i love the black bloody one
she who is born anew every month
like a mushroom in dark soil
Hecate Kali Cerridwen Oya
i follow your phases like the wind
along the contours of a cliff
i borrow your feathered cloak
when my own warmth is not enough.

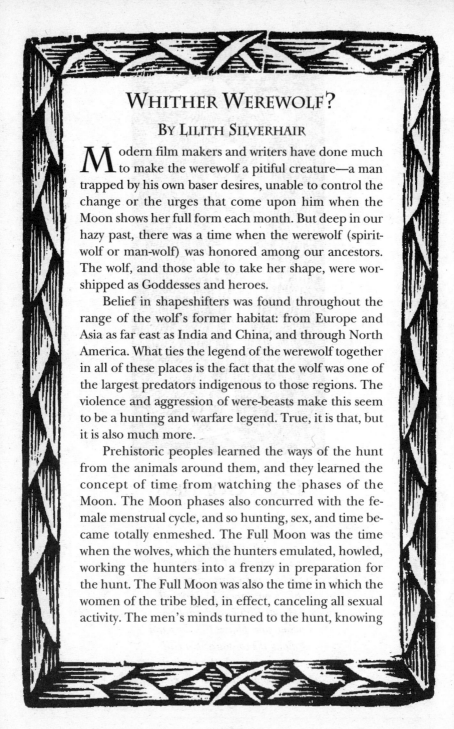

WHITHER WEREWOLF?

BY LILITH SILVERHAIR

Modern film makers and writers have done much to make the werewolf a pitiful creature—a man trapped by his own baser desires, unable to control the change or the urges that come upon him when the Moon shows her full form each month. But deep in our hazy past, there was a time when the werewolf (spirit-wolf or man-wolf) was honored among our ancestors. The wolf, and those able to take her shape, were worshipped as Goddesses and heroes.

Belief in shapeshifters was found throughout the range of the wolf's former habitat: from Europe and Asia as far east as India and China, and through North America. What ties the legend of the werewolf together in all of these places is the fact that the wolf was one of the largest predators indigenous to those regions. The violence and aggression of were-beasts make this seem to be a hunting and warfare legend. True, it is that, but it is also much more.

Prehistoric peoples learned the ways of the hunt from the animals around them, and they learned the concept of time from watching the phases of the Moon. The Moon phases also concurred with the female menstrual cycle, and so hunting, sex, and time became totally enmeshed. The Full Moon was the time when the wolves, which the hunters emulated, howled, working the hunters into a frenzy in preparation for the hunt. The Full Moon was also the time in which the women of the tribe bled, in effect, canceling all sexual activity. The men's minds turned to the hunt, knowing that sexual activity would resume after they had brought enough meat home to supplement the diet of grains and berries the women provided.

It is this circular reasoning that created the association of a female deity concerned with hunting, and in many cultures She was a wolf. Apollo Lycaeus (Wolfish Apollo) was mated to Artemis as the divine Wolf Bitch. The Sabine Goddess Feronia was mother of wolves. Perhaps the most well known of all was Diana, Mistress of The Hunt. Gaulish Diana, under Her totemic name Lupa, "She-Wolf," was mother of wild animals. Young men learned magic and shapeshifting from Her, and She guided and protected them. Her followers' shapeshifting ability followed the Moon phases, and the Moon was another form of the Goddess.

Shapeshifting abilities usually lay within the realm of one person in the tribe, the shaman. It was reasoned that at the moment of death, the animals that the hunters killed took themselves to the spiritual otherworld. For the shamans to "speak" to these animals, so that they could intervene on behalf of humans, the shamans themselves must lose their own bodies and take on the aspects of the animals. And so the first shapeshifters were born.

Down through the years, the werewolf was known in almost every culture. The title of the shaman who held high position in the life of the Slavs was *volkivi*. Variations are the German *volk* (people), and the Russian *vrach* (physician). This indicates that werewolves were healers in wolf masks.

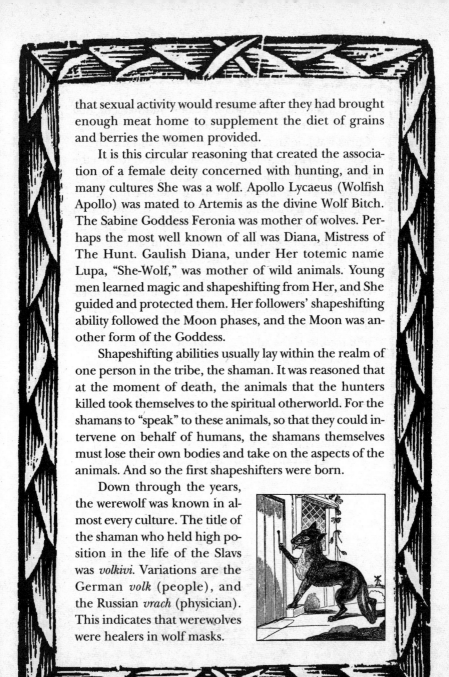

It wasn't until Christianity came on the scene that the werewolf became the demonic creature he is today. Christ was known as the Lamb of God, and the enemy of the lamb is, of course, the wolf. The shift toward the imagery of the lamb as Christ led in natural sequence to the wolf as Satanic. The werewolf, whose first meaning in biblical translations was "outlaw," devolved from that into "ravening wolf," as in Matthew 7:15, "Beware of false prophets, which come to you in sheep's clothing, but inwardly they are ravening wolves."

And so the werewolf descended throughout the centuries; from deity to demi-god, from shaman to satanic. The noble wolf, whose only crime was to howl at the Moon and teach awkward humans to hunt, was demonized by those who would rather be led by a lamb than a true king, or queen, of beasts.

BIBLIOGRAPHY

Douglas, Adam. *The Beast Within: A History of the Werewolf.* New York: Avon Books, 1992.

Walker, Barbara G. *The Women's Encyclopedia of Myths and Secrets.* New York: HarperCollins, 1993.

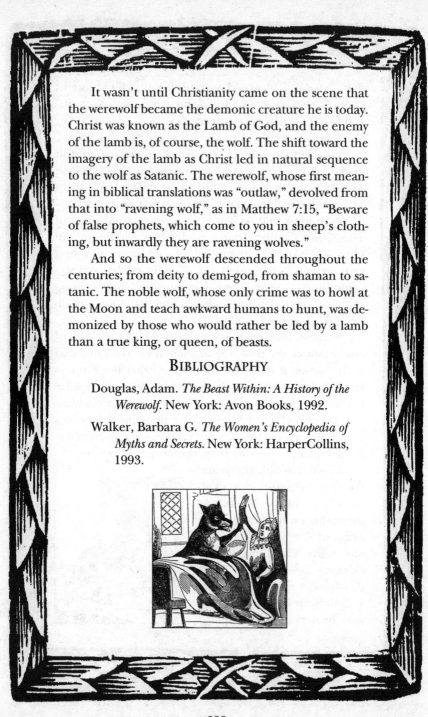

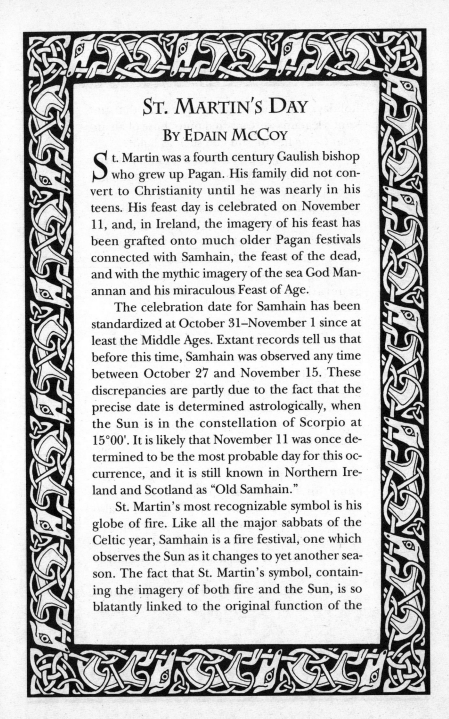

ST. MARTIN'S DAY

BY EDAIN MCCOY

St. Martin was a fourth century Gaulish bishop who grew up Pagan. His family did not convert to Christianity until he was nearly in his teens. His feast day is celebrated on November 11, and, in Ireland, the imagery of his feast has been grafted onto much older Pagan festivals connected with Samhain, the feast of the dead, and with the mythic imagery of the sea God Manannan and his miraculous Feast of Age.

The celebration date for Samhain has been standardized at October 31–November 1 since at least the Middle Ages. Extant records tell us that before this time, Samhain was observed any time between October 27 and November 15. These discrepancies are partly due to the fact that the precise date is determined astrologically, when the Sun is in the constellation of Scorpio at 15°00'. It is likely that November 11 was once determined to be the most probable day for this occurrence, and it is still known in Northern Ireland and Scotland as "Old Samhain."

St. Martin's most recognizable symbol is his globe of fire. Like all the major sabbats of the Celtic year, Samhain is a fire festival, one which observes the Sun as it changes to yet another season. The fact that St. Martin's symbol, containing the imagery of both fire and the Sun, is so blatantly linked to the original function of the

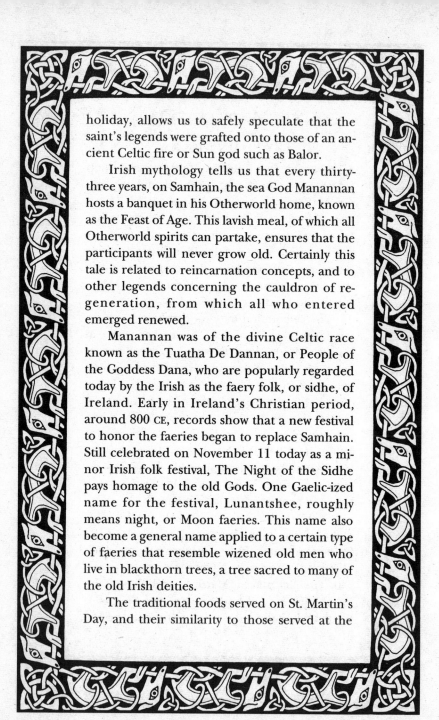

holiday, allows us to safely speculate that the saint's legends were grafted onto those of an ancient Celtic fire or Sun god such as Balor.

Irish mythology tells us that every thirty-three years, on Samhain, the sea God Manannan hosts a banquet in his Otherworld home, known as the Feast of Age. This lavish meal, of which all Otherworld spirits can partake, ensures that the participants will never grow old. Certainly this tale is related to reincarnation concepts, and to other legends concerning the cauldron of regeneration, from which all who entered emerged renewed.

Manannan was of the divine Celtic race known as the Tuatha De Dannan, or People of the Goddess Dana, who are popularly regarded today by the Irish as the faery folk, or sidhe, of Ireland. Early in Ireland's Christian period, around 800 CE, records show that a new festival to honor the faeries began to replace Samhain. Still celebrated on November 11 today as a minor Irish folk festival, The Night of the Sidhe pays homage to the old Gods. One Gaelic-ized name for the festival, Lunantshee, roughly means night, or Moon faeries. This name also become a general name applied to a certain type of faeries that resemble wizened old men who live in blackthorn trees, a tree sacred to many of the old Irish deities.

The traditional foods served on St. Martin's Day, and their similarity to those served at the

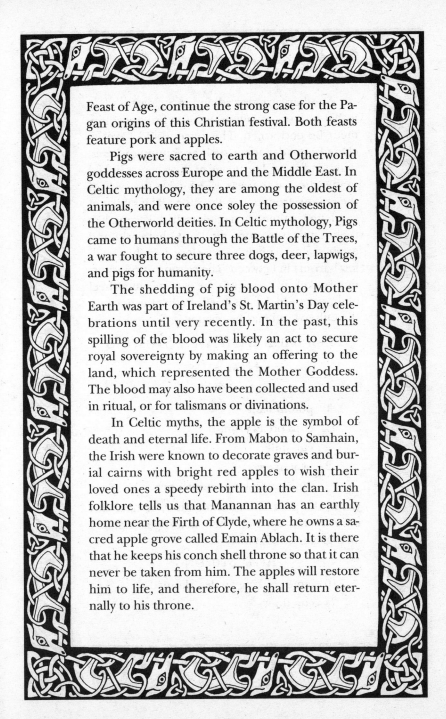

Feast of Age, continue the strong case for the Pagan origins of this Christian festival. Both feasts feature pork and apples.

Pigs were sacred to earth and Otherworld goddesses across Europe and the Middle East. In Celtic mythology, they are among the oldest of animals, and were once soley the possession of the Otherworld deities. In Celtic mythology, Pigs came to humans through the Battle of the Trees, a war fought to secure three dogs, deer, lapwigs, and pigs for humanity.

The shedding of pig blood onto Mother Earth was part of Ireland's St. Martin's Day celebrations until very recently. In the past, this spilling of the blood was likely an act to secure royal sovereignty by making an offering to the land, which represented the Mother Goddess. The blood may also have been collected and used in ritual, or for talismans or divinations.

In Celtic myths, the apple is the symbol of death and eternal life. From Mabon to Samhain, the Irish were known to decorate graves and burial cairns with bright red apples to wish their loved ones a speedy rebirth into the clan. Irish folklore tells us that Manannan has an earthly home near the Firth of Clyde, where he owns a sacred apple grove called Emain Ablach. It is there that he keeps his conch shell throne so that it can never be taken from him. The apples will restore him to life, and therefore, he shall return eternally to his throne.

Another curious tradition of St. Martin's Day is that no work entailing the use of rotary equipment be performed. This once would have included everyday items such as spinning wheels, mills, and carts. The image of the wheel is linked to the wheel of the year, which takes the cycle of the seasons from one to the other. The sabbat of Samhain is a time when modern Irish Pagans, like their Celtic ancestors, see the Otherworld and earth realms as being very close together, with few barriers in between. The ceasing of rotary action is likely in respect to the ever-turning wheel of the year, which halts briefly so that the doors to the Otherworld may be opened.

Ham Balls With Apple Stuffing

Ham Balls

1   pound pork
1   pound ham
1½ cups bread crumbs
¾   cup milk
2   beaten eggs
    Pinch marjoram and pepper

Grind the pork and ham together, or have this done by your butcher. Then, in a large bowl, mix all ingredients together.

Apple Stuffing

10 large cooking apples, skinned
¼   cup flour

½   cup white sugar

½   cup corn syrup

½   teaspoon cinnamon

⅛   teaspoon nutmeg

Chop the apples into pieces about 1" square, making sure no seeds or cores are used. Mix all ingredients together and set aside.

To Prepare:

Take a handful of the pork mixture and make a patty about six inches across and about 1½" thick. Place this in the bottom of a large roasting pan. Spoon up some of the apple mixture and place in the center of the patty. Taking care not to allow any of the apple mixture to escape, pull up the side of the patty and form it into a ball, enclosing the apples. When all the pork has been used, place the balls in an oven which has been preheated to 350°F. Bake for 1½–2 hours.

To Make the Sauce:

Heat the following ingredients together in a small saucepan and pour over the balls about 30 minutes before they are finished baking.

½   cup orange juice

½   cup apple cider vinegar

1   cup brown sugar

1   tablespoon dried mustard

1   teaspoon powered cloves

1   cup water

Pinch allspice

A New Twist on a Wiccan Protection Ball

By D. J. Conway

Witch balls have been around for centuries, but it is near-ly impossible (and very costly) to buy one. These silvery balls were once common fixtures in windows, particularly in England, where they were said to repel evil thoughts and curs-es. Most Pagans don't feel they can spend several hundred (if not more) dollars to purchase such a ball, even if they could find one, but there is no reason you can't make one.

You will need a clear glass ball or Yule ornament with an opening in one end. I don't recommend fishing floats because you need to be able to get paint and thread inside the ball. If the glass ball has some kind of design, choose one you like or one you can change with further decoration. You will also need a bottle of silver paint found in hobby stores, a few drops of frankincense or patchouli oil, a spool of red thread, and a pair of scissors.

Cover your working space with newspaper to protect against spills. Take the metal cap off the ornament. Carefully pour a little of the silver paint inside the ball and swish it around until the inside is completely covered with the silver. Set it aside to dry.

When the paint is totally dry, cut the red thread into three-inch lengths. Carefully poke this thread into the open end of the ball. Continue cutting and putting the thread into the ball until the ball is nearly full. Put in a few drops of the oil. Then put the end back on the ornament. If it has no end, seal it with candle wax.

When you hang the protection ball, chant:

Symbol of the Moon, symbol of the Lady divine,
Reject all negativity, defend this home (car), me and mine.

This protection ball can be hung in the window of your home or in your car. Any negative thoughts or ill-wishes directed against you are reflected back to the sender. I have painted such balls on the outside with appropriate designs and hung them in groups of threes. For spring, decorate them with flowers; for summer, paint butterflies and birds; for Samhain, use bats and ghosts. They can be put onto wreaths without anyone being the wiser, or make them part of a dried flower arrangement. Programmed for protection, these little witch balls do a very good job.

BIRTH PRAYER

BY JIM GARRISON

G oddess of Life and Death and Life again, you whose loving kiss rekindles our memories of the Summerland and whose embrace is the last and first thing we ever know— I call upon you, in this place, at this time, to watch over this mother and to bless this child to be. You through whom all things are possible, I ask for your assistance with this birth; comfort the mother and protect this unborn child. In all your many names, I ask for your blessing upon this.

Father, Lord of the Gates of Death and Life, I ask for your blessing upon this new life we seek to bring into the world. God of Light and Darkness, who dances in the twilight, grant this child and its mother the strength to make this first journey into the world. Bless this mother and child with your protection during this very special time. Grant me, as a father now myself, the wisdom and patience I will need to raise a child to know your presence, and to choose their own path in freedom ,and in love and in trust. Guide my hands, my words, and my deeds that I may shape this new life with integrity, honor, and compassion. This I ask in humility and sincerity, oh God of my ancestors, great one of many names and many places. So Mote It Be.

A Solitary Full Moon Ritual

By Jack Veasey

You will need: Kitty litter in the cauldron; a red candle (to represent the Mother); and an herbal oil appropriate to banishing; two other herbs appropriate to banishing; and a silver coin to offer to the Mother. (If you substitute olive oil for an appropriate essential oil, use three herbs instead of two.) You will also need slips of paper, and a pen with black ink. You may also have your divining tool on hand if you wish to do divination.

Ground and center, devote your altar, cast the circle, call the quarters, perform a working salute, and raise power with "A Verse to Raise Power" (see page 2). Invoke the Mother Battle Goddess, Nemain, saying:

O, Nemain, Goddess of Battle,
Mother of our inner power;
Leather-clad Queen of the field,
Upon your blazing steed whose hooves we hear as thunder;
Ride now in our defense against our enemies,
Who hold us back and down. Oh, Matriarch of Wars,
Our life on Earth, too, has become a battle,
With forces without and within.

Rise up and come between us
And those mortals who won't understand us,
Who stand between us and success,
Who persecute us for our goodness,
Who lay blame anywhere but in the mirror.

Raise up your shield, that they may see their own
Sad faces; that they may feel the sting
Of their own anger; that they be forced
To face their wounds and heal.
Let their eyes no longer fall on us
Till they have seen the truth.

And ride within us, too, Great Mother,
Through the dark terrain behind our eyes

Where illness feeds, where habits dance stale steps;
Where history repeats itself, and prophecies
Of doubt doom our endeavors.
Ride through that terrain and wield your spears,
Slicing all cobwebs from the scene;
Set in your wake a purifying Fire
That will not harm but merely clean.

Fill us with Your fire, Great Mother;
Let its heat drive out the inner enemy
And all his many hidden weapons.
Send down your army of ravens
To pick away the dead debris
That blocks our path to victory.

Harm none, Great one, but come and set us free
From each named negativity!

Anoint the red candle, rubbing oil from the middle to the ends, and energize it by pressing it between your thumb and forefinger until your fingers start to throb, while concentrating on banishing the negative forces from your life. Place the candle in the cauldron and light it. Sprinkle banishing herbs around the base of the candle, and say:

Paper will give way to flame
Let no trace of scar remain.
Fire create and fire destroy;
Burn the wall that blocks out joy.
Fly to the Mother, Fiery Bird;
Dissolve my link with this foul word.

Write the names of things you wish to banish on slips of paper, visualizing yourself already free of them. Let go of your negative attachment to them; let go of their power over you. Ignite the slips in the flame of the candle, and, as you do, imagine the connection between you and the things you've written down going up in flames and being totally burned away. Let the burning slips fall into the mix in the cauldron. As they burn, say:

Truth released from word by flame,
I am free of what I've named!
Mother Fire, bright and hot,
Let what I've named touch me not!
May this spell not reverse
Nor place upon me any curse!

Sit for a few moments meditating, visualizing yourself as free of all negative influences. Say:

Mighty Mother, thank Thee for thine aid
In love and trust, this offering is made.

Pass the silver coin three times through the flame of the candle, then drop or push it into the mixture of the cauldron. Now is an appropriate time for divination, if you wish. Afterward, perform the reverse salute, dismiss the quarters, and open the circle. Leave the candle burning in the cauldron until it is all gone. Take the mixture and bury it off of your property.

A Wreath for All Seasons

By D. J. Conway

Wreaths are usually hung only during the Yule season, but there is no reason that, with a little imagination, you cannot make a wreath for any season of the year. You can give a wreath as an unusual gift, and making wreaths is just plain fun on a dreary day. The foundation of a wreath can be a wooden embroidery hoop, a wire from a lamp shade base, a chicken wire and spagnum moss base from the florist's, a vine wreath from a hobby shop, a styrofoam ring, or even a doughnut-shape cut out of cardboard. Cardboard and styrofoam should be spray painted. Make sure you have the correct paint for styrofoam, or the foam will melt. You will probably want to wind ribbon or yarn around the embroidery hoop and the lamp-wire. Other items you will probably need are florists' wire or fine wire from a hobby shop to tie objects on the wreath; string for the same purpose; and a small glue gun or appropriate glue for non-tieable decorations.

For a Yule wreath, you can use a vine wreath, or wire wrapped with green ribbon, artificial or natural fir boughs, or tinsel rope. Wrap tiny boxes with colorful paper and glue to the wreath. Add a few sprigs of holly and mistletoe. If you use mistletoe, remove all the berries; these are toxic to children and pets! You can also spray little cones in gold and silver and glue them to the wreath. Another unusual Yule wreath can be made from newspaper and a styrofoam ring. Cut out four-inch squares of newspaper with pinking scissors to give the edges a decorative effect. Place two squares together, then pinch the center to form a kind of "flower." Wrap one end of a three-inch-long piece of thin wire around the end of the "flower" and poke the tail end through the styrofoam, bending it back on each side to prevent it from coming loose. Continue adding these "flowers" until the wreath is completely covered. When finished, spray paint the

334

wreath in green, gold, or silver. If you want a variegated effect, spray the wreath green, then lightly spray the edges of the "flowers." Glue on tiny ornaments. Colored tissue paper could also be used instead of the newspaper and paint.

To announce a birthday in the house, you can decorate a ribbon-wrapped wire or vine wreath with tiny stuffed animals, little wrapped boxes, and a ribbon with the person's name on it.

For Ostara, a wreath-base can be hung with decorated eggs. Make a hole in each end of a fresh egg and, holding one end over a bowl, blow out the insides. Allow the eggshell to dry, then decorate. Glue ribbon to the top of each eggshell for hanging. Tiny bunnies and chicks, and even small bunches of artificial flowers can be added.

Another pretty wreath can be made using dried flowers, leaves, and grasses tied to the base with sisal string. To change this wreath for the autumn, add small ears of ornamental corn and little gourds. You can also paint acorns gold or silver and tuck these in among the dried arrangements. You might also attach the heads of dried teasel.

An herbal wreath can be constructed of cinnamon sticks, star anise, and such herbs as bay leaves, sage, and rosemary sprigs. Dried onions and garlic cloves are also nice additions. You can make an unusual kitchen wreath to give as a gift. Simply thread bay leaves on a wire hoop by first carefully making a hole in the center of each leaf. Finish by attaching a little kitchen witch for good luck.

For a baby wreath, wrap a wire base with pink or blue ribbon, or attach bows of these ribbons to a vine wreath. Add small rattles, diaper pins (does anyone use these anymore?), and perhaps even an envelope containing a paper promising the new mother one free evening of babysitting. There really is no limit to what you can do with wreath decorations. Turn loose your imagination, and get your children involved too. This can be a fun family project.

THE FESTIVAL OF THE HAG

BY RHIANNON CAMERON

Hagmenai (Hag's Moon) was celebrated on New Year's Eve in Britain up to the nineteenth century. Fires were set ablaze at midnight, which was the beginning of the Celtic day. Tables were laden with special foods, and the savory aromas mingled with the laughter that filled the air. In the flaring light of the fire, there was dancing and singing and joyous celebration. Groups of people held hands and danced in circles and spirals, reaffirming their connection to the eternal cycle.

The word Hag, from the Greek *hagia*, originally meant "holy one," as in *hagios*, sacred. Most likely, this was derived from the ancient Egyptian root word *heg*, intelligence. Hekat, "vessel of female wisdom," the name of one of the oldest Egyptian Goddesses, was derived from *heg*, as was the name of Hecate, the oldest Greek version of the triform Goddess.

It is interesting to note that the sacred Stone of Scone, which rests beneath the coronation throne in Westminster Abbey, was originally called the Hag of Scone. Medieval legend tells us that this Hag was a Pagan goddess who was turned to stone after being cursed by a missionary of the new religion.

The Stone of Scone casts one's mind back to the time when chieftains and kings were selected by tribal conclaves of elder women and inaugurated over sacred stones. It is said that the stones spoke aloud to proclaim divine acceptance of the new leader.

The ritual of Hagmenai still persists to this day in Scotland. There and in some parts of Northern Ireland, New Year's Eve is called Hogmanay. It is celebrated by the playing of bagpipes, the drinking of whiskey, punch, and hot-pint (hot ale spiced and laced with whiskey). Traditional foods, such as bannock, shortbread, haggis, and Scotch currant buns are eaten. The celebrations go on into the early hours of morning, the next day being a national holiday in Scotland. On the morning of Hogmanay, small groups of children go from door to

door, singing. They are given small gifts, usually a cake. In the Clogher Valley, Northern Ireland, mummers with blackened faces parade around with straw or rabbit skins tied around their legs, and are called Hogmanay men. Cakes are given to them as well.

A bannock is a Scottish and Northern English home-made oatcake or bread. Until this century, bannocks were made for any festive occasion. They are usually oval shaped, and cooked on a griddle. Haggis is a Scots national dish made from the minced heart, liver, and lungs of a sheep, mixed with suet, oatmeal, chopped parsley, and onion. This is seasoned and put into a cleaned sheep's stomach, which is then boiled in salt water. It is served on a large platter, surrounded with mashed turnips and boiled potatoes. Haggis means "hag's dish." Some researchers say that this is a remnant of the prehistoric rite of communion, when women ate the flesh and blood of the dead so that they could be "born again" as new children.

Shortbread was originally a large round cake, notched at the edge, probably a descendant of the Yule bannock, which was notched to symbolize the Sun's rays.

TRADITIONAL SHORTBREAD

1   cup unbleached all-purpose flour
1   cup rice flour
1   cup sugar
2   cups butter
    Milk, if necessary

Mix together the flours and sugar. Work the butter into the flour mixture with your fingers until it is well mixed. If the dough is too crumbly, it can be moistened with milk (use the milk sparingly). Roll dough on floured board to about 3/4" thickness, and cut as desired. (You can cut small shapes, or form the entire recipe into a circle.) Flute the edges and prick all over with a fork. Bake at 350°F for 35-45 minutes until light golden brown.

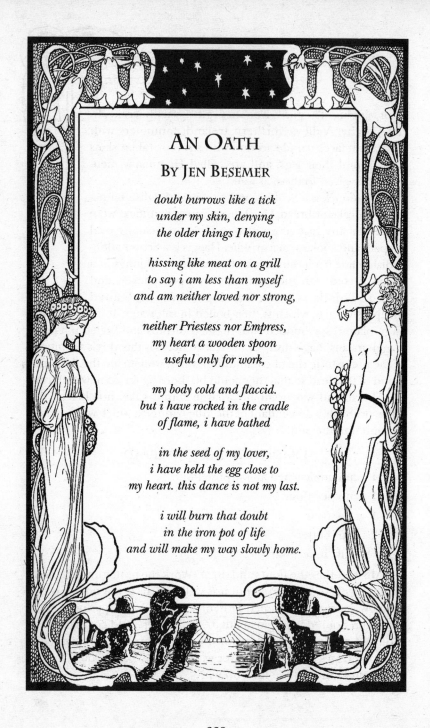

An Oath

By Jen Besemer

doubt burrows like a tick
under my skin, denying
the older things I know,

hissing like meat on a grill
to say i am less than myself
and am neither loved nor strong,

neither Priestess nor Empress,
my heart a wooden spoon
useful only for work,

my body cold and flaccid.
but i have rocked in the cradle
of flame, i have bathed

in the seed of my lover,
i have held the egg close to
my heart. this dance is not my last.

i will burn that doubt
in the iron pot of life
and will make my way slowly home.

DIRECTORY OF
PRODUCTS AND SERVICES

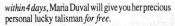

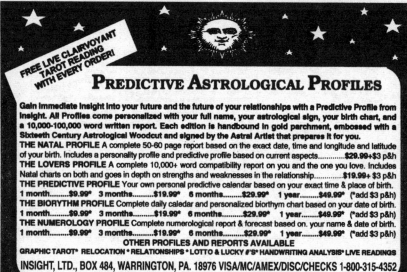

Cloister Wear

Clothing &
Other Things
For the Enlightened

™

In this age of an enlightened society, when minds, bodies, and souls unite to continue the quest for wholeness, natural fabric garments designed to capture the mysticism of the sages of old, the roots of religion, and Karmic truth came to be. Romantic and mysterious, flowing with the tides of emotion, braced with fibers from the earth, burning with firey passionate intent, and full of magickal ideas, this line of esoteric clothing was created in peace, love and harmony by artisans who share in the quest for enlightenment. Each garment was designed to assist you in your karmic path, and is accompanied by the warmest wishes for a successful journey while on this plane.

Visit our Internet site at:
http://www.lightworks.com/Connections/CloisterWear
or e-mail Cloistrwr@Aol.com

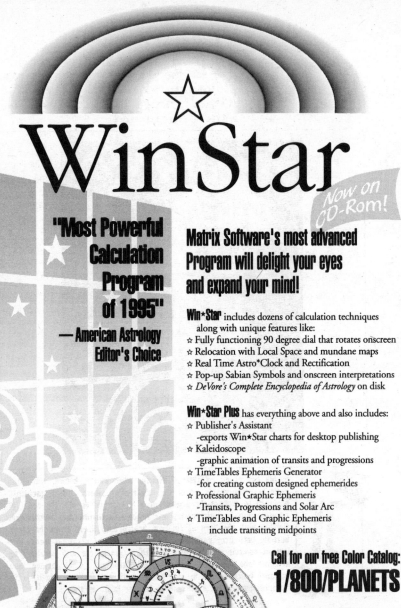

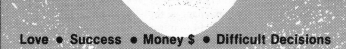

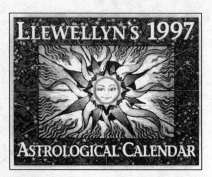

The Gods and Goddesses Are Alive Within You!

12 Horoscopes for the Price of 1

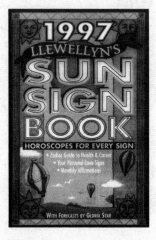

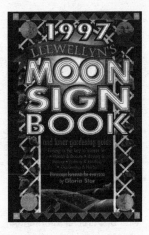